Seeds of the Kingdom

Seeds
of the Kingdom

Notes
from Conferences, Spiritual Directions, Meditations

by ALMIRE PICHON, S.J.
Spiritual Director of St. Thérèse of Lisieux

Edited and Translated by
LYLE TERHUNE, T.O.C.D.

The Newman Press · Westminster, Maryland
1961

Nihil obstat: *Imprimatur:*
    Edward A. Cerny, S.S., S.T.D.   Francis P. Keough, D.D.
    Censor Librorum   *Archbishop of Baltimore*

April 24, 1961

The *nihil obstat* and *imprimatur* are official declarations that a book or pamphlet is free of doctrinal and moral error. No implication is contained therein that those who have granted the *nihil obstat* and *imprimatur* agree with the opinions expressed.

Foreword

Father Almire Pichon, S.J., providentially chosen to be the spiritual director of St. Thérèse of Lisieux, is described in her autobiography as "a director such as our Mother, St. Thérèse, desired, that is, one combining virtue with knowledge." Louis Martin, father of the saint, held the zealous priest in highest esteem, referring to him as "the friend and director of the Martin family." Father Pichon was a lifelong spiritual director of St. Thérèse's three sisters, Pauline, Marie, and Celine, as well as of the saint herself. Marie Martin declared that "to me he was an angel of the Lord."[1] Celine at one time considered establishing herself in Canada in order to assist the Father in his missionary labors.

"God's traveling salesman," was Father Pichon's description of himself, in humorous depreciation of his gifts as professor of philosophy, Greek scholar, pulpit orator, senior missionary-in-charge, retreat preacher, and spiritual director. For forty years over two continents he journeyed in pursuit of souls for the Kingdom of Heaven, scattering wide his priceless wares of peace, joy, confidence in the

[1] *Copie d'une lettre circulaire envoyee aux monasteres du Carmel,* written by Mother Agnes of Jesus, dated February 22, 1940, and sent to Carmelite monasteries throughout the world upon the death of Sister Marie of Jesus, January 19, 1940 (translated by Lyle Terhune), p. 15.

love of God, and absolute surrender to His guidance.

This was a man who went the whole way; who was content with no divided loyalties, no evasions, denials or surrenders, yet who praised laughter; who knew how to jest at the opportune moment; who illustrated the sublimest truths by homely anecdotes and dialogues; and who knew how to die to self with an *Alleluia, Deo Gratias*, upon his lips. His favorite virtues were love, joy, and peace; his favorite maxim was: "Love your neighbor *just as he is.*"

The Father's acumen was sound as he probed the souls to whom he ministered. He spoke out boldly in condemnation of mediocrity and faint-hearted compromise, yet always with the undercurrent of sensitive love and profound understanding of the human heart that distinguishes the true prophet from the zealot.

So great was the veneration in which he was held that religious communities as well as individuals preserved notes of his conferences and spiritual directions. The translator, through a series of unusual circumstances, discovered certain of these treasures, researched for others, and has rendered this compilation into English, as an answer to numerous inquiries received following a series of magazine articles covering his life.

There is unanimous agreement that the Father always spoke extemporaneously; this accounts for his vigorous, colloquial style, and for occasional interpolations, even repetitions. His words are presented as delivered, with no attempt to smooth them into a formal literary style. Editing is limited to deletion of certain remarks wholly personal to those addressed and to the more orderly arrangement of a few passages. His words answered the exigency of the moment, the spiritual needs of his hearers, rather than the sustained exposition of a thesis. Their immediacy lends them vitality and urgency. His exhortations were delivered to religious or laymen present before him in all the tension of definite spiritual problems upon which their eternal salvation might depend. Thus, at times, he adopted the colloquial dialogue as most suitable for communicating his thought simply, emphatically.

Father Pichon and St. Thérèse of the Child Jesus present a new interpretation of our relationship with our Father in Heaven as a childlike way of love, confidence, joy, and peace. "It is the same journey to the same city, but the map is improved; it is easier to read and to travel by."

LYLE TERHUNE

Feast of All Saints
Washington, D. C.

Acknowledgments

DEEP gratitude is here expressed to the Very Reverend Father Provincial of the Jesuit Province, who gave permission for the translation of this compilation of notes and quotations from Father Pichon's conferences and spiritual directions; to Father Paul Vanier, Rector, College Jean-de-Brebeuf, for his sustained interest and his reading of the manuscript; to Father John J. Heenan, S.J., Georgetown University, for encouragement and kindness in offering invaluable suggestions, incorporated into the text; to Père Guillaume Hitter, S.J., Superior, Jesuit Residence, Angers, for valuable data; and to Pére J. Dehergne, S.J., Archivist, Seminaire Missionaire, Les Fontaines, Chantilly (Oise), France, for furnishing invaluable data from the archives of the Paris Province. (Pére Dehergne writes that he would be most grateful for receipt of any letters and documents relating to Father Pichon.)

Sincere thanks are also extended to Father Angelus M. Kopp, O.C.D., and to Brother Vincent Madden, O.C.S.O., whose initial interest encouraged the translator to proceed with the necessary research despite other arduous duties and unavoidable delays.

To the Carmelites of Lisieux, who have never wavered

ix

in their devotion to the memory of their revered spiritual director, the translator offers her profound gratitude for their interest, their prayers, and their loan of a treasured photograph of Father Pichon as he appeared at the period of their first acquaintance. From Mother Agnes of Jesus, since deceased, came a precious note containing family data concerning the relations of the Father with her family.

The translator is indebted to Madame de Salaberry Archer and to Madame Georges Vanier for encouragement and cooperation in making their former venerated spiritual director and his luminous spiritual doctrine more widely known.

Thanks are also due to the following for permission to quote from copyright works: Sheed & Ward, *Collected Letters of St. Thérèse of Lisieux;* McMullen Books, Inc., *Life of the Little Flower,* by Monsignor August Pierre Laveille; Burns, Oates, & Washbourne, Ltd., *Holy Wisdom,* by Augustine Baker, O.S.B.; P. J. Kenedy & Sons, *St. Thérèse and Suffering,* ed. Abbé Andre Combes, and *St. Thérèse of Lisieux, the Little Flower of Jesus;* and L'imprimerie du Messager, material from their publication, *Un Directeur d'Ames, le Pére Almire Pichon* (1921).

The translator also extends her gratitude to the editors of the following publications, who have granted permission to use material adapted from her articles: *Mount Carmel,* issues of January-February, March-April, May-June, July-August, 1945; *Messenger of the Sacred Heart,* November, 1950; *The Little Flower Magazine,* November, 1949, November, 1952, October, 1953; and *Social Reign,* August-September, 1950.

Table of Contents

"The Lamb . . . is the Lord of lords, and King of kings, and they who are with him, called, and chosen, and faithful."

APOC. 17:14.

Seeds of the Kingdom

Biographical Introduction

S T. THERESE of Lisieux and her spiritual director, Father Almire Pichon, S.J., were both of Norman birth, descendants of the sturdy Northmen, the Vikings, the monarchs of the sea who in the ninth century overran northern France to make themselves masters of the province which later came to be known as Normandy. Both were born in the same township, Carrouges: Thérèse Martin at Alençon, civic center of the township, and Almire Pichon at Sainte-Marguerite, a rural village a few miles distant. There were similarities in their temperaments and even in their physique. Both were tenacious; both invariably told the truth. Their emotional pitch was similar: both responded with keen sensitivity to affection. To the more stolid Anglo-Saxon this reponse might seem at times over-emotional, but its origin lay in the delicacy of sensitive hearts keenly alert to the reactions of others and intent upon spreading good-will and contentment about them. Both were tall, of robust physique, with fair complexions, light hair, and blue eyes, and both possessed an innate dignity of bearing.

Father Pichon regarded his birth on a First Friday, February 3, 1843, as a happy coincidence, if not presaging his lifelong devotion to the Sacred Heart.

1

Jean-Baptiste Pichon and his wife, Marie Augustine Anger, often recounted the story of his birth. Following the death of two daughters at an early age, no other children came into the Pichon home. After several years had elapsed, Jean-Baptiste and Marie, longing for a normal family, made a pilgrimage on May 3, 1842, to the five-hundred-year-old shrine of Our Lady of Deliverance, petitioning for a son. When, exactly nine months later to the day, a son was born, the joyful parents presented him to God, christening him Auguste Theophile Almire. The infant was baptized on February 6, in the church of Sainte-Marguerite by the Abbe Hodiesne in the presence of a joyous concourse of relatives and friends.

The Pichons would seem to have been both industrious and intelligent, since they had acquired sufficient capital to purchase a homestead, La Gringoriere, near the village of Sainte-Marguerite. This was a considerable undertaking for French farmers during the turbulent 1800's, when a succession of widely disparate forms of government was the political expression of an unsatisfied nation which had lost the secret of continuity.

The economic crisis which began, halfway through the century, with the widespread blight on the potato crop, had ruined whole countrysides, had caused industrial markets to shrink, and had resulted in over-production, unemployment, and unrest, but seems not to have affected the Pichon family greatly.

From early historic times, Normandy has been noted for its lush meadows, in which prize-winning horses, cattle, and sheep graze, and for its abundant orchards with apple, pear, and cherry trees growing in profusion, their branches trimmed high that the fertile soil might produce, even in their shade, its quota of nourishment for the livestock.

Jean Pichon followed the Norman pattern of cattle raising. In addition, he had developed a side line of traveling over northern France buying up scrawny cattle, fattening them at La Gringoriere or on rented pasture lands, then reselling them at the great provincial fairs or the Paris market of La Villette. Since he was away from home the greater part of the time, the management of La Gringoriere devolved upon the capable shoulders of Madame Pichon. Rigorously just to children and domestics, Madame Pichon had little time, and perhaps little inclination, for demonstrations of affection.

Almire tenderly loved his mother, but his childish love was not always evidenced, for he related in after years that his chief characteristic as a child was stubbornness, and that he was addicted to lying on the floor, kicking and screaming, until his hard-pressed mother, vanquished, gave him whatever he had set his childish heart upon.

Only the firm devotion of the hard-working woman saved the child of her prayers for his predestined vocation. The boy's early years at the parish school nearly ruined his vocation. There, in accordance with the Jansenistic trend of that era, he was taught facts about God and His Church, but not the essential core of religion, the participation in the life of the Holy Trinity by love.

How nearly Father Pichon came as a child to missing his life's fulfillment is revealed in the vigorous exhortations given in later years to retreatants: "You have a false idea of God; you believe Him to be a hard Master! How well I understand you, for I, too, once trembled before Him. As a child I hated God! I said to myself, 'They want me to love God, but I see nothing lovable about Him.' I thought Him to be a savage God, constantly threatening me with hell. 'He can cast me into hell,' I said, 'but He will never win my heart,'" Then he added: "But since that time I 'changed my religion.' It was in the Jesuit novitiate that I became acquainted with the true God. I began there to learn something of His love, His goodness. The grim god whom you are trying to serve is a false god, a counterfeit god!"

What an ascent, an immensity of spiritual distance, separates the child who hated God from the venerable missionary of seventy-six, who wrote, three days before he passed from earth: "Death is but the leap of a child into the arms of his Father."

At eleven years of age, the stubborn little Norman was hustled off to the preparatory seminary at Sees by his much-enduring mother—probably with a sigh of relief, for she could not have been unaware that the gift which she had so happily presented to Our Lady was fast becoming a problem child.

Schoolmates prophesied that Almire would never become a priest because he loved his mother too much to leave her. The valiant mother's devotion to her first-born son is indicated by her perseverance in visiting him each Thursday and Sunday for the nine years he remained at Sees. Came rain, storm, blizzard, or summer heat, the faithful mother never failed to appear at the seminary door, although other sons and daughters had since been born.

The first conversion of the little rebel occurred at Sees. There he came under the salutary influence of the renowned blind prelate, Monsignor de Segur. The latter recognized the spiritual potentialities dormant in the bright, earnest child at his first confession and thereafter guided him to devotion to the Heart of Jesus and to a love of frequent Communion, both of which Almire made the basis of his interior life. Later, it was Monsignor de Segur who gently guided Almire, in his twentieth year, into the Jesuit novitiate then at Angers.

The great moral crisis of Almire Pichon's adolescent years, the change which marked the dawning upon his consciousness of an experiential knowledge of God, as revealed in the tender love of Jesus, occurred during his novitiate days.

Throughout his student days at Sees, Almire's record had been excellent; we find him appointed as monitor to assist in keeping order among the students. But the Jesuit novitiate was another matter. The French have a saying: as stubborn as a Norman. Because he was naturally tenacious of his own opinion, reasoned out in the exact Norman fashion, Almire suffered extremely when called upon to obey orders blindly, orders, perhaps, from those less capable than himself. It was only through a painful death to self that he would learn to obey.

In addition to his struggle with the Rule, Almire found another cause for distress. "When I entered the Jesuit novitiate," he confided to confreres, "I was suffering from scruples until I was almost distracted."

Death to self can be a long drawn-out process, so wearing that the warrior loses courage. A new principle of divine grace was now to be instilled into the young novice's heart which would hasten the process immeasurably. Psychology describes this new principle by the classic phrase: *the expulsive power of a new affection.*

"The story of the dawning and development in my life of devotion to the Sacred Heart of Jesus is very dear to me," he once wrote. "It was in listening to the man whom I have most loved in this world, my novice master, expound the Gospels, that I came to know and to understand our Lord and His way with souls. Then it was that I made a resolution to fight all my life against Jansenism, which so harms souls, especially generous souls who have given up all to follow our Lord, but who follow Him as servants, and not as friends and brothers, as He would have them do." This revelation of the God of love that came to him through study of the Gospels was in later life to be the basis of his sermons, retreats, and spiritual directions.

Almire Pichon had entered the Jesuit novitiate at Angers, on October 21, 1863. In 1866 he was a student in the Juvenat at Amiens. In 1867 he was elevated to the sub-diaconate at Laval by Monsignor Languillet, Vicar Apostolic of Nanking, who had come to Europe to take part in the Vatican Council of 1870.

After teaching in various schools, he was assigned, in 1871, to the scholasticate of Laval for courses in philosophy and theology. His proficiency in Greek is indicated by his assignment to preside over the Greek Academy.

Almire Pichon's ordination, September 8, 1873, marked the third great step in his ascent up the Mount of Perfection. His singular fidelity to divine grace was rewarded by the fullest measure of sacerdotal grace. Of this experience, he wrote in his journal: "The change in me from one day to the next was miraculous. . . . Between the vigil of my ordination and the moment when I stood before the altar, a priest of God forever, the gentleness of Jesus was revealed to me, and how it is to be our model in dealing with souls."

The first confession that the Father heard, following his ordination, left its mark upon the whole future course of his priestly life. Offering a few kind words to his penitent, the Father was startled to hear her weeping. Fearing he had inadvertently pained her, he sought to excuse himself. "Oh, no, Father," she answered, "it is not that. For fifteen years I have lived in great trouble of soul. With a few words you have lifted my burden. These are tears of joy." Greatly touched, and instantly responsive to divine grace, Father Pichon knelt before the altar and consecrated his ministry anew to the Most Sacred Heart of Jesus, promising that in all times and places, in season and out of season, he would thereafter preach the infinite goodness and mercy of God. Never was a promise better kept!

After the Father's ordination he was appointed President of the Greek Academy, a position he held until 1875, when, in accordance with Jesuit custom, he was returned to the rank of a student of philosophy at Vals, under Père Ramiere, co-founder of the Apostleship of Prayer.

During the troublous political period of 1870-1881, there arose in France a violent persecution of religious orders. Jesuits were ordered to close their Houses.[1] Father Pichon had been assigned to the Jesuit House of St. Germain, in Paris, as preacher and retreat master.

In 1880, when police assembled to eject the Jesuits from this House, Father Pichon decided to seek shelter at a hotel owned by one of his penitents. Some two hundred Catholic men gathered as an escort. The cortege set out, Father Pichon in the lead, surrounded by a cordon of police. Gathering momentum as it proceeded, the procession was followed by a hooting mob of anti-Catholics. When they arrived at the hotel, the proprietor, alarmed by the turbulent mob milling about in the narrow cobblestoned street, rushed to the door. The Father explained his predicament, asking for shelter. The hotel proprietor cried out: "My hotel will be ruined forever, but *Alleluia, Deo Gratias,* Father, come on in. This is the happiest day of my life." The man had learned his lesson well. One of Father Pichon's most characteristic utterances was: *Alleluia, Deo Gratias.* He explained it thus: "Holy Indifference replies to suffering: Amen, I accept! Holy Love cries out: *Alleluia, Deo Gratias,* I accept with joy!"

Of this period the Father wrote: "We are still in Paris,

[1] "On March 29, 1880, a decree signed by Jules Ferry brought about a new dispersion, and the substitution of staffs of lay teachers in the Jesuit Colleges. The law was not strictly enforced after the initial expulsion in 1880, and by 1881 the Fathers returned to their posts. Then followed the law of Waldeck Rosseau in 1901 against unauthorized congregations, which closed all their Houses. . . . The communities were, therefore, scattered in various Houses of Europe." Thomas J. Campbell, S.J., *The Jesuits, 1534–1921,* II, 761.

formally proscribed by the Government and tracked by police. We hope for and await the martyrdom they have promised us. If our prayers are granted, you must sing a joyous *Te Deum*."

The famous Jesuit "Third Year" of spiritual formation was passed, with twenty-six confreres, at Hadzor, England, and Hunans, Scotland, in modest and barely adequate lodgings. At Hunans, located at the lowest level of a deep gorge, surrounded by craggy mountains denuded of vegetation, the young Jesuits found a veritable Thebaïd. The Father wrote: "Do not look for any melancholy here. The most fraternal gaiety seasons and sweetens all our sacrifices. We laugh with all our hearts. For all that, the life that we lead is all prayer, solitude, and penance."

The French Government had permitted, in 1881, the reopening of Jesuit Houses and churches. Father Pichon was assigned, as preacher and retreat master, to the Jesuit House of St. Germain in Paris. He was praised for his eloquence, his impressive bearing, and his cordiality. He became a popular preacher. It appeared that he would live and die in Paris, beloved, acclaimed. But the designs of divine Providence are farseeing. This tool was of precious metal; it must be tempered lest its edge become dull.

Father Pichon of the robust physique suddenly became gravely ill, was given the last sacraments, and as suddenly recovered. A young Parisian working girl, one of his numerous penitents, called to see him. "Father," she said, "when I heard that you had received the last sacraments, I offered my life to God, if He would spare your life. You are doing so much for Him—I would not be missed." Greatly disturbed, the Father endeavored to induce her to withdraw her offering. The girl refused. He visited her mother, insisting that the latter order her daughter under obedience to retract her holocaust. The mother likewise was adamant. "No," she replied, "I gave my consent. What is once offered to God, must never be withdrawn."

When, less than a month later, the little working girl lay dead, another milestone was passed in the interior life of the young priest. Two lives were now scored up against his life: the life of his beloved Master and that of a young girl, obscure as a grain of sand blown about the streets of Paris, whose name is recorded only in heaven.

Father Pichon, apostle of peace and joy, became troubled. The device of Norman knights was engraved in his heart: *Noblesse oblige*. He had long ago detached himself from persons, places, things. But one possible sacrifice remained: his native land, beloved France, where his future field of service was opening so auspiciously. Never again, perhaps, to see Normandy of the fragrant apple blossoms in springtime, the lush meadows, flowering hedges, picturesque streams, the low-lying farmhouses. Never, perhaps, to see his mother again, that valiant, hard-working woman for whom he was the center of life.

"Something is lacking to my happiness," the Father wrote at this period. "I shall die with uneasiness if I do not sacrifice my native land for God." He offered himself for the mission fields in China, but was rejected. He persisted. Finally, his superior offered Canada as a substitute, an offer eagerly accepted, and in February, 1883, he was professed in the Society of Jesus, preparatory to embarking upon his apostolate as a missionary.

Before Father Pichon left for Canada, an event occurred which was significant in the lives of the Martin family of Lisieux. They became acquainted in October, 1882, with the young Jesuit who would become known, in the words of M. Martin, as "the friend and director of the Martin family." This first encounter with the Martins is described by Marie Martin in a short autobiography written at the request of her sister, Mother Agnes of Jesus. This account was edited by the Carmelites of Lisieux and distributed to Carmelite convents throughout the world, upon the death of Marie, then Sister Marie of the Sacred Heart, January 19, 1940.

The account proceeds: ". . . a person known to us spoke with enthusiasm of a Jesuit Father, the Reverend Father Pichon, who had come to preach a retreat in the neighborhood of Lisieux. 'He is a saint,' she said, 'a real saint such as we never meet with nowadays. You will be able to see him, for he is soon to give a mission in Lisieux.'

"Through curiosity I went to see 'the saint.' I assisted at his Mass; then . . . I entered his confessional, asking myself, 'Should I tell him the true purpose of my visit?' 'Father,' I said, 'I only came to see a saint.' He smiled at my simplicity, then said, 'Very well, my child, now make your confession.' I made my usual confession, then left without speaking to him further. Walking along I thought, 'Had I known in advance what it would be like, I should not have troubled myself.'

"But behold, that evening a lively desire to return to see the good Father took possession of me. . . . I overcame all obstacles and the next day I assisted again at the Mass of this holy religious. Then I entered his confessional and said, 'Father, I came back, irresistibly impelled to see you again. The reason I do not know.' He asked me some questions, among others, if I desired to become a religious.

" 'Oh, no, Father.' 'Do you wish to marry?' 'Oh, no, Father,' I answered again. 'Do you wish to remain a spinster?' 'Oh, no, not that either!' 'What then? . . . I am pressed for time,' he said, 'as I leave for the railroad station in a few minutes, but I shall return to Lisieux within fifteen days to preach a retreat at the Refuge. I will make an appointment to see you there. Write down for me all of your impressions about the religious life, with your reasons for not desiring it, and, lastly, all that you will have thought about your vocation during the intervening time. For myself, I hope to give you to Jesus!'

"I was caught in his nets," Marie continued, "caught in his nets of kindness. I returned to Les Buissonets with a heart as light as air and filled with a great joy. Jesus, therefore, had cast upon me a special glance of love. I assure you, I had no temptation to imitate the young man of the Gospels and 'go away sorrowful.'

"On the appointed day I went [to the Refuge] to meet Father Pichon, with my eight big pages in which I revealed the most intimate thoughts of my heart. In order not to influence him unfairly, I took care not to reveal what I had actually been thinking about since my first visit to him. After my confession, I passed my manuscript through the confessional grill and rose to leave, but he detained me for an hour reading my paper aloud and making comments. I can tell you that I passed a troubled hour.

"I, who had never before wanted a director, now had one! And I had chosen him of my own free will. Or, rather, it was the good God who had chosen him for me. He arrived in my life at the moment when I was about to lose my dear Pauline (Sister, later Mother Agnes of Jesus). I avow that to me he was an angel of the Lord. And he did good also to our father who received him many times at Les Buissonets, calling him 'the friend and director of the Martin family!'

"He wrote me fatherly letters from time to time, but, overwhelmed by his correspondence and his retreats, . . . he sometimes left me for a long period without a letter. I have written him as many as fourteen times before receiving a single word in reply. . . . In 1884 Father Pichon was called to Canada and the good God alone knows how I suffered over his departure."[2]

---

[2] *Copie d'une lettre circulaire envoyee aux monasteres du Carmel*, pp. 14–16.

Father Pichon once related an incident which occurred during this period and which indicates his friendly intimacy with the Martin family. On one of the Father's visits to the Martin home, M. Martin, to whom he had rendered a favor, called little Thérèse, then nine years of age, and said, "Thérèse, thank good Father Pichon for me. I do not know how to thank him enough." Little Thérèse ran to his side and, standing on tiptoes, kissed him lightly on the cheek. The Father added: "It was the only kiss I ever received in my whole life."

It was M. Martin who accompanied the Father to Le Havre on October 4, 1884, as he sailed for his mission field in Canada. Before his departure, he had fulfilled the prayers of his valiant mother in closing her eyes in death. He had now no personal ties to France.

The zealous missionary notes in his journal: "On October 22, 1884, I took possession of my small cell at the College Sainte-Marie, Montreal. . . . I shall make my first appearance in the pulpit of the Gesu on All Saints' Day. Within three days (following my arrival) I have been engaged to give four retreats and to preach the series of Advent sermons." In his first sermon at the Gesu, he announced: "You are come here to learn to know Jesus Christ better. My sole glory is to be able to preach Jesus and Him crucified."

In Canada, as in Paris, his ardor, his simplicity, his unaffected eloquence, inspired by his love for Jesus, attracted large congregations. His sermons were reported in the press. Churches were soon crowded when he preached; his confessional was besieged with penitents. His labors became prodigious. Contemporaries relate that on retreats and missions he made a practice of spending seventeen hours daily in preaching, hearing confessions, giving spiritual directions, and similar apostolic work, with but seven hours for sleep, food, his breviary, and particular examen, which no pressure of activities ever caused him to omit. Retreats to religious were given for from eight to ten days, with three or four sermons daily. All were preached extemporaneously. During the forty years of his ministry, the Father preached 1,015 retreats, an average of more than two monthly, in addition to other priestly duties. Complicating his ministry was a vast correspondence following him from Europe, Canada, and New England, where he gave retreats to religious communities in New York, Rhode Island, and Massachusetts.

This correspondence originated in his ardent spirit of service, his apostolic absorption in the problems of each soul that appealed to him for spiritual aid or consolation. He answered letters on trains, steamships, in country railroad stations, and while awaiting interviews. Each query he looked upon as coming directly from his Master. Each was answered as soon as was humanly possible.

Consonant with his trained mind, he organized missions and retreats in advance, down to the most minute details. The first step was to enlist the prayers of religious communities for their spiritual success. At some point within the first few days of a retreat or mission, he would announce: "All that is good and true in what I say comes from the Sacred Heart. All that is banal and stupid is the work of Father Pichon."

Religious and priests who were personally acquainted with the Father relate that the consensus of opinion was that Father Pichon always walked in the presence of God. Souvenirs of him and his words of direction are still treasured by venerable religious who, as novices or professed, based their interior life upon his direction. Many communities and individuals took careful notes on his sermons and spiritual direction, to which they still refer as treasured instructions inspired by the Holy Spirit.

One such religious, who, in early youth, had entered

her community upon the advice of the Father, relates this incident of what she considers his remarkable foresight. While she was a novice, her mother died. Greatly attached to her father, she felt her duty might lie in returning home to care for him. Presenting the problem to Father Pichon, she relates that he gazed upward for a few moments, then replied: "No, my child, remain where you are. When the time arrives that your father will really need you, you will be enabled to go to him."

She remained in her convent. Her father remarried. After she had spent forty years in a semi-cloistered community, her father, then a widower, alone and ill, needed her care. The religious applied to Rome and was granted permission to leave her convent, resume lay dress, care for her father until his death, settle his affairs, and then resume her life as a religious—a literal fulfillment of the Father's prediction.

An eminent member of the laity, another of the Father's spiritual daughters, shares her experiences under his spiritual direction, as follows: "I shall have to say that no one whom I have ever met has exemplified so profound and penetrating an impression of saintliness as did Father Pichon, who was my spiritual director for more than twenty-five years. He always appeared to me to be the personification of his Divine Master, especially in His infinite goodness, always accessible to all who appealed to him. His native dignity, his simplicity, his firmness enveloped in kindness, were only equalled by his profound knowledge of the Heart of Jesus whom he loved with such generosity.

"I was sixteen years of age when Father Pichon preached a retreat at my boarding school. Having early lost my parents, I was reared in a narrow environment, devoid of emotional warmth. Of a naturally ardent temperament, I had turned inward as a result, and my interior suffering had caused me to live a somewhat lonely life. The first words of this ardent apostle of Divine Love were to me a revelation.

"When I presented myself in his confessional, not only did I find that, for the first time in my life, I was thoroughly understood, but I found that my problems and their solutions were divined in advance. I was given to understand, from my first interview with him, that God was giving me a father and a guide, and that it was, above all, God Himself for whom, in my loneliness, I was athirst. The Father inspired me with the certitude that, with the grace of God, he would assist me to begin the ascent toward the Divine Light. How well he kept his word! With what patience he resolved the scruples that tortured me! And at long last he succeeded in eradicating these scruples which were blocking my interior life.

"Many years later he made a remark that impressed me: 'When for the first time I saw you enter my confessional at the boarding school, I had the distinct impression that I was to become a support for you throughout your life.' A presentiment that became fulfilled.

"In the Father's advanced age I was privileged to see him in Paris, so feeble, so weak, worn out by his incessant apostolic labors, but with his saintly soul and his good heart unchanged. I found him almost wholly recollected and lost in God. He promised to let me know immediately of any change in his health. Some days later I was obliged to leave with my family for Italy, hoping to see him upon my return.

"A few days later the only person in Paris who knew our Rome address was unexpectedly advised of his death and sent me word.

"Since that time (1919) innumerable have been the spiritual favors, the providential protections, the temporal assistance, that have been accorded to my family, relatives, and friends, to those in distress, and to myself, through the prayers of Father Pichon."

A priest in whose rectory the Father spent some weeks drew this picture of his guest: "Having closely observed his spirit of prayer, his assiduity in ministering to souls, his forgetfulness of self, his courtesy to all, especially to servants, his constant care to glorify God, I must admit that I prize his memory as much for his personal qualities as for his instructions."

There was nothing morose about his spirituality. The same priest continued: "I admired his exuberant high spirits, his conversations, which he always took care to make entertaining, and which were as interesting as college courses on account of his varied and inexhaustible fund of knowledge."

Father Pichon, faithful to the example of his Master, was not to be denied the boon of persecution. Jansenism, against which he waged warfare implacably, was rife in Canada at this period. For two hundred years it had influenced religious thought in France, and despite papal condemnation it accompanied French colonists to the New World.

Jansenism was spiritually, but not doctrinally, akin to Puritanism. The movement had arisen in protest against laxity in morals. The protest had overshot the mark and developed into a self-righteous rigorism. It had obtained learned adherents in some influential quarters. It taught, among other things, that the sacraments are to be received only after a long and rigorous preparation; that Holy Communion is a reward, not a remedy, and should be received but rarely; and that God should always be addressed as a monarch, in fear and trembling. Thus, in the name of high holiness it blocked one of the chief means of sanctification. Clement XI definitely condemned the movement in the Bull *Vineam Domini Sabaoth*, issued July 16, 1705, but its influence was widely felt until Pius X's ruling on frequent Communion in 1905.

Thus it was considered presumptuous, in regions under Jansenist control, to receive Communion more often than once or twice monthly. Priests were known to refuse Communion to women as they knelt at the altar railing, because they wore feathers or flowers in their hats. To a Jansenistic mind this indicated pride, hence, unworthiness to receive the Body and Blood of their Saviour.

It was into this gloomy, rigoristic atmosphere, charged with fear and austerity, that "God's traveling salesman" brought his precious wares of humility, love, and joyous confidence in God's eternal mercy, with, as a corollary, frequent, even daily Communion.

Critics in high places began to charge that the Father was "diluting religion" with his new-fangled ideas about frequent Communion and his constant emphasis upon "love, joy, and peace."

To this the Father replied: "People came to our Lord, sinful, sick. They left His presence, forgiven, healed. What He did then, He does today at the altar. Those who come to Holy Communion today and believe they will return tomorrow, will be on guard against sins and imperfections. Dare we forbid the people to come to their Saviour?"

But the love, joy, and peace to which he directed his auditors were not a superficial "sweetness and light," as they soon found out. It was a doctrine of "blood, sweat, and tears," in the most profound spiritual sense of those words.

First, he exhorted the acceptance of the cross of absolute self-surrender, with every fiber of the heart consecrated to Jesus. Self-love must be pursued into the remotest citadel of the soul and relentlessly sacrificed.

"Christ invites you to His Heart, His table, His cross," he cried out to retreatants, lay or religious. "Turn neither right nor left; break every bond that binds you to worldly things. You ask how to advance in divine love? I reply, immolate yourself with Jesus; offer yourself to Him as a victim of love. When Jesus does us the honor to nail us to the cross beside Himself, we must remain, not seek to descend. . . . The will of God must be our unique joy, our sole source of contentment."

There were jeers, also, in high places. "This Father Pichon is too naïve; it is time he grew up. At forty he still has the outlook of a child." To which we may be sure the saintly missionary would have replied, "*Alleluia, Deo Gratias.*" For the latter charge was true.

The following description was written about this time by one of his penitents: "Father Pichon combined in his person two usually opposite qualities, a gracious simplicity with a marked distinction of bearing. His expression habitually reflected a spirit of recollection combined with an expression of supernatural joy. His most outstanding characteristics were a certain candor, the naïveté of a child incapable of suspecting evil from any source, a tender charity for all, with an unmeasured zeal for God and souls. From his ardent devotion to the Sacred Heart of Jesus, he absorbed that implicit confidence which he preached to others, and which was the foundation of his apostolate."

A priest to whom he confided that he was praying for a certain grace replied: "I am certain that it will be granted you. You have such confidence in Almighty God that He would be ashamed to refuse you anything."

But now "the child who hated God," the richly-endowed man who had sacrificed a brilliant career in France that he might carry his Master's message to the mission fields of the New World, was about to receive a signal reward. The philosopher's words might have been written of him, so fitting they were: "How cautiously men sink into nameless graves, while now and then one forgets himself into immortality."

Back in Normandy, God was creating a unique master-piece of His grace. The time was come for His cherished handiwork to be placed in the frame decreed for it from all eternity. A collaborator was desired, for, in the divine economy, God wills that His grace operate through the unity of the members of the mystical body of Christ, since it is through this collaboration that love is communicated, that love which is the sole medium of exchange in the Kingdom of Heaven.

Almire Pichon was found to be an ideal collaborator: the priest whom divine grace had made over into an un-assuming missionary of childlike spirit so forgetful of self that the Lord of the Universe could use him as a delicately adjusted tool, a tool so perfect that He knew it would leave no false or careless line to mar the perfection of His workmanship.

In April, 1886, Father Pichon was unexpectedly re-called to France by his superiors, who, unknown to them-selves, were likewise cooperating in the designs of Divine Providence concerning a certain Thérèse Martin, a thirteen-year-old maid of Lisieux, whose few, almost casual words about Father Pichon in her autobiography would reward him with an imperishable memory in the annals of the church.

Marie Martin describes the return of the Father to France in these words: "He returned [to France] in 1886, and I desired to go to Calais to meet him upon his arrival. When I asked our father if I could make the trip, he replied: 'I can refuse you nothing, my daughter.' We awaited the boat at Calais for two days, then at Dover, but in vain: we had been misinformed.

"Returning to Paris, we found Father Pichon there. I complained bitterly at missing him on his arrival, but papa answered me like a saint: 'We must not murmur, my Marie; the good God deemed that you had need of this trial. As for me, I am happy to have been His instrument in making this trip with you.'

"Oh, Mother, it was true. The good God wished to detach me even more from earth, and even from its most innocent joys. . . .

"Without doubt I was very near to entering Carmel, unknown to myself. One day in the parlor you remarked that it was high time I thought about it. As I felt no attraction for a religious vocation, I replied that I would enter when the good God spoke to me, but that so far He had not revealed His will clearly enough. You replied: 'Do not expect Him to appear to you. You are now going on twenty-six years of age. It is high time you made a decision!' 'I shall not make a decision,' I replied. 'The good God knows well enough that I only desire to fulfill His Will. So He will, Himself, send me a celestial messenger to advise me.'

"Soon after that I received a missive from Father Pichon. He inquired how soon would it be possible for me to respond to the call of God. . . . I was thunderstruck! The hour of sacrifice had then rung for me! I beheld that hour approach, but without enthusiasm. I, the independent one! I who have always had the air of being unable to endure convents! I, to become a religious! . . .

"I entered Carmel, October 15, 1886. . . . How austere I found it! Yet I was well aware that I had not come hither expressly to view pleasing scenes. I asked myself how I could ever spend my entire life within those four bare walls. Behold how low was my enthusiasm!

"But, oh Mother, I have found Jesus within these four bare walls, and in finding Him, I have found Heaven. Yes, it is here that I have passed the happiest years of my life. . . ."[3] In entering Carmel, Marie took the name of Marie of the Sacred Heart, a name well calculated to please

---

[3] *Ibid.*, pp. 16–17.

her spiritual director. Thus did the zealous missionary make conquests for the Sacred Heart of Jesus and the Kingdom of Heaven.

The Father had arrived in France on October 2, 1886. Stationed temporarily at the church of Gesu in Paris, he was soon assigned to Rouen as preacher and retreat master. The Martin family took the initiative in resuming relations with their beloved spiritual director.

Thérèse Martin, now fourteen, and confirmed in her conviction that her vocation would only be fulfilled in Carmel, wrote the following letter to Father Pichon on October 23, 1887.

Reverend Father,

I thought, as you have concerned yourself with my sisters, that you would be kind enough to take the youngest too.

I wish I could tell you all about myself, but, I am not like my sisters, I am not very good at expressing all I feel in a letter.

I believe, Father, that you will read me aright all the same.

When you come to Lisieux, I hope that I may be able to see you at Carmel and open my heart to you.

Father, God has lately granted me a great grace: for a long time now I have wanted to enter Carmel: I think the moment has come. Papa is willing to let me enter at Christmas. Oh! Father, how kind the Child Jesus is to take me so young, I don't know how to thank Him.

My Uncle thought me too young, but yesterday he told me that he only wanted to do God's will.

Father, I ask you please to pray for your youngest child. I am just back from the convent: my sisters there told me that I could write and tell you quite simply all that was going on in my heart. You see,

Father, I have done so, hoping that you will not refuse to take me as your little daughter.

Bless your second little lamb, Thérèse.[4]

Thérèse had written to him just before her First Communion to commend herself to his prayers, saying that soon
she would be a Carmelite and that then he would be her
director. He had replied under date of 7 May 1884 (the
eve of Thérèse's First Communion and Pauline's profession): Tomorrow I shall go to the altar for you and
Pauline."[5]

Monsignor Laveille, Vicar-general of Meaux, a member
of the pilgrimage to Rome in November, 1887, which
numbered among its pilgrims Louis Martin and his daughters Céline and Thérèse, relates that "Father Almire Pichon, S.J., was an eminent religious, especially qualified for
the preaching of retreats, in which he excelled. Upon the
advice of her sisters, whom he directed, she (Thérèse) confided to him her desire for a religious life. He was probably
the only ecclesiastic to encourage her project of entering
Carmel without delay, even if it were necessary to appeal
to the Sovereign Pontiff for authorization."[6]

The Father, from his headquarters in Rouen, traveled
throughout northern France preaching retreats. Thus it
was that in June, 1888, two months after fifteen-year-old
Thérèse Martin had succeeded in entering the Carmel of
Lisieux, he was called there to preach the annual ten-day
retreat, and so renewed direction of the young postulant
soon to be Sister Thérèse of the Child Jesus.

St. Thérèse and Father Pichon were pioneers blazing
new paths of confidence in God's merciful love amid the

[4] *Collected Letters of St. Thérèse of Lisieux*, ed. by the Abbé Combes,
trans. by F. J. Sheed. (New York: Sheed & Ward, Inc., 1949), p. 29.

[5] *Ibid.*

[6] Monsignor August Pierre Laveille, *Life of the Little Flower*, trans.
by Rev. M. Fitzsimmons, O.M.I. (Mineola, L.I.: McMullen Books, Inc.,
1952), p. 155.

general gloom and austerity of the Jansenistic spirit that permeated the France of that era. As is the usual lot of pioneers, they were often misunderstood by their fellows, devoted and sincere as these might be according to their more meager light.

When the young Sister Thérèse had said to Father Blino, S.J., a spiritual director currently esteemed for his learning: "I want to love God as much as St. Teresa loved Him," he replied, scandalized: "What pride! What presumption! Limit your aspirations to correcting your faults, ceasing to offend God. Moderate your rash desires."[7]

Father Pichon, on the contrary, having already sown seeds of love of God, abandonment to His guidance, and joy in suffering in her young heart, approved the path by which she was being led and encouraged her to even more generous aspirations.

St. Thérèse, in her autobiography, which within a few years has become a classic on the interior life, describes Father Pichon's directions in these words: "Two months after I entered Carmel, Father Pichon was astonished at the workings of grace in my soul; he considered my path most peaceful. I made a general confession to him and when I had finished, he said: 'Before God, the Blessed Virgin, the angels, and all the saints, I declare that you have never committed a mortal sin. You must thank God for this favor which He has bestowed upon you without any merit upon your part.' . . . this assurance coming from the lips of a director such as our Mother, St. Teresa, desired, that is, one combining knowledge with virtue, seemed to me to come from God Himself."[8]

An elucidation of this episode is given by the Abbé Andre Combes. Discussing the mysterious illness to which

[7] *Summarium* of 1919, p. 208.

[8] *St. Thérèse of Lisieux, The Little Flower of Jesus,* ed. by the Rev. Thomas N. Taylor (New York: P. J. Kenedy & Sons, 1926), pp. 123–124.

Thérèse was subjected from March 25 to May 13, 1885, which so seriously threatened her reason and her life, Abbé Combes has this to say: "She (Thérèse) could not bear to think of herself as the child whose words had not been controlled by her thoughts, and whose actions had not been controlled by her will. She was afraid she had been untruthful and that she had exaggerated her illness. 'For a long time after my cure I believed that I had deliberately pretended to be ill. It was a real martyrdom for my soul' (unpublished documents at Lisieux, p. 55). Moreover, as regards the vision itself [of the Blessed Virgin's smile] the indiscreet questions that were put to her caused her a similar fear. From this twofold distress of mind, even her regular confessions could not free her. The second trouble was set at rest only in November, 1887, when she made her pilgrimage to Our Lady of Victories (in Paris on the way to Rome); the first not until 1888, with the help of Father Pichon."[9]

So the ardent missionary fulfilled the delicate task that had been entrusted to him, and four months later, the purposes of Divine Providence accomplished, Sister Thérèse wrote: "Hardly had Father Pichon undertaken the direction of my soul than his superiors sent him (back) to Canada."

From that time on, Father Pichon's highly prized spiritual directions to Sister Thérèse and her sisters were given by correspondence. How extensive these directions were and how completely the young saint assimilated them is revealed through the numerous quotations from the Father's directions to be found in her letters.[10]

The golden thread of Father Pichon's spiritual directions is visible throughout Thérèse's writings. A theologian-writer might analyze the impact of each upon the

[9] Abbé Andre Combes, *St. Thérèse and Suffering*, trans. by Msgr. Philip E. Hallett (New York: P. J. Kenedy & Sons, 1951), p. 16.
[10] *The Collected Letters of St. Therese of Lisieux*.

other. Their spiritual doctrine is so similar as to be identical.

Monsignor Laveille describes the Father's direction of
· Sister Thérèse at this time thus: "Père Almire Pichon was an eminent religious who excelled in his particular work as preacher of retreats. . . .

"During the year 1888 (in June and October), Père Pichon came to give the *Exercises* at the Carmel of Lisieux where he again met Thérèse, and he thought that he had only to encourage her in the way of trustful love, the safety and efficacy of which he everywhere dwelt upon in his preaching. This was, also, the time when the poor child, plunged as she was in aridity, asked herself with bitter disquietude if she were worthy of love or hatred. The Father commenced by restoring peace to her soul. . . ."[11]

Father Pichon, called as her former spiritual director to testify at the process for Sister Thérèse's beatification, said: "It was very easy to direct this child. The Holy Spirit, Himself, directed her. I never even once had to warn her against illusion. What impressed me most were the spiritual trials through which she passed. I had then a most lively impression that God designed to make of her a great saint."[12]

Father Pichon and St. Thérèse are the apostles of the Way of Perfect and Joyous Acceptance, in which everything in our lives, great or small, must be surrendered to accord with the will of God. Likewise, everything must be accepted, joyously, as coming from Him. It is the way of absolute giving without evasion, reservation, denial, or demur, a heroism of self-surrender, commensurate, in proportion to our gifts of nature and of grace, with the gifts bestowed upon us by our Creator. Father Pichon bridges

[11] Laveille, *op. cit.*
[12] *Summarium* of 1919, p. 20.

the gap between the God of the theologian and the God of the layman, simple, courageous, and faithful. St. Thérèse described her inability to understand the ponderous terms of theologians as "giving me a headache." She found Father Pichon's direction couched in words as simple and direct as those of the Gospels—and as uncompromising.

The identity of spiritual doctrine between St. Thérèse and Father Pichon may be explained in the words of an early English mystic: "Souls which were of quite different, even contrary, disposition, after such supernatural unions [with God] do come to a near resemblance to one another. . . . And the reason thereof is, that nature and its particular affections and inclinations are now so worn, and even burnt out by the fire of Divine Love that has become the principle of all their actions, which, therefore, must be uniform and like to one another."[13]

St. Thérèse wrote one of the last letters of her life to her beloved director. It was written between August 3 and August 10, 1897, and is listed as No. CCXXXIV. In this long letter, written on her deathbed, St. Thérèse "told him all that God had done for her, all her thoughts upon His Love and Mercy. She also laid before him her hopes and especially her desire to do good upon earth. She based her letter upon Psalm xxii on which she made a brief commentary. . . . It was intended to make a copy of the letter, but the post went before it was done. When Thérèse learned of this, she said simply, 'My whole soul was in it'; and her sisters realized that she would have been glad to leave it to them as a spiritual testament. . . ."[14]

The Father was recalled to Canada at the urgent solicitation of religious communities and Père Turgeon, rector of the College Sainte-Marie. He sailed from Le Havre on

[13] Augustine Baker, O.S.B., *Holy Wisdom* (London: Burns, Oates & Washbourne, Ltd., undated, edited from the Douay edition of 1657, by the Right Reverend Abbot Sweeney, D.C.), pp. 546–7.
[14] *The Collected Letters of Saint Thérèse of Lisieux*, p. 366.

November 3, 1888. Again stationed at the College Sainte-Marie, he journeyed throughout eastern Canada, New York, Rhode Island, and Massachusetts, preaching and giving retreats. In 1901 he was appointed superior of all French-speaking missionaries in Canada.

Now he entered upon the most fruitful period of his long apostolate—nineteen years devoted to zealous and incessant labors. Up to the age of sixty-five "God's traveling salesman" journeyed to cities and distant villages by dusty roads under the searing summer sun; over snowy wastes in sub-zero winters; by slow country trains, by horse and buggy, always with a cordial smile of greeting and never-failing absorption in the problems of retreatants and penitents.

Again he adhered to his schedule of seventeen hours daily reserved for his ministry to souls and but seven hours for repose, refreshment, and personal devotions. The sturdy physique inherited from clean-living ancestors stood him in good stead. At sixty-four, a confrere noted: "Age has not weighed down those robust shoulders; occasionally his head bends forward a trifle, but one does not notice it, fascinated by his eyes so fine, so good, and by the kindly smile always hovering about his lips."

An eminent priest closely associated with the Father for many years writes: "The gift of selflessness that he possessed to a rare degree was practiced without one day's failure for forty-six years. Heroic fidelity to the confessional, unfailing patience in listening to moral grievances heard a thousand times over, constant readiness to repeat the luminous word of comfort, a persevering interest in the progress of those who addressed themselves to him, fatherly delicacy in consoling their grief without ever appearing bored—these qualities demand an uncommon share of renunciation and self-abnegation. And what a lesson he gave us, when, advanced in age, he still traveled widely to hear confessions in various places at the appointed hours, never failing to arrive on time! One of his penitents remarked to me: 'Whether it snows or rains, if he be alive, Father Pichon will arrive on time.' "

"In the confessional," said one of his penitents, ". . . he was a man transformed; the man proper vanished and only Jesus seemed to remain, so well did he show forth the goodness and gentleness of the Good Shepherd. His sole presence recalled to us the presence of God. . . ."

These qualities, precious as they are, do not suffice fully to explain the Father's ascendency over souls and their remarkable devotion to him even thirty-seven years after his death. His spiritual children unanimously witness that "the secret of his influence over souls is to be sought in his whole-hearted devotion to the Heart of Jesus."

"How happy I am to have found that devotion," he would say, "and how I thank God for it! . . . All is there! Alas! We believe in His justice, in His mercy, but not in His love. If His love were truly known, what generosity it would inspire! Poor Jesus, You so good, so loving, how You are disfigured!"

Loving the Heart of Jesus, he loved the Eucharist, and to him, gaining souls to the Heart of Jesus meant also gaining them to frequent, even daily Communion, and that in a period when it was the custom for religious to approach the Holy Table but once or twice monthly.

To religious he would say: "My Sisters, I will go before each one of you if necessary, begging you never to lose one Communion. . . . I speak frankly just as I think. I would weep all of my life over one Communion lost through my own fault. One Communion the less is a great loss in the life of a religious. Go to Holy Communion for our Lord's sake if you do not wish to do so for your own sake."

This doctrine at that time appeared to many as an innovation, and he was severely criticized for his persistence in recommending it. When the decree *Sacra Tridentina Synodus*, counseling frequent Holy Communion, appeared on December 20, 1905, the good Father was jubilant: "It is one of the greatest joys of my life," he wrote to a confrere.

When the Father reached the age of sixty-four, he was recalled to France, his long apostolate in the New World definitely ended. He sailed from New York on the *Savoia*, on April 18, 1907, after having visited all the religious communities in Canada, Rhode Island, New York, and Massachusetts to whom he had given retreats, and had given one last interview to each of his spiritual children down to the newest novice and humblest lay Sister.

As the *Savoia* bore him irrevocably from the beloved scenes of his labors, for the first and only time on record, a cry of pain escaped his lips: "This morning," he wrote in his journal, "I offered Mass for all those dear children whom God had confided to my care. The sacrifice is consummated. Surely God cannot be displeased if I love my adopted country so truly! Never has He asked of me a greater sacrifice—never! He knows that I accept this sacrifice for the souls which are His and mine. May my sacrifice bring them an increase of His love."

Some years later he confided to a brother Jesuit: "I dare not say that my sacrifice is consummated because I must still make it anew each day."

His Jesuit superiors sent him to preach missions and retreats, not only throughout the Paris province, but to the Jesuits, dispersed through political machinations, in England, Holland, Italy, Spain, and Hungary.

During the year 1909, Father Pichon had a serious illness. He attributed his unexpected recovery to "my little Thérèse," as he termed his favorite spiritual daughter. In a letter describing his recovery, he added: "It is not the first favor she has obtained for me. . . . how many

favors do I owe to her." He wrote at this time to Sister
Geneviève of the Holy Face (Celine Martin, who had entered the Lisieux Carmel, September 14, 1894): "Yes, God
wills to glorify His humble little saint. After that how can
we fail to strive to become as little children? At sixty-six
that is my constant endeavor."

One of the last joys of his life, as he neared seventy,
was an invitation from Mother Agnes of Jesus (Pauline
Martin) to preach a retreat at the Carmel of Lisieux.

Gradually his robust health had been declining; he was
obliged to conserve his strength, limit the number of retreats to be preached. A former penitent who visited him
a year before his death was struck by his continuous recollection. He who had been so adept in conversation now
spoke slowly, in a subdued tone, as if loath to interrupt his
interior prayer. It was during this time that he wrote:
"Appearances indicate that the eternal farewell is at hand.
Death is but the leap of a child into the arms of his Father."

Father Pichon wrote in his journal during 1919, his last
year on earth: "My Mass is the great work of my day; it
is my life; the rest does not count. O my God, never deprive me of my altar. My child," he continued, addressing
"my little Thérèse," "obtain for me that I may say my Mass
up to the moment of my death. To die at the altar would
be so beautiful." His prayer was generously answered.

On November 14, 1919, the venerable priest, then assigned to the Jesuit House at 10 rue de Dantzig, Paris, rose
as usual at 5:00 A.M. for his customary hour's meditation
before the altar in preparation for his Mass. In deference to
the infirmities of age, he had, in late years, divided the hour
between sitting and kneeling. It was in the former position
that the Brother sacristan found him—with eyes closed
as if in sleep. Touching him gently on the shoulder, the
Brother said, "Father, you are late for your Mass." But the

saintly man of God had already sung his *Ite, Missa est,* and had passed on to chant his eternal thanksgiving before the great throne of God—that thanksgiving that he had passed a lifetime in perfecting.

LYLE TERHUNE

May Your Heart, O my
Jesus, be the support of my
helplessness, the strength of
my weakness, and the joy of
all my weariness.

ST. MARGARET MARY

1. *Hidden Treasure*

THE HIDDEN Treasure, to gain which
we must sell all, sacrifice all, is the Heart of Jesus. It is He
who does all. We cannot depend upon ourselves.

Whatever of truth or virtue is to be found in my words
comes from the Sacred Heart. Whatever there be of dull-
ness, banality, is the work of Father Pichon.[1]

I desire that all those who follow this series of conferences endeavor to live this prayer: "To the greater glory
of God, through aridity, tedium, distaste, bodily discomfort. Through rebellious movements of the memory, the
intelligence, the emotions, I ask only for the greater glory
of God, and not for the absence of distractions or of temptations. That I may experience no consolations, even that
I may be wearied, means nothing to me provided that God
be glorified. I shall concede that others may glorify Him
to a greater degree than I, and I shall rejoice in their
good qualities."

Oh, our crosses! If God lifted them from our shoulders,
we should have to go upon our knees to beg them back.

Monsignor de Segur, member of an illustrious family,
on the day of his ordination petitioned God that if he were
ever to be advanced to honors in the Church, he would be

[1] Father Pichon always prefaced the opening conference in a series
with this declaration.

33

sent a great trial to offset the honor. He was called to Rome to accept a post of distinction. Within the year he became totally blind. Thereafter, he always celebrated the date of the onset of his blindness by a solemn High Mass and a banquet to which he invited all the members of his family, asking them to rejoice with him.

"My dear Cecile," he wrote to a child who was praying for his recovery, "when one is raised to the cross with Christ, the safest way is not to descend, but to remain beside Him."

We never leave a series of conferences exactly as we enter upon them. If the word of God does not enlighten us, it leaves us more blinded. If it does not touch our hearts, it hardens them.

Doñoso Cortes once listened with respect and interest to the sermon of a simple country priest. A friend expressed astonishment. "At his side," replied Cortes, "I see Christ." So much the better if you can see Jesus at my side. I shall try to efface myself that He may speak to you.

We are egoists. We always seek our personal pleasures. St. Catherine of Siena reproached herself on her deathbed for having sought consolations in her thanksgivings. Failures, defections, have become more numerous. To be saved requires effort. Instead of praising, glorifying God, do I live a purely natural life that would be reprehensible in a pagan?

A visiting confessor startled Blessed Hyacinth Scotti by inquiring: "Do you imagine you are headed for heaven with that wholly natural behavior?" The question engendered a train of thought that ended in his conversion and, ultimately, in his beatification.

During these conferences, our particular examen must be upon the seemingly little things: punctuality, custody of the eyes, silence of the lips, of the imagination, of our memories, of the heart. Our basic meditations:

1. All things have been created that I may fulfill the individual design that God had in creating me.

2. All things have been created by God. They issued forth through His power, His wisdom, His love.

3. They were created as a remedy and an aid in order to help me attain my goal, and not to satisfy my curiosity or my whims.

SPIRITUAL READING

The Imitation of Christ: Book I, Chapter 20
Book II, Chapters 9, 10, 15

2. Recreation: Tool of Sanctity

A FAMOUS archbishop of Reims, deceased a few years ago, had a favorite prayer: "My Jesus, heart for Heart! Give me Your Heart to love, to savor. Behold my poor heart to nourish, to adorn with Your virtue."

Heart for Heart! Happy exchange! Our Lord is faithful; He asks but for that.

In one of the first general meetings of the Society of Jesus, this question was debated: would it be advantageous to suppress the recreations provided for by the Rule? Were not recreations lost time? It was brought out that during recreation it is easy to give way to sallies of self-love, to words that might prove painful to susceptible persons. Yet, all present unanimously voted that recreations be preserved. Certainly there are dangers to be avoided during recreation, but how many excellent occasions are presented for the practice of the virtues! It is an incomparable means of advancement. When one truly desires to die to oneself; when one aspires, in all sincerity of heart, to advance spiritually; when one seeks to abandon oneself to the Divine Will in all of its exigencies, one will come to love recreations. A soul that seeks perfection will find there great, ready-made opportunities for augmenting its virtues, the degrees of glory to offer to our Lord.

St. Teresa of Avila, while visiting her daughters, arrived at a convent where the superior, a serious, austere person, had forbidden all jests during recreation under the pretext that self-love entered into their recital.

"My good God!" cried St. Teresa. "What are we coming to? We are fools enough by nature without also becoming fools by grace."

Recreation, especially in religious communities, is for many the most difficult hour of the day. But often a good conversation carried on during recreation will be of greater profit than a meditation or a sermon.

Sometimes we hear this: "Father, recreation is painful to me." Yes, for certain dispositions, it demands definite renunciations. But you tell me that you observe your rules faithfully.

"It is true, but I always have a hundred pretexts for being absent from recreation."

"Father, I have little talent for conversation: I am unable to converse interestingly."

There is something better than a talent for conversation: to understand how to listen, to listen with warmth, with an animation that inspires others, to take actual pleasure in what is being said, to become a part of the group not necessarily through words but through an interested expression. This requires that one should not act as though one were a stranger, and not cast gloom upon the group by wearing a long face. Learn how to jest, how to joke during recreation. Humor is a necessary element in life. It lubricates emotions, eases tension, drives away sadness and discouragement, and even aids good health.

Our recreations must be veritable re-creating exercises. If we are not naturally light of heart, we must learn how to rejoice. There are gifted temperaments who have the talent of inspiring a certain warmth, a heartiness in recreation. I congratulate them. I beg of them never to permit their talent to become rusted from disuse. Doubtless, we should never permit foolishness or trivialities to mar our recreations. Even in enjoyment, one should always maintain a certain modesty of demeanor. I will emphasize my meaning: there should never enter into our recreations anything that savors of a deficiency in education, nothing that might cause pain to others.

St. Teresa of Avila cultivated a spirit of joy in all of her monasteries. One Easter day the dear saint rang the bell for an extra recreation. Each Sister left her cell. One of the religious joined the saint to say: "Mother, would it not be preferable on Easter day to meditate rather than to make merry?" "Remain in your cell, if you wish," replied the saint, "but permit your sisters to rejoice, to expand their hearts in the Lord."

3. Alone with Jesus

OUR LORD does not dwell within the tabernacle solely to immolate Himself upon the altar, but also to abide in the midst of His people. We should be assiduous in our visits to the Blessed Sacrament made with profound respect and love. Our Lord repeats, ceaselessly, "I have not wanted to leave you, to leave you orphans."

There is no need for a servant to announce your visits, as the rich of this world require. You will always be welcomed at the Court of Christ. There are no other nations so privileged as to have their gods so near to them. It is here that our Lord is truly *Emmanu-el:* God-with-us. It is here that we fully comprehend those words: "Behold, I am with you even to the consummation of the world."

How many Christians only appear before our Lord on Sundays! It is a marvelous privilege to have our Lord, not at our door, but under our very roof.

The foundress of the Religious of Marie Reparatrice was an important personage in the world. One day, as she lingered at the church door after Benediction, she met an intimate friend who began to make light of her devotion. "For whom do you pray, and why for such a long time?"

"I pray for sinners," was the reply.

"And then—"

"And then? Our Lord is alone and I keep Him company."

How consoling it is to find oneself alone in a deserted church, alone with our Lord. For myself, I admit that I experience a profound joy in reciting the formula of my vows in a secular church, a little church in the country, perhaps. I say to myself: "The good God has never, doubtless, heard anything of the kind here. What an intimate joy it is."

A sick man was in a hospital. Everything possible was being done for him, every attention was paid to his needs; yet he was sad at heart. His family had deserted him. One day, being alone, he held in his hand a photograph of his children.

"Ah," said he, "they do not visit me." Then, as if to excuse them, he added with a sad smile, "They lack the time." Poor father! By that he meant to say, "They have the time to work, to enjoy themselves, to rest, to pile up wealth, but to their father they will not give even a quarter of an hour."

I hope our Father will never have need to make such reproaches to us. May our assiduity be redoubled; may our zeal be increased.

The Master is here and calls for you.

A religious once expressed, in the presence of St. Teresa of Avila, a regret that she had not lived in the days when our Lord traversed Galilee, remarking how happy she would have been to have accompanied Him. St. Teresa, with a shrug of the shoulders and a glance in the direction of the tabernacle, replied, "Do we not live in His presence? Do we not converse with Him and attend to His responses?"

Yes, He is always there. He is there to listen to us. He has said: "My delight is to be with the children of men."

St. Teresa put all the fervor of her heart into this exhortation: "Abide with a good heart in our Lord's presence—He, who says to us, 'Do not leave Me so quickly. Remain here with Me.'"

"What happiness," said St. Francis de Sales, "to be there alone, alone with God, without anyone's knowing what passes between Him and us, in that heart-to-heart communion in which we share our most secret thoughts and desires." He continued, "You come before our Lord hoping that He will speak to you, but that is seldom. Ordinarily it is to speak to Him, to tell Him your troubles, your sorrows. But very often we come before Him to witness by our presence that we desire to belong to Him."

While in secular life, St. Margaret Mary, still a young girl, loved to be near the altar. "I could not be content to remain in the back of the church. Despite embarrassment at being conspicuous, I could not refrain from placing myself as near the Blessed Sacrament as possible." She often rose at five on a cold winter day that she might be at the door of the church when it was opened. She adored our Lord.

Père Eymard, while a small child, disappeared one day and could not be found. After a long search, he was discovered in the village church with his head closely held against the tabernacle. Asked what he was doing there, he replied: "I am near Jesus and I am listening to Him speak."

St. Bernard, having renounced family, wealth, and all worldly goods, repaired to the altar where he repeated those memorable words: "Jesus, You are now my father, my mother, my brother, my sister; You are to me all in all."

O Tabernacle of Jesus! How I love there to retire, to hide, to take my repose; there to share my joys! I find no roof so hospitable, no family more gracious and welcoming. There is the support of my weakness, the consolation of my griefs. On this earth, it is the richness of my poverty, the treasure of my indigence, the garment of my nudity, the crown of my happiness. My God and my All!

In our visits to the Blessed Sacrament we must always observe a profound respect. There is the living God, the soul of our souls, the object of our love, of our faith. Of our faith, yes! Let that be shown in our attitude. He is there!

At the Eucharistic Congress held at Brussels some years ago, the resolution was passed to take note of an abuse that might interest you. There are some devoted people who, upon entering a church, make a brief gesture toward the tabernacle, then quickly go over to a statue of St. Anthony or some other saint, where they prostrate themselves fervently to recite their prayers. Their prayers ended, they leave as they entered, that is to say, neglecting to adore our Lord upon the altar. This is false piety. Everything in its rightful place. Every Christian should be convinced that divine grace comes from God alone.

Bossuet once had a long discussion with a Protestant

named Claude. On another day, the latter observed Bossuet leaving the cathedral hurriedly, with several buttons on his cassock missing, and gave him a good lesson.

"Monsignor," remarked Claude, "you do not really believe in the presence of God in your church."

"But, assuredly, I do believe," Bossuet answered, indignantly.

"Monsignor," replied Claude, "if you truly believed, you would not appear before your God with your cassock in disarray."

A living faith must be shown in your attitude before the altar. You are in the presence of your King—your Divine Captive. Do you recall the reply of the conquered Eastern king to Alexander the Great: "How do you want to be treated?" "Like a king," was the reply. Our Lord desires to be treated like God.

Louis XV lay dying. The Viaticum was brought to him. Raising his hand, the monarch made a salute. His physician entreated him to lie quietly: "In your present state, the least imprudence may hasten your death." "What," the king replied, "my God lowers Himself to visit a wretch like me and I should fail to salute Him?"

The essence of our faith lies in the Real Presence of our Lord in the tabernacle. A Protestant once said: "If I had the faith of you Catholics in the Holy Eucharist; if I believed in the Real Presence of our Lord, it seems to me that I would never quit that holy place. I would want to pass all my life in His presence."

When Moslems visit the tomb of Mahomet, all, even children, preserve absolute silence. A Moslem ambassador at the court of King Ferdinand said: "I believe in the presence of God in your temples. Whenever I enter one, I kneel before the altar to adore the one God."

We must pray with all our hearts at the foot of the tabernacle, in response to the tender invitations: "My

children, give Me your hearts. Come to Me, not as a servant, but as a friend. Come to bring Me your love, to share
with Me your most intimate secrets." If you desire that
our Lord treat you as an intimate, then you must be confi-
dential with Him.

Let us heed the loving invitation of Christ: "You who
are weary and heavy-laden, come unto Me and I will give
you rest.

"O hearts wounded, forgotten, neglected, I call you to
Myself. I open to you My own Heart. How often have I
longed to enclose you within My Heart, as the hen gathers
her little ones beneath her wings, but you would not. Come
now, throw yourself into My open arms!"

Can you be lonely when this loving Heart awaits you?

Are you friendless, while He begs for your love?

4. "Forgive Us Our Trespasses, as We Forgive . . ."

T HE CONSISTENT effort to be virtuous
is painful to nature. It involves the exercise of our moral
fiber. But let us not be frightened so quickly at the vigor of
the fray, nor at the length of the combat. One must learn
to eat dry bread in the service of God and not look with
a critical eye upon the fare that He serves us.

My dear friends, I come to you with a very simple subject which I hope will be practical. I come to speak to you
of confession.

Confession, first of all, presents something of repugnance, of the disagreeable. It goes against the grain to

testify against ourselves, to unveil our faults, our miseries, to a man equally inclined to evil as ourselves. However, there are souls who make a veritable hell out of confession. They torment themselves when this religious duty becomes necessary. But our Lord said, "My yoke is easy; My burden light."

Two categories are carried to equally dangerous extremes: those who are too broad in their views and those who are too narrow. Among seculars, the former extreme is the most frequent, among religious, the latter.

Confession was established for the self-accusation of our sins, not in order to expose us to temptation. The demon has it greatly at heart to render the service of God insupportable. His ambition is to make us discontented and anxious.

It is painful to find certain persons so enmeshed in thorns at the moment of their examination of conscience. My friends, you have the wrong idea of the good God if you believe Him to be hard of heart, a Master difficult to please, who weighs you down with heavy burdens.

Oh, permit me to say that, even before you, I became acquainted with that view of a rigorous Master. I also trembled before Him. I calumniated Him in my failure to appreciate His goodness when I was a child. I said to myself, "They want me to love and serve so terrible a Master, but there is nothing attractive about Him. He is a harsh and terrifying God. I might tremble before Him, yes, but love Him, adore Him? Fear Him? Oh, yes. Fear Him, above all! But love Him? Impossible! Show me a whip? Menace me with hell? Oh, no, no, it is not in that way that my heart can be won. No, I refuse to have anything to do with such a god. He is harsh! He is a caricature of the true God! He is a false god! A counterfeit god!"

But after that period of my life I came to know another God; I changed my religion. Upon entering the Jesuit novitiate, I was shown the true God. I there learned to serve, in joy and peace, the Author of peace. It was there that I learned to understand something of His love, His gentleness, His goodness, His mercy.

I beg of you, my dear friends, encourage all those with whom you come in contact to know the true God. In order to do that, study Him in the book which He Himself opens before you, and of which the reading is accessible to all: the book of His Divine Heart.

Let us examine some points on confession which may make it less onerous.

Why do you make yourselves so uneasy over confession every eight days? Four minutes of examen is sufficient. If you question that, I shall change it and say three and one-half minutes. A little work recently published tells us, "Scrupulous souls never improve their judgment of themselves after their first glance at themselves."

We have the same experience in a general confession, spontaneously made. The confessor questions the penitent. His response, based upon judgment of himself at first glance, is always excellent. When the penitent goes over and over his past, he gets a headache, becomes confused; and all is lost.

A member of her Carmelite community complained to the superior, Madame Louise of France, that she never had time enough in which to make her examination of conscience. "Remember," replied Madame Louise, "that a Carmelite ought always be ready to confess, to communicate, and to die."

An examination of conscience must never leave us disquieted, especially when it is concerned solely with venial sins. One is not obliged to accuse oneself of venial faults, be they deliberate and with malice aforethought. You are only obliged to accuse yourself of all mortal sins. If you have actually committed a mortal sin, you will know it well in advance of confession. Examen will not make it any clearer than the testimony of your own heart. Who, I ask you, could poison himself unknowingly?

The demon cunningly works out his strategy. He arouses worry and trouble in order to disquiet us. Once he accomplishes this, I see him applauding himself for his achievement.

The difficulty in examination of conscience is to determine the exact evaluation of our faults. I hear of persons who present themselves for spiritual direction and then traduce themselves as criminals for what are, in reality, light imperfections.

"Father," they will say, "I was voluntarily distracted during Sunday Mass." That is a venial sin.

"But, Father," they will insist, "it was during the elevation." Still a venial sin.

"But it was during the most essential part of the Mass. I have been told that is a mortal sin."

An erroneous doctrine! The Commandments of the Church oblige us to assist at Mass on Sundays. They do not oblige us not to have distractions. The precept was fulfilled when you assisted at the Sacrifice. You are culpable with separate culpability for faults committed during this time, be they irreverence, voluntary distractions, or lack of respect.

Again a person will say: "I have calumniated my neighbor, with grave consequences. . . ." There is here a matter of which one must accuse oneself.

It is necessary to be forearmed against scruples, an ordinary ailment of devout souls. We must develop a well-balanced conscience through study of the obligations of our state of life, of our responsibilities. These we must check against theological truths.

One subject upon which many who believe themselves to possess most delicate consciences are not scrupulous enough, and which easily lends itself to illusions, is charity.

Before a gathering of the General Council of the Society of Jesus, this question was posed: "In a religious community, on what point is it most easy to sin mortally?" The seventy or eighty senior professed there present replied unanimously: "On charity in words."

Two conditions must be present to make uncharitableness a grave sin: a serious matter and knowledge of the harm caused to the person under attack, whether it be to his honor or to his reputation.

Another snare into which it is easy to fall is particular friendships, too emotional, too natural. Particular friendships constitute a danger to fraternal charity. Such friendships may seem, at first, to be based upon motives of devotion, of zeal. Yes! But little by little, there arise certain regrettable familiarities. One must be on one's guard in these matters. They are, if not always grave, at least dangerous, depending upon the character, habits, and moral strength of the individual whose personality may seem to you to be so congenial.

A subject to which one must pay attention is that of certain conversations. Here there may be consequences that are fatal. One sometimes meets with thick-headed persons who have been reared in a lax, worldly atmosphere. In such an atmosphere it is possible to be initiated into many things that are best kept to oneself. The veil of unworldliness should not be lifted from souls that have been sheltered from laxity. The calm of their hearts should not be troubled.

Another point upon which one can easily cultivate a false conscience is that of jealousy. This fault is rarely confessed, though frequently committed. We would prefer to say, "I have committed a sacrilege," rather than, "I am jealous." This is a serious fault. Not, perhaps, if it exists solely in sentiment. But how often does jealousy inspire sinful words and acts. How many disastrous faults it brings in its train! We make nothing of it. We fail to reproach ourselves for it; nevertheless, it is an evil that reigns everywhere.

We may place ourselves in a false position to evaluate our faults. That lie, told ten years ago, did not, at the time, require a high degree of contrition to efface it. But, by this time, how many graces have been bestowed upon you, how much light has been shed upon your conscience, so that, today, the same lie seems almost criminal. God has spoken. He has revealed Himself to you more clearly. He has shown Himself to you in all of His magnanimity. You now realize how deeply you wounded His Heart in permitting yourself so to dishonor His justice, His holiness, in so seemingly small a matter. Let us flee all faults that dishonor our vocation, our state of life.

Avowals in confession may be free, obligatory, or even insufficient. Confession was established for the avowal of faults, not of temptations. Temptations are the work of the demon. They are not proper subjects for confession, except in asking for advice. You have only to place yourself above the importunities of that miserable being.

There are some souls always ready to calumniate themselves, to point out the equivocal, the stain, in their conduct. They bring to their confessor a litany of temptations, not of faults committed. One should not accuse oneself of imperfections as if they were venial sins.

Here is an ardent nature, subject to sallies of vivacity, carried away, sometimes, by impulse. Would you consider it culpable in the sight of God? Sometimes, yes, but more often, no. Let us learn how to take our own part, not make ourselves into pitiless dictators in dealing with our own conscience.

There are three kinds of doubtful sins, depending upon whether the doubt concerns the act, the gravity, or the confession. The doubt may concern the act itself. Did I really commit that fault?

"It seems to me that I did." Are you sure?

"No." Then you need not accuse yourself. The act is doubtful.

"Yes, Father, I committed that sin. I am fully convinced of it." Did you realize at the moment that you were offending mortally?

"Father, I only saw that afterward." One does not sin after the act is committed. At the very time of the act did you realize that you were sinning mortally?

"No, Father." Then it is a doubtful sin and you need not accuse yourself.

"Father, I am certain that I committed that sin and I knew it was serious, but I am not sure if I accused myself of it. Perhaps I did, perhaps not." It is a doubtful sin according to the principle: the doubtful does not oblige confession.

In order that one commit mortal sin, it is necessary that the conscience speak clearly. When the conscience hesitates, it is a good sign. We can never be in the state of mortal sin without being aware of it. When we do not hear the voice of conscience clearly condemning us, we can remain at peace.

What are the obligatory avowals in confession? Mortal sins, certainly. The exact number must be given. One must not say "four or five" when one is well aware that the correct number is five. This is important and absolutely necessary. We must also mention any circumstances that change the nature of the sin. Some people give their confessor a lessson: "Father, you have not asked me about this or that circumstance." He may reply: "Those are not circumstances that change the nature of the sin." Time, for instance, does not change the nature of a sin.

There are also confessions that are insufficient. Often,

it is difficult to distinguish between real sins and imperfections.

Sometimes we hear people say, "Father, I am happy: I have just received a general absolution." That is not an extraordinary privilege. You can have the same privilege at each of your confessions provided you take care to add, "I accuse myself of all the sins of my past life."

Dear friends, profit by all of these means to purify your souls more and more fully.

St. Teresa of Avila said to her confessor: "Please, Father, I beg of you, preach about poorly made confessions. Through them hell is peopled."

Permit me to add something about the formation of the conscience. At the moment of Holy Communion you may experience a serious uneasiness of conscience. You are not, perhaps, positive of this. You cannot determine the exact degree of your culpability in a certain circumstance. At this point the demon intervenes and places within your imagination a certain determination of which you must take no notice. Should you succumb to his suggestions, it may appear to you afterwards that you said to yourself: "Even were I certain that I had committed this fault, I would communicate this morning just the same."

Wait a moment. Take the devil in his own trap. It is not your doubt that is your undoing, but the attention that you pay to the devices of Satan. Turn the question around: If you had eaten this morning, would you go to Communion? "Oh, no, no, Father." Well, you see plainly that you are not in the disposition to commit a sacrilege.

"Father, I touched the Host with my teeth. Is that a sin?" We shall see. Are your teeth in any way more profane than your tongue? Not to touch the Host with the teeth is a counsel that the Church gives out of respect for our Lord. But there are always those who go farther than the counsel and make a travesty of the precept. Why not remain within the limits of prudence and common sense?

How is it that so many do not know that the penance given is obligatory? It is an integral part of your confession. If you have accused yourself of venial faults, then your penance obliges under pain of venial sin. If you have accused yourself of serious matter, then your penance obliges under pain of mortal sin. Penance is a serious matter, a sacramental work. Penance is of incalculable value. The rosary that you recite as a penance is of far greater value than the one you recite from simple devotion. It is a praiseworthy practice to fulfill your penance immediately upon leaving the confessional, while you are still bathed in the blood of our Lord, all impregnated with the divine pardon. To forget to carry out one's penance is not a sin, but a misfortune, a loss. Our good works are minor in comparison with sacramental penance.

A person comes for spiritual direction and says: "Father, I am so afraid of minimizing my sins that I prefer to tell more rather than less." It is as wrong to exaggerate as to minimize. There are some persons who, if they realize what they are doing, make bad confessions. They exaggerate their faults, blacken their own characters, and calumniate themselves unmercifully.

Thoughts and desires are two different things. There is an abyss between them. What is a bad thought? It is the arresting of the imagination voluntarily upon something wrong, something forbidden. It means to see, to comprehend, with the imagination. There may be a desire, but with the imagination only, to commit evil solely for the pleasure of dreaming about it, thinking about it, but not with the determination to carry out the thought in action. This is a sin of thought. To entertain such thoughts with the determination to commit the evil, if or when the opportunity presents itself, is a sin of desire.

The success that the devil has with his temptations is

unbelievable. He is a clever actor who plays out a comedy at the expense of poor souls who never imagine the source of their difficulties.

The spiritual director meets with the souls who describe themselves as having failed in charity. He asks, "Have you had thoughts against charity?"

"No, Father."

You have, then, given way to rash judgment?

"No, Father."

You have harbored resentment?

"No, Father."

You have wished evil to your neighbor?

"Oh, no, Father, not that."

You have rejoiced in the misfortune of another?

"No, no, Father."

You have struck some one? You have spoken humiliating words?

"No, Father."

You have spoken evil of your neighbor?

"Yes, Father."

But you used terms that were too vague. "To fail in charity" is not only what one does, but it may be all that could wound the love due to our neighbor.

"Tell me, Father, could one fail in charity to the neighbor in thought?" Yes, we have people so naïve as to ask that. Our neighbor has a right to his reputation. We must not fail in our esteem for him. We must not impute intentions to him which he does not have.

"Father, I have despised my neighbor, and, often, I have spoken ill of my neighbor." But they are not the same thing. One can despise by words, by feelings, or by emotions.

There are people who believe that it is permissible to fail in respect for the dead. But the dead have as much right to their good reputation as the living. To disparage the dead is even more odious than to speak ill of the living.

The spiritual director often hears small self-criticisms that are entirely out of place. "I failed to make the sign of the cross upon awakening; I failed to go to Communion on a First Friday; I ate between meals on a fast day." Or, "I am not mortified." The last is a counsel, not a precept. Or, "I did not make the act of contrition in the confessional." That is not strictly necessary. It suffices to have had a moment of contrition during confession or preceding it. The moment preceding confession, the accusation of faults, the absolution, and the satisfaction are all parts of the sacrament of penance. It is important not to make the accessories of more importance than the obligation.

Do you obey your confessor?

"Oh, yes, Father, I do all that he tells me to do." That is not sufficient. You must also believe what he tells you. How many deluded souls make themselves unhappy because they will not renounce their self-direction! Remember the words of St. Ignatius: "He who directs himself has a fool for director." No one is a good judge of himself. You, my dear friend, appear to be wise, experienced, competent. I would willingly confide children to your instruction. There is one soul that I would never confide to you: your own. You are, for one thing, a tormentor, a persecutor, of your soul. I would want to snatch it out of your hands.

And for confession, you need but four minutes. Yes, no more. It is wise to have a certain method: our duties toward God, toward our neighbor, toward ourselves. We should go over the order of the day, the different places where our life is passed, the cell, the chapel, the class, the community room, the refectory. Four minutes of examen for confession is sufficient.

There are weightier elements that influence our reactions in the confessional. Woe is us if we fix our eyes to right or left, if we seek to retrieve worldly goods, pleasures that we had once renounced, seek to examine, through human motives, the difficulties that surround us! That is how we come to feel all the weight of our human nature and to lose our footing amid the storm. There will be no danger for us as long as we keep our eyes centered upon Jesus. Our danger, our unhappiness, begins the moment we lose sight of Him.

There are times when we must repeat the cry of Peter, "Lord, save me or I perish!" It is the cry of the soul experiencing its innate weakness, its helplessness.

"Lord, when we can do no more; when our miseries overpower us; when all without betrays us; then we learn the cry of the heart: 'Lord, save me or I perish.'"

Prayer! It is our great strength, our only strength. The soul that prays, said St. Alphonsus, will most certainly be saved. And St. Teresa of Avila went further to say that, for the soul that prays, salvation is no longer problematical: it is assured.

One who follows his exercises of piety through routine, who cites certain formulas of devotion without feeling in the depths of his heart the need of God, does not pray. He will almost inevitably fall, and most grievously, into serious sin, in order that he may come to realize his powerlessness and need of God.

Oh, Peter had no need of a formula for prayer when he found himself sinking beneath the raging waves. His cry rose from his heart, ardent, imperative. It was not a form; it was truly a cry: "Lord, save me or I perish!" Our Lord awaited only those words. He stretched out His hand to Peter. He raised him above the waves with these simple words: "Oh, man of little faith, why do you doubt?"

How we shall tremble before the tribunal of God, confused and ashamed at our disbelief! We who understand so many varied and unimportant things, but fail to understand the one thing necessary—the love of God for us and our own relationship to Him!

"Oh, had I but known how Your Heart loved me, watched over me, I should never have experienced those useless fears, those discouragements!"

5. Have I Contrition?

My very dear friends, St. Augustine has a word that merits our deepest thought: "The Heart of Jesus is the source of graces from which one may always draw without exhausting its riches." Let us, therefore, during these conferences in which we have more need than ever of the grace of God, drink from this Blessed Source.

If these conferences are to be, as we hope, the starting point for an entirely new life, that point will not be our work but the unique work of Divine Grace. Of ourselves, we can but impede the divine action. May it, therefore, be the work of God alone.

St. Francis de Sales said: "We must never speak of God or of the things of God in such a banal manner as to bring them down to the scale of the trifles that fill our ordinary conversation. It is a lack of respect toward a sacrament which one has no more right to touch than a sacred vessel, a ciborium or a chalice." What we have said as well as what is said to us in confession must be enveloped in a sacred respect.

The Venerable Bede said that confession is the summary of all religion. Behold a sign that will not deceive us. Often we stop at certain appearances and believe that we have done our duty. Where do you stand in relation to sin? Do you find hatred for evil growing within your heart? Congratulate yourself if you do. You are on the right track. You are making progress. The best confession is not the one in which the fewest sins are unveiled, but the one in which there is the greatest sorrow for offenses committed. A confession is to be evaluated by the degree of contrition experienced.

Two conditions must be present if contrition is to fulfill its purpose: its degree and its perfection. I find a multitude of souls, good and sincere with God, who torment themselves. "Have I contrition?" they ask ceaselessly. My dear friends, you are wasting your time. I will guarantee that you possess contrition. It is the intimate disposition of the heart that loves God. Perhaps in confession you experience no sensible pain, but, tell me, would you be capable of saying to God, "I am happy that you were crucified"? No. That is certain. Then, knowing that your sins were among those that caused Him to die for our salvation, it follows that you are contrite. But there must also be actual contrition. Habitual contrition resides in the heart in a latent state. The habit of regret and sorrow for sins is good, but for the forgiveness of sins something further is required. A formula is not sufficient. There must be an actual sentiment within the heart.

Here is a person who possesses noteworthy historical knowledge. When he is asleep, he is not thinking of his knowledge of history. Has he lost the historical facts? Ask him a question the next day, and instantly his knowledge passes from a latent state into a conscious state. In a similar way, a good religious, or a devout lay person, always regrets his faults. An act of the will is sufficient to awaken contrition. A penitent says to his spiritual director:

"Father, I fear that I do not have sufficient regret for my venial sins to assure the validity of my confession." Do you accuse yourself of all the sins of your past life? You are surely contrite for your past mortal sins.

"Yes, Father." Therefore that is sufficient.

There are those who are plunged into sadness because they never experience a lively sorrow for their sins. They say to their director, "Father, I am afraid." Why do you fear? You should rather thank God for having preserved you and given you the grace to live for so many years in a state of habitual contrition.

They insist: "But, Father, I do not shed tears." It is not necessary to experience a crisis of the nerves in order to be contrite. Without a flow of tears it is possible to experience great and authentic interior sorrow. If God grants you the gift of tears, accept it, but perhaps you will at the same time experience sentiments of pride. You will believe yourself to be a candidate for canonization. What is needed for contrition is fewer tears and more supernatural sorrow.

Supernatural sorrow! It must needs be prayed for. Without the grace of God, you will never, of yourself, experience this sovereign supernatural grace.

Priests often hesitate to cause the divine grace of absolution to flow over a soul when they recall these formidable words: "There must be contrition, a sovereign sorrow, exceeding all other sorrows. Each sin must be repented of; and we must be willing to accept all possible misfortunes and be willing to sacrifice all the goods in the world, rather than to commit it again."

That is not to say that I shall be as sensibly affected over each mortal sin as I would be over the death of my father, my mother, or of the loss of all my fortune. No, but according to the spirit of theologians who say: a mother loves her child; she must love God more than her child in order to be in the state of grace. What does that mean? That the love of God will cause her to thrill with emotion as does the love of her child? Does it mean that the love of God will necessarily take up as much of her attention, create as much of a stir in her heart, as the love of her child? Obviously not. The mother thinks more often of her child than of God. The least ailment of her child causes her a sensible pain, while the crimes of sinners against God may induce but slight emotion.

How, then, could the love of God be stronger than love for her child? If it came about that some day the mother would have to choose between God and her child, she would have to sacrifice the child to God, in spite of her repugnance and her suffering. It is in this sense that sorrow for sin must be sovereign. It is not in the sensible part of our soul that we must experience sorrow for sin, but in the higher part, the superior part.

My dear friends, I want to enlighten your minds on these points so that never again will you have to torment yourselves to find out if you have sufficient contrition.

"Oh, Father, I am afraid. I do not know if I have sufficient contrition. But it seems to me that I have. Have I sufficient contrition?" A devout life consists in tending toward perfection. You are devout, not in order to do as others do, but to act more perfectly. On the question of confession, which is the résumé of religion, are you going to be content to be commonplace, ordinary? To have a bare contrition? No, no. You must have something more perfect. Try, then, for perfection in contrition.

The demon is a clever strategist; he attempts by every subtle means to keep us from mounting the mysterious ladder of perfection.

The penances given today are mere nothings; they are out of all proportion to the sins committed. They are less designed to pay the debt incurred than to cause us to recall that we are under obligation to acquit ourselves of it. I beg of you, let us not believe that with one rosary said we obtain the remission of our temporal punishments. Would you like to consider some samples of penances formerly imposed? Had a penitent spoken a word against charity? Three days fasting on bread and water was his penance. In the morning, nothing; at noon, some dry bread and cold water. A confessor who would give such a penance today would be looked upon as excessively severe. If such penances were meted out today there would be those who could not find time in the year in which to carry them all out. In any case, tongues would be less active and reputations safer. For a sin against holy purity, thirty days of fasting on bread and water. For such a sin with another person, three years of penance, the person in the meantime being excluded from the assembly of the faithful. During religious exercises he had to remain at the threshold of the church—at the portals of the holy place. If it concerned married persons, the penance lasted for ten years. For a religious man or woman, the penance lasted a whole life through. These penances now appear to us to be astonishing.

During the first centuries of the Church, penitents condemned to those rigorous expiations had one means by which to redeem themselves. It was in the days when so many Christians sealed the confession of their faith with their lives. When a martyr was to die, a penitent could beg him to sign a petition addressed to the Sovereign Pontiff begging him to remit the penance due, and it was rare that the favor was not granted. We have a martyr who is of our family: He is our Friend, our Brother, our Father—the King of Martyrs. His merits are not lost. They are enclosed within the treasure-house of the Church. The pope imposes certain conditions for their fulfillment, upon which are accorded forty days, five hundred days, seven years or seven quarantines, the merits of which the early Christians would have acquired in the same periods.

We must not understand this as though we were to be dispensed from suffering for seven years or so many days in purgatory. A plenary indulgence does not always guarantee full compliance with all the conditions. It requires a perfect disposition: death to venial sin. If one has the least attachment to venial sin, one is not able to gain a plenary indulgence. Some day, through persevering prayer, the soul may arrive at the point of making a perfect act of contrition which will earn a plenary indulgence. And oh, what debts we shall have to pay!

One sole act from the heart suffices to cause all our sins to be pardoned and our debts acquitted. Why not profit by the generosity of our God so rich in mercy? You who are dragging yourselves along the beaten path, you do not know the riches of the Heart of God who makes us to thrill with joy and happiness.

I long so greatly to be able to place within your dear souls the means to grow, not only today but every day, every week, every month, in the perfection of contrition.

In your creation, God said: "I design this soul for a life of perfection. I will accord it great graces in order to conduct it to that end." At your baptism you received all the graces designed for the Christian soul. Later, at your confirmation, you were dowered with the graces designed for the perfect Christian. Over and above the ordinary habitual graces, behold one day there comes to birth a whole system of mysterious conditional graces.

Our Lord said: "If this soul does not offend Me by mortal sin, I shall shower upon her choice graces, decisive for perfection, graces which she will not receive if she offends me mortally. If this soul never offends me mortally by a serious fault, behold the delicate favors that will be her recompense." And there is still more.

"Behold yet higher privileges, graces most special, which will be the recompense of this soul, if, beginning on the day on which she gives herself to Me, she never commits a mortal sin." But, alas! What happens? How many faults? Is all thereby lost? Have I lost all those precious graces beyond recall? Alas! Alas!

No, no, all is not lost. All may be recovered through reparation. In your heart resides an admirable resource, incomparable, heavenly. It remains for you but to make an act of contrition so intense, so perfect, that God in an excess of tenderness will embrace you and will say: "All is repaired. I restore to you your former vigor of soul. I shall cause the stains of sin to vanish. I shall restore your former delicacy of heart, just as if your life had been immaculate. I shall even restore those privileged graces that were yours before your fall." It is in this sense that it is possible to say that one can recover baptismal innocence. It will always be true that you have sinned, but also true that you are a masterpiece of Divine Compassion.

God starts all over again working in your soul just as if you had never sinned. How beautiful to behold the riches of divine mercy flowing down upon your heart, so narrow, so despoiled. It only remains for us to attain to such a degree of contrition. We obtain it through prayer. You are designed for perfection—patience, perseverance.

It will always be true that St. Mary Magdalen is Mary Magdalen, but what incomparable grace was granted to her! All can aspire to the same degree of grace; all can achieve it. All, without exception. We must aim at nothing less. Patience and perseverance! To attain this grace by years of prayer and mortification, is it to buy it too dearly? Confidence! Confidence! Some happy day from our heart will arise a flame of love so intense that it will attract to itself a mighty blaze of benedictions from God. We are incomparably rich. We have but to weep over the ruins of our spiritual life—our Lord will come to repair all.

Let us range ourselves anew, then, in the ranks of those

following our Lord. Let us meditate upon His first steps in His life upon earth.

6. The Mass: Mystery of Divine Charity

Now I would like to say a word to you about Holy Mass. The Mass, my dear friends, is the greatest treasure of our lives, along with Holy Communion. We should be very happy to have the privilege of assisting at it. It is one of the great privileges of our lives. We must, therefore, renew our fervor as to the manner of assisting at it. How, then, should we assist at Holy Mass?

Holy Mass is the most beautiful of all prayers. It is the prayer of our Lord Himself. In comparison with it, all other prayers are as nothing. It is an offering worthy of God. Holy Mass! It is more than a prayer; it is a sacrifice, the Sacrifice of God, and worthy of God. It is the same sacrifice as that of Calvary.

The Curé of Ars said: "All of our good works united do not equal the offering of one Mass. Martyrdom is little in comparison with the Mass. In the Sacrifice of the Mass, God offers for men His own Body and His own Blood. Martyrdom is but the sacrifice of a man offering himself to God."

Holy Mass! Nothing on earth is greater because it is the commemoration of the Passion of Christ. The Mass! It is the ineffable mystery of divine charity: God communicating Himself to us, bringing us His graces and His favors.

The Sacrifice of the Mass is not only offered by the

priest who celebrates, but is also offered by all who assist. You, also, are priests. Does not the priest say, "Pray, my brothers, that this sacrifice, which is also yours, may be agreeable to God?" We should assist at Mass with the greatest devotion. It is one of the most precious privileges available to us. People in the world often cannot assist at Mass so frequently as they desire. Children, husbands, households, occupations of many kinds, conspire to prevent them, even when they desire with all their hearts so to assist. Many people in the world look upon religious with envy of their happiness in going to Mass each day.

St. Jane de Chantal, while living in the world, inquired of her director, St. Francis de Sales, "On weekdays, if I have not time for both, should I sacrifice mental prayer to assist at Mass, or should I leave Mass to make prayer?" The saint replied: "My daughter, it is far more beneficial to assist at the Holy Sacrifice than to remain alone with yourself."

A problem arises: "Father, when many Masses are being said at the same time, for example, if five priests are at five chapels in a church, should I unite my intentions to the five Masses to benefit from them all?" Theology says on this point that you are not obliged to assist bodily at all the Masses being celebrated. You can unite your intentions with all the Masses being said over the four quarters of the globe. A priest may be far distant from you, yet may say a Mass for your intention. You are not present physically, yet that Mass is no less precious to you than if you had actually assisted in person. When your intention is united with that of the celebrant, you are one in spirit with him. When you assist at five Masses at the same time, five priests offer the Holy Victim, five priests pray for all those assisting, and their prayers are yours. One hears, properly speaking, but one Mass. One can, however, recommend oneself to all the prayers of all the priests present, and so one does, truly, assist at all the Masses being offered. One must not be content merely to hear Mass; one must hear it with the right intentions and in the right way.

I counsel the laity to take good places in church. They should not be so modest as to sit always in the rear or behind a column. Sit near the altar. If there is only the communion rail between you and the altar, you can more readily follow the celebrant's movements. You will not so readily be distracted by what goes on around you. You will be oblivious to those who come and go. We thus avoid distractions, and remain in recollection and fervor of spirit.

In what attitude should one hear Mass? The best way is to hear it kneeling. Monsignor de Segur recommends that we hear Mass on Catholic knees. However, often our knees may demand to be respected. We should, then, not exceed the rule of prudence and common sense. In the novitiate we were put on guard against an excess of fervor. Once an ailment of the knees is contracted, it generally remains throughout a lifetime.

We should hear Mass with the same recollection that we would have had on Calvary. St. Francis de Sales wrote to St. Jane de Chantal: "As soon as I turn toward the altar, I am no more distracted."

While I was in college, I was acquainted with a saintly religious. He was the spiritual Father of the students, and he had been the confessor for generations of Jesuits. We beheld him each morning shedding tears before the holy altar during his Mass, and we were always edified. "Oh, that priest!" we said. "How devout he is; what consolations he is granted!" After his death, his spiritual director disclosed to us that, at the holy altar itself, he had, for many years, been assailed by terrible temptations: frightful temptations of unbelief, of blasphemy, of despair. It was, for him, a desperate struggle each day to celebrate Mass, a struggle against powerful and evil invisible adversaries that brought the tears to his eyes which we mistook for tears of devotion. We must not be astonished, then, if we experience temptations even before the very altar of God. At those moments the demon is more highly enraged and revengeful. He vents his rage through tormenting the souls of the good, especially those who aspire to perfection.

In what spirit should we hear Mass? It is a good practice to unite with the celebrant, to appropriate his intentions to ourselves. To unite with Jesus Christ—this is the best and highest exercise. We must follow the attraction of our hearts in all simplicity. These attractions vary for each soul, and vary at different times for the same individual. The best method for you today might not be the best method one year from today. You should follow the Mass prayers, or, if it appeals to you, say your own preferred prayers.

"On Sunday is it necessary to read the Missal prayers?" No, it is not absolutely necessary. Do you find devotion in the practice? Then continue it.

"Sometimes I do, and sometimes not. At certain times I prefer to hold a colloquy with our Lord." Very well, follow your attraction. An excellent way of hearing Mass is to unite with the purposes of the Holy Sacrifice. In this way we unite ourselves with the dispositions of our Lord.

"Father, may I prepare for Holy Communion during Mass?" Certainly! The priest helps prepare you. He asks for you, in certain prayers, the dispositions required for a good Holy Communion. The reason is this: one must, as often as possible, communicate during Mass, not before. Communion before Mass is tolerated by the Church for good and sufficient reasons, but it is certainly not encouraged. In former times it was not permitted to communicate before Mass.

"Father, sometimes I experience consolations in continuing my meditations during Mass. I may have a subject for meditation that does me good." Very well, that, also, is permissible, providing you unite your intentions with those of the Mass. Thus you are speaking to our Lord according to the leading of your heart.

Let us examine ourselves to see if we have not something to reform in our method of hearing Mass. Let us see if we have not lost much from the Masses we have heard throughout our lives, and through our own fault. What an incomparable blessing is one Mass! Let us profit from this transcendent grace.

> My God, You will bless these conferences, for we have taken for our motto Your own words, spoken to those who honor Your Sacred Heart: "I will shower abundant blessings upon all their works."

7. Self-Surrender

PREPARATORY PRAYER: "To the greater glory of God, through aridity, tedium, distaste, bodily discomfort. Through rebellious movements of the memory, the intelligence, the emotions, I ask only for the greater glory of God, and not for the absence of distractions or of temptations. That I may experience no consolations, even that I may be wearied, means nothing to me provided that God be glorified. I shall concede that others may glorify Him to a greater degree than I, and I shall rejoice in their good qualities."

We must bend every effort to discover the will of God in our regard, His designs of mercy and of love for us, that we may correspond with them.

Above all, therefore, we must establish ourselves in a state of loving indifference, as a condition indispensable to our spiritual advancement. We must not be surprised if we do not always find ourselves *feeling* indifferent. We may not always *be* indifferent, but we should attempt to control our reactions so that we shall at least always try to preserve an *attitude* of indifference, of abandonment to the holy will of God. Herein lies the work of a lifetime.

What is self-surrender, or holy indifference? It is nothing else than conformity to the will of God, a generous and gracious acquiescence in the divine good pleasure. Holy indifference is the state of a soul that is well-balanced, that inclines neither to the right nor to the left so long as God has not manifested His will.

Self-surrender is the state of a soul disposed to say, "Yes, oh God, so be it!" of a soul always ready to adhere to the good pleasure of the Master. After the example of St. Margaret Mary, this soul always says, "It suffices, oh my Well-beloved, to be what You wish for me! I accept and embrace all the decrees of Your providence in my regard." It is the state of a soul that does not know how to say, "I would prefer."

There are those who say to God: "May Thy will be done, Lord—and my own, also." Is this submission to the Divine Will? Extinguish, oh Lord, all self-will within me! I wish, at last, to abandon myself to Thy Love. St. Francis de Sales gave the wise counsel to his daughters, to refuse nothing coming from God, to demand nothing except that His Holy Will be done.

How many prayers we send up that arise out of purely

human motives! How many prayers are in conflict with the will of God! We must add to each of our petitions: "Close Your ears to my prayer, Lord. Do not grant it; do not incline to my will. Perhaps what I am asking of You would be to my great loss, if granted. Oh, of Your mercy, dispose of me and of all my affairs according to Your divine Will."

What is the extent of self-surrender? It extends to all that is neither God nor sin. Sin is the loss of God; I must, therefore, hold it in horror. I must hate it with a hatred that grows stronger, more unyielding, every day. All that is neither God nor sin must remain a matter of indifference to me.

Should I desire a long or a short life? I would probably make a choice that would result in spiritual bankruptcy. There are saints who, had they lived one more year, would have found themselves at death in the depths of hell. There are those in hell, who, had they lived one year less, would have had high places in heaven. Holy Indifference, then!

What kind of death shall be mine?

Will it be a lingering or a violent death? After a long illness or a few days of pain? Shall I die tranquilly in my bed? The answer I know not. The will of God must find me ready to acquiesce in all of His decrees, however rigorous they may appear.

There must be indifference in regard to the employment that is given me. "But it seems to me that there are valid reasons why I should be given other work. I think that thereby I would be more successful and be able to work for the glory of God more efficiently. I would be in a state of life in which I would advance more rapidly in the perfection that God asks of me." How do you know this?

There must be indifference to the kind of mission to which I must devote myself. "But it seems to me that, were

I in other surroundings, another occupation, there would be more helps to fervor." How can you judge, never having been in the other situation?

"I wish to live in that place and with that individual whose personality seems so akin to my own. I believe that with her I would find wonderful aids to my spiritual advancement." How do you know this? Holy Indifference!

Self-surrender involves submission in accepting spiritual trials, desolations, repugnances, weariness, temptations. Père de la Colombière, in his spiritual notes, said: "I have delivered myself over to our Lord to be the plaything of all sorts of temptations."

"Oh, Father, I used to have sensible consolations in my religious exercises. I was filled with devotion. Now I am plunged into the darkness of aridity, pain, anguish. Oh, if God would but give me back my first fervor!" Holy Indifference! Were your prayers answered, it would perhaps be a danger for your soul, a hindrance to your perseverance. God sends exactly what best suits our needs at that particular time.

I hold to only one thing: the will of God. I abandon myself to this adorable Providence. I make the sacrifice of every preference, of every "I would prefer."

There are three degrees of Holy Indifference. The first consists in permitting God to weave the web of our lives freely, according to His divine purpose. In this degree I always raise my eyes on high and remain submissive and confident in the situation in which Divine Providence has placed me, without ever departing from this disposition.

But if each day I judge things from a purely human standpoint, then I am not practicing self-surrender. Let us not confound indifference of will with that of sentiment. To feel nothing, to experience nothing in our emotional life, is impossible. The greatest saints have never arrived at this point. On the contrary, the greater their advancement, the more their sensibilities became refined, delicate. God permits this in order to multiply, along with their repugnances, the merits of His true servants.

The saints! Day by day they became more and more indifferent, yet they are the true sensitives. They had to fight against themselves, and endured frightful combats. The saints! They battled face to face with their natural repugnances and some of them with personified evil. They experienced all the resistances of the flesh, and felt their wills rise in rebellion, in spite of themselves, against the will of God. Their human will revolted against its Creator. All the trials of nature, of the flesh, of the spirit, of the heart were theirs. Certain people imagine that the saints were marble statues, naturally docile, naturally endowed with all the virtues that characterized them.

But the saints *were made* into saints.

In the degree that they approached God, they became more and more refined and delicate, until, at last, nothing was able to divert their will from its object, God. While the hearts of sinners become hardened, coarsened with time, the hearts of saints develop into more exquisite sensitivity.

St. Margaret Mary left us these words: "How consoling it is to examine the lives of the saints, and to find them so great, but with natures so similar to our own."

It may be difficult to understand, but in the degree that they advanced in perfection, they experienced stronger repugnances in their work, their devotional exercises. St. Margaret Mary knew something of this herself. Our Lord said to her one day: "My daughter, promise Me never to refuse any employment. Promise Me never to refuse to go to the parlor." This was torture to her, but as mistress of novices she was obliged to accompany them to the parlor.

"Promise Me never to refuse to write a letter." All correspondence was to her an occasion of interior suffering.

The saint was greatly disquieted. "Lord," she answered, "do not require these sacrifices of me." "My child," was the reply, "I shall multiply your repugnances. I shall redouble your sensitiveness."

Upon reflection, the good saint said to herself: "My repugnances, therefore, are not faults. Our Lord would not multiply my faults. They are, therefore, not even imperfections. Our Lord would not multiply my imperfections. My repugnances, therefore, are only means," she said, "of proving my love for my good Master." What a beautiful and joyous discovery this was for St. Margaret Mary! It was worth all it cost her.

"My Well-beloved has given me to understand," she said one day, "that He wills my life to be a continual sacrifice so that I shall never act except with extreme repugnance."

Hear St. Teresa of Avila cry in a transport of love! "To suffer or to die!" But the good saint did not always recall this prayer. Another time, overwhelmed with suffering, she laid her sorrows at the feet of our Lord. Her good Master appeared to her and said, "My child, you ask for sufferings; but when I send them to you, you refuse to accept them? But know that I am not offended because your refusal was but the cry of nature; your will did not enter in."

It is not always within our power to prevent our repugnances from appearing exteriorly, on some extreme occasions. They are messengers who appear without having been called and who will vanish of themselves provided we do not magnify them by our conscious attention. Holiness is more practical than we can imagine. It is not necessary for us to become either marble or ice.

"My God, redouble, if You wish, my repugnances." This wholehearted acceptance relieves the self of waves of repulsion once the resolve is undertaken with the whole heart. "I protest that I shall not draw back from any sacrifice, that I shall walk with a firm step in the path You have marked out for me. With eyes fixed lovingly upon my divine Model I shall advance into the fray. I beg of You, take no notice of my interior rebellion. I will what You will, cost what it may."

Such a disposition of soul brings with it happiness, perfection, perfect security of heart. We are so prone to seek our own happiness, our own peace, as if there were no other in the world. Yes, they are unhappy who do not love the will of God above all else. Even when they come to have everything that they think they desire, they are still unhappy. There is no way to be happy in this life except to accept what God sends us and to will what He wills.

Let us approach that person who smiles, not only when she is with others, but also when she is alone. Let us approach. We find her murmuring these words out of a sincere heart, "May Thy will be done, O God! In everything that happens to me, I experience only the joy of all that You do—for You always do only what is best for me."

Announcement was made to a devout person of the death in an accident of an only sister, tenderly loved. "It is as I would wish, my God, because it is Your will." That was the first cry of her heart. One who studies in this way to love the will of God, prepares for himself a heaven upon earth.

Do not attempt to impose your little plans, your little ideas, upon God. He is more farseeing than you. He knows infinitely better than you possibly could of what you stand in need. How sad it is to observe souls in perpetual discord, at constant cross purposes with the Providence of God! Each time they scan their past lives, they do so with lifted eyebrows. There is no doubt that in many lives there are pages we would wish to tear out, to disclaim. But God thought it well to bring us into that danger, that situation.

Do you dare to say that He did wrong? He bears great responsibility, and your mercy toward yourselves is extremely limited. You concede no rights to Him in the direction of your lives.

Look upon the mother of this family, wearing herself out to provide for the well-being of her children. To what end do all her sacrifices, her devotion, tend? To make discontented beings? To see around her long faces? Children who are contented with nothing that is done for them? Who find everything bitter or insipid? This is the experience of the good God. Surrounded by His immense family, He labors to make them happy, but more often succeeds merely in making them discontented. How satisfying it must be for God to meet, now and then, with one of His children who is always smiling, always abandoned to His will, always ready to say YES! Who never says, I would prefer! Who always says, Do not trouble Yourself about me, oh, my God; give me what You will!

The good God troubles Himself often over us. Sometimes He says, "How will this soul take this remedy of which she has such great need? Will she murmur against Me? Accept it unwillingly? Will she draw any good from it?"

My God, I have but one ambition: to deliver myself over to You without reserve. Do not listen to my murmurings. Pay no attention to my repugnances. Close your ears to my cries. Accomplish in me Your divine Will.

A penitent of St. Francis de Sales wrote to him one day: "Whatever sauce the good God serves me, it is all the same to me." The good saint replied: "You say, my dear daughter, that whatever sauce God serves you, it is all the same to you. This is a marvelous saying. Take care to digest its meaning well. Often we make such statements through habit and a certain lightness of temperament, and it seems to us we are saying them from the depth of our hearts. This sometimes is not true, as we find as soon as we attempt to put them into practice. You say that whatever sauce God serves you is all the same to you. But you know well in what circumstances He has placed you—in what state and what condition—and tell me, is it all the same to you? How much self-love insinuates itself among our affections, however devout they may appear to be! Here is the great word! We must do what God asks of us and do it joyously, or at least courageously, and not only that, but we must love the will of God and all the obligations that this entails, whether it be to tend pigs all of our lives, or to do the most abject thing in the world, if need be. For in whatever sauce God places us, it must be all one to us. In this lies the height of the perfection to which we must tend, and he who most nearly approaches it carries off the prize."

The good God has a great variety of sauces. . . . Oh, He has a magnificent assortment: white sauces, sauces sweet, spiced, pepper-laden, piquant, bitter! He knows how to serve them at just the right time with a profusion worthy of His liberality. He excels in choosing precisely the sauces that we do not want, those that are most bitter to our taste. "Whatever sauce God serves us, it must be all the same to us." I know religious who believe themselves confirmed in Holy Indifference, yet who would rebel if asked to tend pigs for even a day. I beg of you, abandon yourselves to the loving Providence of God.

Let us abandon ourselves, therefore, to the will of God. Great is this virtue, worthy to capture the heart of God. It consists in suffering with patience, above all, our own weaknesses, our own miseries, our own moral infirmities.

Self-surrender is the perfect conformity to the will of God in all that happens to us. Woe to us if we hinder the work of God within our souls, if we oppose His designs, if we dare to attempt to make our personal ideas prevail!

Oh, my dear friends, how happy is that soul that abandons itself to God, delivers itself entirely over to the designs of Divine Providence, depends upon His Divine Heart as its sole support. Such a soul can be certain that it will never be deceived, will never be the victim of the assaults of the demon.

"When God does us the honor of nailing us to the cross beside Himself, the safest way is not to descend, but to remain beside Him."

To each of our prayers, we should add: "Oh, my God, do not listen to me; do not answer my prayer. Follow the designs of Your Wisdom. Do not accommodate Your Will to mine. Had You answered all of my prayers up to today as I originally requested them to be answered, I should already have been plunged into hell."

No, we do not know how to pray. That for which we pleaded would often have been our worst misfortune had God inclined to our will. Let us repeat with St. Augustine: "Cut, burn, slay, Lord, do not spare me in this world, if that I can be happy with You in the next."

My very dear friends, the time has arrived for us to practice self-surrender. You are not to begin practicing this virtue within eight days, a month, or a year, but today. More than ever we are at the mercy of God.

"My God, I deliver myself over to You. I abandon myself to Your Divine Providence. It suffices for me to be and to do what You will for me." Tomorrow, perhaps, this prayer will not be sufficient for you. God has in store for us certain surprises, joyous or sad. Tomorrow may be more than you hope for—or less. Holy Indifference!

SPIRITUAL READING

The Imitation of Christ: Book I, Chapters 2, 24

BOOK III, Chapter 54

BOOK IV, Chapter 7

8. Prince of Darkness

Preparatory prayer: "I will the glory of God, however much it may cost me." During the first week of the *Exercises* of St. Ignatius, he asks us to consider ourselves as the sinners that we are. It is true that the blood of Christ has washed away our sins, but we are to consider what we are of ourselves and in ourselves, as if we had not been pardoned. "But," you will say, "if during these days I am to consider myself as a sinner, how shall I dare turn my eyes upon the Sacred Heart?"

Is not this devotion intended for sinners? Our Lord has taken the initiative. He has made a promise especially for sinners. "Sinners will find in My Heart an infinite source of mercy." At the moment that I am most culpable, even before repentance has touched my heart, You, even then, invite me to have recourse to You. Does it require an ocean to wash away my sins? Your Heart is that boundless ocean, without shores, without limits. As a spark thrown into the waves of the sea disappears without leaving a trace, so it is with the transgressions of the most culpable soul, once embraced within that Divine Heart.

In order to fix our imagination, let us behold our soul enclosed within the prison of our body, our soul degraded by sin, our body and soul exiled amid ferocious animals unleashed against us—surrounded by nature in revolt against mankind. I ask for the graces that I wish to obtain, not only for sorrow, contrition, the firm determination to avoid sin, but above all for shame, confusion. My degradation began through pride; my perfection must be initiated through humility.

My dear friends, I invite you to listen for an instant to the most horrible of all beings: the prince of the damned. Approach nearer to him; he wants to make you join in his sentiments. "In heaven I was the Prince of Light, the model of divine beauty. I was raised high above my fellows in glory. I was at the head of the angelic phalanxes; I was radiant. The cherubim admired the marvelous beauty with which the Creator had endowed me. I was crowned with glory in the midst of the seraphim. And now! Behold to what an abyss of shame I have descended! Behold how I am degraded! I am horrified at my own self. I spread terror and fright everywhere. I am the most hideous, the most despised being in all creation.

"Oh, if you could only realize to what a summit of happiness I had been raised! I was surrounded with delights; God refused me nothing. I was submerged in happiness, inundated with glory. Now, behold into what a deluge of misfortune I am plunged. All the powers within me are objects of indescribable torture. I am plunged into flames that burn but never destroy. I know only rage and despair. I am he who cannot love. I detest my Creator, now become an implacable enemy. I detest myself, but lack the power to annihilate myself.

"Oh, if you but knew to what a summit of virtue God had permitted me to ascend. All within me was innocence and wisdom. I knew only holy thoughts. No temptation had ever assailed my heart. I was the most holy of all the angelic choirs. And now! Behold into what evil estate I am plunged! What degradation! And all this for a sin of thought that lasted but an instant. A thought of pride! I turned against God with a jealous eye. I am a rebel.

"I lifted myself against Him, my Creator. I desired to elevate myself above Him. In my folly, I said to myself:

Non serviam, I will not serve Him. I willed to be equal with God. I disdained to bow down before Him. Fool that I was! God is just; God is holy; God is redoubtable. My sin condemned me to this eternal abyss!"

My friends, we can all say: "I am more culpable than he is." This angel committed but one sin—one sin of thought. He only abused his liberty once. And I? Look at me! How many times have I transgressed? He did not abuse the sacraments—but I, how many times? He did not behold Innocence expire upon a cross for him—and I? I am more culpable than he.

You will find that sometimes you will not be treated according to your merits, real or supposed. Sometimes you will not have proper respect paid to you, to you who are a refugee from hell. If God had treated you as you deserve, where would you be today?

Let us interview Adam, expelled from the earthly Paradise, tearful, sad, somber, ashamed. Let us approach and share his painful thoughts: "Oh, if you could but know the glory with which God had clothed me in the earthly Paradise! All animals recognized my dominion over them. And now! Behold how I am fallen, uncrowned. Now all Nature revolts against me. I am plunged into ignominy.

"If you could but know to what a summit of happiness God had raised me! Yes, if you could but know my former happiness! I did not know suffering. All the powers of my being enjoyed unalterable happiness. My heart overflowed with the most holy joy. Now I am condemned to the sorrows of earth while awaiting the eternal flames. So it is: regret devours my heart and mind. There is no remedy. Behold the ills which assail all of my children. Look within the hospitals and behold the marks of suffering: the innocent children, the aged, all victims of diseases brought upon them through me. Consider the shipwrecks, the epidemics, the conflagrations, the victims on the field of battle! All evils that followed in the wake of my sin. The deluge of maledictions that weighs upon the world as a result of my sin!

"Ah, if you but knew how holy I was, how immaculate! No stain had ever, even for an instant, tarnished the radiance of my soul. Only the purest thoughts filled my imagination. And now! I am delivered over to assaults of the most shameless passions. Look upon the degradation of my children. I beheld the dead body of my son, Abel, slain by his brother, perfidious Cain. How many shameful things have disgraced my children. Look within the prisons; behold degradation on every side. All, all is the work of sin . . . the result of my one sin. My punishment is just."

Let us, for an instant, observe a soul in hell for only one mortal sin. Many people consider it a scandal that there is a hell for souls guilty of but one mortal sin. Let us reflect upon a soul that dies on the very day on which it has committed one mortal sin. That does not mean that God awaited the consummation of that first sin to withdraw that soul from the time of mercy. God is not to be thought of as one seeking His prey in order to precipitate it into eternal suffering. No! But there is a moment when, according to the laws laid down by the Creator, the thread of an existence is to be severed. That moment is not known to us; it will, therefore, always take us by surprise. "If thou failest in thy watch, I will come upon thee like a thief; thou shalt never know the hour of my coming to thee."

Are you demanding that God perform a miracle to prolong a life against the laws of nature, because this person has committed a sin? "Be ye always ready," said the Master. Nature obeys laws marked with the seal of her Creator. It is true that God knows the hour and the minute when your life will be cut short. If you have the misfortune to commit a mortal sin just before that supreme instant and you do not have the mercy of receiving pardon, you will, alas, go into eternal fire. That sudden death might even be a last mercy from God. He may foresee that that soul, instead of committing but one mortal sin, might continue on and commit thirty, forty, or more mortal sins and thus deserve to be condemned to an increase of suffering. We must try to understand the ways of Divine Providence which are always based upon mercy and forbearance.

Let us represent to ourselves this person in the depth of hell for just one mortal sin. Let us approach and listen: "Oh, if you but knew with what glory God had crowned me! My youth was so fair, so pure. I was venerated as promising to become a saint. And now! Behold how I am dishonored. I, who was once surrounded by honor, by respect. Now I see myself among the damned, the prey of Satan. Demons pursue me with indescribable rage. Consecrated souls arouse their rage and animosity more than any other of the damned. Oh, if you but knew how happy I was in the religious life. I experienced days of radiance, of heavenly peace. And now? Behold to what an excess of misery I am doomed for all eternity. See the fire that tortures me; see the pain of loss, of regret, that will never end.

"If you but knew what was my perfection, my virtue, at one time. For years my soul knew only holy thoughts. I made progress in perfection. I aspired to holiness of life. And now? I, beloved of the God of all holiness, I chose evil, knowingly, willingly. How I boast of sin amid the mire of vice. For one sole sin God justly chastises me. He has placed me at an inexorable distance from Himself for all eternity. He is justified!"

My dear friends, let us close with a fervent prayer to our Lord to aid us in acquiring the virtue of perseverance in His Divine Grace.

9. That Rebel—Myself

PREPARATORY PRAYER: "My God, do
not see anything in my heart except the desire to work for
your greater glory." I ask for the grace that I wish to
obtain.

We have asked for profound shame and humiliation.
Now we shall ask for contrition, a sincere sorrow, ever
deeper, even more heartfelt. Our contrition of a year ago
will not suffice; neither will that of yesterday.

"My God, grant me a hatred for sin—a strong hatred,
a hatred as deep as the grief that it caused You."

I am going to glance over my whole life, survey the
past, see again all the various phases of my life, from infancy through childhood and adolescence, up to the present. I shall survey the places where I have lived, my family
home, the schools I have attended, the social groups in
which I moved, the world, the novitiate, my religious life
or my occupation, my interests, my friends. I shall pass
in review all the places in which I have lived, the work in
which I have been successively engaged, all the charges
entrusted to me.

I see faults, clouds of sins that pass back and forth before my eyes, in the home, the street, the countryside, the
city, the religious house. Everywhere I behold faults;

everywhere remorse rises up to accuse me. It is a frightful picture. The eyes of my conscience bring all of that before me. What will it be when I am confronted with such a hideous revelation before the tribunal of God? What day is there in my whole life in which I have not, in some way, offended God? There is not even one.

I shall consider my faults in themselves, independently of the pardon accorded them by God. Even when a certain fault is not forbidden by a definite precept, is it not, in itself, repulsive, ugly? The least falsehood, is it not as repulsive as the greater one? Should I not regard it with horror? What would be my confusion if, one day, I were to be looked upon as a liar? Falsehood! How repulsive I find it! How I despise a person known to be a liar.

The sixth commandment: how shameful, infamous, are such faults. Even those who have no faith instinctively loathe such sins. To accuse persons of them is to bring against them revolting, odious insults.

To belittle one's neighbor! What is more detestable, evil? To misinterpret his intentions! What pettiness, baseness of heart is concealed in uncharitableness? Such is sin in its intrinsic ugliness.

What am I in the face of all these faults and sins? If I should disappear from the earth, who would miss me? Am I really good for anything here below? I am lost in the anonymous mass. What am I in comparison with the billions of people who inhabit the earth? I am but a miserable atom lost in the multitude. What am I in comparison with all the children of Adam? I do not count. What am I in comparison with the angels? In relation with God, before whom angels and men are as nothing? What am I? A poor nothing, doomed, of myself, to weakness, to misery, who dares to despise, to violate, the divine law of my Creator.

Who is this offended God? This God of infinite grandeur, of adorable majesty, who is all-powerful, could have destroyed me at the moment of my sin as easily as I destroy an insect under my foot. He is a God of glorious majesty, of sanctity, who has a horror of the least stain, of the least defilement. He is the God who has loaded me with benefits, the God who has every right to my gratitude. It is He whom I have outraged. It is He whom I caused to suffer and to die. I am surrounded on all sides by the humble creatures of God who serve me, as well as by the angels on high who protect me. I ask myself: "How is it that the creatures of God have not leagued themselves against me to destroy me? How is it that the angels continue to bring me good thoughts, inspirations? How is it that my patient guardian angel consents to remain by my side when I have outraged him a thousand times? How is it that he has not drawn a flaming sword with which to destroy me?

At the moment of sin, my soul, which the waters of baptism had rendered so beautiful, so immaculate, emerges with the most infectious evil. My soul becomes vile and repulsive. And God? This offended God is my Saviour. It is He who commanded all creatures to serve me, to befriend me. It is He who infused so much compassion into the hearts of his priests and religious and inspired them to devote their lives to my welfare.

My very dear friends, here is a sentence seemingly simple, but which contains profound significance: "My daughter, the least faults of souls consecrated to Me pain Me infinitely more than do the crimes of great sinners."

This is proof of the tenderness with which our Lord loves us. It proves that we are the cherished ones of His adorable Heart, that we are in very truth members of His family. This thought should suffice to inflame our hearts, to awaken a lively horror of the least imperfection. "My daughter, the least faults of souls consecrated to Me pain Me more than do the crimes of great sinners." There speaks the voice of love.

Is it not true that when we love, that person can cause us pain in many and unexpected ways? A cold glance from a friend is felt far more keenly than recriminations from a stranger.

Let us close with a colloquy at the foot of the cross. There, prostrate at the feet of the adorable Victim, let us ask His pardon. Let us ask of Him that degree of humiliation, of confusion, of contrition, that He wishes to find in us. Let us thank Him for our faith in His holy cross.

It is told of a criminal who, upon mounting the scaffold, was handed a crucifix to kiss, that he refused it, saying, "I have never believed in that. Had I believed in it, I would not be where I am today."

My God, I am at the foot of Your cross, at Your Calvary. I weep over my sins, my ingratitude. Now I comprehend all their ugliness, their enormity. I beg You, oh, my God, to give me an ever-increasing sorrow for them, and the grace in the future to avoid the least imperfection.

10. Abode of Darkness

My DEAR FRIENDS, we have already asked for shame and confusion over our sins. The starting point of conversion is the overthrowing of the vessel of our pride, the principle of all evil. We have asked for contrition—hatred of our faults. We must now make a firm decision; we must find the means of strengthening, of fortifying our souls, communicating to them a holy energy. That is the reason why we are about to meditate upon hell. It is of the highest importance to give a little ballast to our resolutions in order to guarantee them against our own weakness. There are certain times in our lives when it is indispensable for us to know how to tremble.

"There are hours," said St. Teresa of Avila, "when the most perfect souls, souls prepared to accept any torture rather than to commit sin, are so assailed by temptations that they appear to themselves to be weakening, that it seems they will succumb in spite of themselves. They must, then, tremble in fear; if not, their fall is assured. The eternal abyss is opening at their feet."

This horror of hell is so necessary that St. Ignatius prostrated himself before God saying, "My God, penetrate me with such fear that if, one day, in a moment of folly, I come to forget Your love, at least the memory of Your justice will hold me back from the edge of the abyss."

St. Paul says: "I fear that, after having preached to others, I myself may become a castaway." Do I not have to tremble? Am I more sure of myself than St. Paul?

Let that one arise who is able to say, "As for me, I am sure of not going to hell." St. John Chrysostom kept in his sleeping room a canvas depicting the torments of the damned. Every morning upon awakening he paused a moment to consider that picture, in order to excite himself to constancy in the service of God. He, the great servant of God, trembled for himself, and I, do I dare feel assured of my perseverance?

Listen to St. Bernard speaking to his religious: "Descend, while alive, into hell, in order not to descend there after your death."

I shall imagine myself to be on the brink of hell. I measure its length, its width, its depth. I hear horrible cries. I see the whirlwind of flames. . . . This is not a vain imagination. While I am speaking, there are legions of souls tortured in the flames. Others, now falling into the infernal braziers, are, at this very moment, becoming acquainted with the never-ceasing torments of hell.

"Oh, my God, grant that, if I should ever come to forget Your love, that at least the memory of Your justice will hold me back from the abyss."

In these meditations, St. Ignatius taught a new method: the application of the five senses. This method is suitable for a certain type of person in whom the imagination is very active. Generally speaking, it is the easiest method. It is we, ourselves, who are to make this meditation. I shall simply discuss the points. It is a personal work for each one.

Sight! What is it that we see? I see the somber dungeons of hell, eternal horror. I see whirlwinds of fire and smoke. I see the damned lying upon burning coals. I see demons throwing themselves avidly upon a religious or upon a devout lay person fallen from the arms of God into hell. I see the accomplices in my sins: companions, friends. I see Satan, prince of the damned, tormenting the poor despairing souls. I see the damned whom I have known, with whom I have lived; upon their features I can trace the maledictions of God.

How terrible it is to fall into the hands of an avenging God! I see the damned, their hearts torn by remorse. . . . They long to annihilate themselves, to disappear forever. Mountains fall upon us! Hills destroy us! Horrible spectacle! Bodies that have sinned, victims of voluptuousness, expiate by their eternal sufferings the pleasures of a moment.

Hearing! What do I hear? Blasphemies, sarcasms, cries of rage and of despair. I hear Satan who repeats his *Non Serviam*—I shall not obey—the cry of revolt. I hear the Jews who cried, "May His blood fall upon us and our children." I hear these words: "Woe to him who scandalizes the least of my little ones. It would be better for him if a millstone were placed about his neck, and he were cast into the depths of the sea." I hear the selfish rich who cry:

"I am tormented in this fire; give me but a drop of water to quench this thirst which devours me. My tongue and my body dry up, but are not consumed." I hear all the damned who cry: "The worm that devours us will never die. We have merited our punishment." I hear the sacrilegious: "He who eats the flesh of Christ unworthily, eats to his own condemnation! Cursed be the day of our birth."

I hear the eloquent voice of God, penetrating even into the depths of hell: "How many times have I desired to save you, and you would not? Away from me, evil ones, into eternal fire!" I hear the "Always! Never!" Always to suffer! Never to be comforted! Always to curse God! Never to love Him! Always to be plunged into despair! Never to have even one ray of hope!

Smell! I experience an insupportable odor which makes my very heart turn over. I am there in the midst of corruption, of slime. This delicate organ of sense that has always willed only to breathe delicious perfumes is now plunged into an atmosphere of corruption, of putrefaction.

Taste! I taste the bitterness of sin, of remorse. I taste all that is horrible in the malediction of God. I taste the bitterness of despair.

Touch! Approach this bed: it is marked with your name. Touch these glowing coals! Extend yourself upon this white and red bed—the white and red of coals glowing with greater heat than you have ever experienced. Touch the blazing feet, the flaming hands of the damned, cursing and blaspheming God, although they know full well that only their obstinacy in sin has brought them to this terrible condition.

We shall close this colloquy by throwing ourselves at the foot of the cross of our Lord. We shall inquire of ourselves how it is that we are not yet in hell. We shall hear our guardian angel reply to us: "If you are not now prey to the flames of justice, you owe it solely to the Heart of

your God. How many times would justice have thrown
you into hell, but His Heart has intervened. He has allowed mercy to triumph over justice." What have I done
to repay so incomparable a blessing? What am I doing today during this series of conferences? What shall I do for
the future?

11. The Sins of Consecrated Souls

PREPARATORY PRAYER: The same, but
made with more fervor, more sincerity. We can demand
the third grace we have solicited: contrition, a firm purpose
of amendment.

It is easily our own fault if we tremble before the
thought of hell. There is a practical way in which to reassure ourselves. Our Lord said—and He cannot deceive us—
"None of those who are especially devoted to My Heart
shall perish."

Is it difficult to be devoted, to be consecrated, to the
Heart of Jesus? A pledge of predestination is offered to us.
Many souls before the tribunal of God will send up cries
of astonishment: "Oh, had I but known. It would have
been so easy and so sweet to have devoted myself to the
Adorable Heart of Jesus."

Now do you understand why, before each conference,
I direct your thoughts and your hearts toward the Heart
of our Lord? How happy I should be if this series of conferences would be, for some of you at least, the starting
point, the revelation, of a more intimate devotion, and
one more practical, toward the Sacred Heart of Jesus.

To fix your imagination, represent to yourself the

chapel where you made your vows. There you prostrated yourself before the altar, at the feet of our Lord, offering Him your promises.

At the same time, the demon, driven back into an obscure corner, ground his teeth and prepared a plan that promised him revenge for this victory over him. It is certain that your vocation excited his rage, and is worth the many temptations that you would not have had in another vocation. Yes, on the day of your vows, the devil was angered, exasperated. He sought to know your weakest points in order to prepare his traps, counting upon the most vulnerable places in your armor to aid him in achieving success. From that moment he has not ceased to prowl about your soul, to circulate around you, like a roaring lion seeking a prey to devour—a delicious prey—the soul of a religious. The sins of a religious are more grievous in relation to himself than sins of the people in the world.

The sin of the religious is more grievous in relation to God because it betrays His more sacred rights. You belong to Him; and not only because He created you, redeemed you; not only because through baptism you have become the temple of the Holy Spirit; not only because He placed His seal upon you at confirmation; not even because He has visited you and vivified your heart in Holy Communion; but because He claims full possession of your heart, because He has chosen you, because He has placed sacred vows upon your lips.

The Church has consecrated you. If anyone strikes you, he commits a sacrilege, he profanes a holy thing. If a spot of earth appears upon your clothing, it is a small thing. If it is thrown upon a ciborium or an ostensorium, it would be a horrible desecration. That is another reason why the devil is so enraged against you; he sees in you something that belongs to God. He sees in you the seal of God. You are consecrated to God; you belong to Him by a special right. When a religious falls into the depth of hell, the demons shout with joy. That is the sole pleasure that demons are enabled to experience: they count it a princely success to be able to drag into the mire a soul consecrated to God.

The sin of a religious is more grievous against God because He has dowered him with greater blessings. Have you ever realized what you owe to God? It is amazing that so few recognize their debt to Him.

At your birth, God, so to speak, leaned over your cradle. He saw in you a future religious. How many graces has He royally bestowed upon you since that moment! You owe your vocation to Him. He has always dealt with you as with a future religious, inasmuch as He had a predilection for you. From your infancy He has watched over you with jealous love, up to this moment.

Our Lord said to Himself: "This soul will console Me for the others who fail." Alas, Lord, what actually happened? This favored soul outraged You, became Your executioner.

The sin of the religious is more grievous because it wounds a more sensitive love. Our Lord is especially sensitive to all that comes to Him from a consecrated soul. The sacrifices of others are acceptable to Him, but they do not touch His Heart as do your sacrifices. He reserves His tenderest regards for you. He turns toward His spouses: "My son, my daughter, you at least will console My Heart. The consolations that I receive from those in the world are, for the most part, colorless, insipid. You, at least, I count upon to console My Heart." Jesus is sensitive to all that comes to Him from us. Above all, He is sensitive to sin, to offenses. This thought should penetrate our hearts with deep emotion. "The least offense from the soul of a religious, a consecrated soul, causes Me more pain than the crime of sinners." It is the cry of love.

The treasure of a vocation belongs not only to you, but also to your family, to your neighbors. It was given to you for the salvation of the souls confided to you. If you become culpable, you will be, not their salvation, but their damnation. What responsibility!

The sins of a religious are more serious as regards himself or herself. Who falls from the highest point, falls the lowest. A religious who falls makes a frightful descent. One of our Fathers gave a mission to some thousand women in prison for divers crimes. All followed the exercises assiduously; many were touched by his words and expressed themselves as determined to lead a good life thereafter. That is, all but one. Her companions sought to influence her with words, advice, examples; all were useless. Then the Father learned that she was a former religious who had been in an austere Order for twelve years. She had appeared to be fervent. One day she abandoned her vocation. Once back in the world, passions carried her away. She then came under the equally austere rule of justice. She had resisted divine grace.

My God, protect me! Prostrate at the foot of the cross, let our hearts speak of the past that we may ask for pardon. Let us express our sincerest gratitude to God for having supported, pardoned, loved us, so far. Let us speak of the future to ask our Lord to preserve us from every fault, however slight, and to grant us that delicate and sensitive love which He has the right to expect from us.

Blessed is that weakness
which nourishes humility
and obliges us to place all
our confidence in God.

DE LA COLOMBIERE

Those hours in which we
despair are the hours of
God.

ST. SOPHIE BARAT

12. Our Spiritual Temperature

MY DEAR FRIENDS, the saints know
our combats. They also had repugnances, interior struggles,
failures. St. Margaret Mary, being no longer able to struggle against herself, one day breathed out her plaints at the
feet of Jesus: "I can go on no longer, Lord. My will is too
weak to overcome these attacks." Our Lord replied to her:
"Hide your will in the Wound of My Side. From thence
you will draw the force to conquer. It is there that wills
are tempered."

It is well for us to experience our weakness. Our Lord
knows this and sometimes takes the liberty of testing us to
permit us to find out who are His real friends. But then,
when that happens, how we sulk! Instead of suffering in
silence, instead of smiling, we frown. We become disillu-
sioned, discontented. "It was not in this spirit that I expected to attend these conferences." But smile, therefore,
at God. Be content with Him. "It suffices me, oh, my Beloved, to be what you wish me to be." Am I just the contrary of what I would wish to be? It is well. The less there

is of our own choice in ourselves, in our spiritual exercises, in our lives, the more there will be of true devotion.

"If it were not for Your will, oh, my God, I would give up these conferences. But I desire to suffer for You; therefore, I accept the present moment with all its sufferings, its disappointments. Content Yourself at my expense. Glorify Yourself through my afflictions."

We have already learned, in the school of St. Ignatius, of three little practices designed to reform our spiritual exercises. Here is another. Père Chaignon, preaching a retreat to us students, told us: "My children, do you wish to be saints? Then always make the sign of the cross well." I opened my eyes wide. Was I dreaming? Become a saint through making the sign of the cross well? I did not, at that time, understand his meaning. Later, I understood it.

I believe that if our signs of the cross were always made as if in the presence of God, rather than as if we were chasing away flies, they would open for us the Heart of God. Each sign of the cross brings us nearer to God. For each sign of the cross, well made, there is one added degree of eternal glory. Each sign of the cross, made with devotion, deposits within your heart another degree of love, which you would not have had without it.

During the *Exercises* of St. Ignatius for the first week, devoted to the past days of our lives, our hearts may become narrowed. It is but natural. While there is much fruit to be drawn from these meditations, not all of it is bitter. There is also much of sweetness to be extracted from them. Let us realize that our Lord counts upon our generosity to expiate the sins committed by our families, our neighbors, the entire universe.

Do you desire to be victims of the Heart of Jesus? Could you desire a greater honor? Our Lord said to St. Margaret Mary, "My daughter, I seek a victim for My Divine Heart." During the carnival, when so many sins of all kinds were committed, our Lord said to her, "My daughter, behold days of sin, days of hell. You, at least, console My Heart." Could I, even I, console the Heart of God? Why not? Is our Lord any the less sensitive to your reparation than He is to your faults?

What are you doing to save souls? To expiate the sins of the world? To repair the outrages offered to our good Master? What are you doing to prevent sin? To make reparation for sin is good—to prevent it is better.

Good is done without any commotion; noise never helps. Good is performed gently, quietly. It is difficult for you to see the good you are doing to those with whom you come in contact. Years must pass before it becomes apparent, before it blossoms upon earth. Do not seek to discover the good you are doing. Priests see that in the confessional. There is no comparison between the soul that has received a Christian education and one that has had only a secular education. How much easier it is to bring the former back to Christian principles! There is another consoling side to the vocation of those who teach youth. It is that each day you are preventing many mortal sins. How precious this is! It is worth all that it has cost.

St. Ignatius had a hospice built to shelter some women of disorderly lives. People said to him: "You are wasting your time. These women are under your supervision at night; but when daybreak comes, they will return to their vices." St. Ignatius replied, "I would exchange the labor of all my sons throughout all time, to prevent one mortal sin." Each teacher can say: "However many may be the disagreeable features that I encounter in my life, in my work, I am certain that I have, at least, prevented one mortal sin." To save souls takes its toll of us. It is worth all it costs.

St. Francis Xavier was walking through a forest one day with a man whom he sought to convert, but his efforts had been in vain. Suddenly, the saint said to him, "Wait here for me just a minute." A few moments later his companion heard unusual sounds. Suspecting that the Father had met with robbers who were maltreating him, he ran to find him. What did he see? St. Francis Xavier was lacerating himself with the branches from a thorn tree. "Father, Father, what are you doing?" cried the man. "I am accepting, in your place, the strokes of divine justice. Go back now to your sinful pleasures, to your forbidden amusements." The man was conquered. The words he heard, the abnegation he saw practiced for his sake, won his heart to God. What are you doing to prevent mortal sin?

During the French Revolution, St. Gaetano expired from grief at thought of all the souls being precipitated into hell. St. Ignatius said, "May my body be rent into a thousand pieces; may I be detained in purgatory until the end of the world, providing that one sinner might thereby be saved."

One source of reparation, sweet in itself and at the same time agreeable to God, is gratitude. There are certain persons who never commit mortal sin, yet who are ungrateful. They complain to their spiritual directors. They behold their lives in a somber light, enveloped in a dark cloud. They are bored in the service of God. My dear friends, you should thrill with joy, should fall upon your knees to send forth your *alleluias* of gratitude to the God who has accorded you the greatest of all graces—the grace to live in His love. But you, you complain. You are sad, discontented. Leave tears to those who have had the misfortune to offend God.

Our Lord said to Himself: "This soul I shall treat as a privileged one. I have confidence in its gratitude." Instead, see how that soul conducts itself—as if it were disinherited. Ah, at the last day you will say: "Had I but known how good God was to me."

There are souls who would be consumed with envy at

the sight of your privileges. How is it that you have so
low an opinion of what God has done for you? Your resistance to sin? To what do you owe it? Do you think it
comes from your own will power? Is it due to your great
love of virtue? To the energy of your character? To the
elevation of your sentiments? What a mistake! The best
endowed natures fall into the most abominable sins.

Render thanks, therefore, to God, to whom you owe
your state of grace. The demon has nothing so much at
heart as his endeavor to throw a veil over the better side of
our natures. Then behold the poor soul swimming in bitterness, in rancor, all aspirations lost, all impetus for good
nullified. How satisfied is the demon when he beholds a
soul playing his own game! How he applauds himself!
Only the devil has a right to be sad. And what a good
right he has!

The first day was given to the study of the lesson of
indifference; the second day, to the study of mortal sin;
the third day was devoted to the lesson on contrition. Today we shall consider tepidity. We shall examine its precise nature, its effects, and its remedy. Tepidity is the
intermediate state between hot and cold, heat and frigidity.
God says, "Because you are lukewarm and neither hot nor
cold, I will begin to spew you out of my mouth."

Spiritual warmth is charity which expresses and main-
tains itself through the medium of actions. God is charity—
pure love. In the degree in which we approach Him we
become conscious of this warmth. The soul that is plunged
into mortal sin is plunged into an icy coldness, far, far
from the ardent flames of His Love. This is the state of
coldness toward God.

But here is a soul that is not living in mortal sin, that
is not given over to the demon, but which oscillates between the demon and God. It is tepid. Divine grace is
diminished little by little. A mysterious descent begins,

leading into mortal sin. Nature invades the whole of the spiritual life. Tepidity is that state of the soul in which it habitually gives itself over to venial sin. I know well that I have this or that bad habit, or that I tell small falsehoods, that I neglect my exercises of devotion, that I waste the time God has given me.

"Oh, I fear mortal sin, but these shortcomings are only venial." Venial sins committed of deliberate purpose, habitual venial sins which one does not take the time to correct: these are the acrid fruits of tepidity.

We must, of course, distinguish between deliberate venial sins and those committed through fragility, through a kind of surprise, not complete, perhaps, but of which the knowledge is not exactly foreseen. Suppose that I am about to say a word against charity. When it is already upon my lips, my conscience utters a cry of warning; but I seem to be urged on by a certain curious necessity. The propriety of the moment, of the situation, impels me not to forego my words. I lack the moral force to check the uncharitable expression.

There are other venial sins more striking. Conscience speaks well in advance. I have some revenge in my heart that demands expression. I think it over and accept the responsibility for this fault. I have had time to reflect. The occasion presents itself. I take advantage of it to let it be known that I have been offended, wounded, in order to get even with the perpetrator of the offense against me. I say to myself: "This is not a serious sin; it is only a venial sin."

St. Francis de Sales said: "One venial sin committed through malice and of set purpose causes more injury to the soul than a hundred venial sins committed through fragility."

This understood, what then is the state of a soul which commits venial sins through fragility? The Blessed Virgin

alone escaped these miseries. The fervent soul may sometimes fall into deliberate venial sin. But the fervent soul
has no excuses to make for its faults. "I have committed
many venial sins," said Père Dupont, "but I have never
lived in peace with them."

St. Teresa of Avila was once asked what constitutes a
fervent community. She replied, "A fervent community
is not one in which there are never any violations of
the Rule, but one in which such breaches are noted and
punished."

Here is an exact description of tepidity: boiling water,
in cooling, goes through a succession of phases, a progres-
sive diminution of heat, a series of mysterious alterations
gradually effected. The demon and our own concupiscence
impel us gradually into tepidity. He knows better than to
try, at the beginning, to bind us with the chains of hell.
He seeks first to bind us with a silken thread, then with
a cord, until one day the soul finds itself bound by a chain
to hell. It may be a natural antipathy not repressed. There
are some natures so poorly suited for living together that
it takes almost a miracle for them to live in peace. Let us
watch out for this. It is easy to let antipathy ferment,
though it be but an atom's weight. Later, uncharitable
thoughts arise: this is the silken thread. Then, one refuses
to speak—behold the cord! At last the sentiment has grown
so strong that it refuses to pardon; hatred has come to life
within the heart. Behold the chain.

An identical danger may be found in the opposite excess. Here is a person whom I esteem, I admire. This sentiment takes on too natural, too emotional a shade. Caresses
follow: this is the thread. Later on, one frequently seeks
out that person. There are intimate conversations alone.
Mutual admiration increases until at last the day arrives
when both are bound in the chain from the abyss.

When the demon wants to conquer a soul, he does not

at first propose that it commit mortal sin. He knows well
that such a proposal would be repulsed at once. First, he
studies the weakest point of that soul in order to open a
breach there. He presents natural satisfaction, causes it to
commit what appear to be minor faults for which the same
soul would have vigorously reproached itself some months
previously. Now, under the insinuating influence of Satan,
they appear as mere nothings. Our comprehension of spiritual things, of those values which were so well understood in
the beginning of our conversion, is now obscured.

A veil develops between things spiritual and the soul.
Faults persisted in enervate the will. Little by little, the
soul loses its delicacy of conscience; remorse itself is dulled.
Let us be on the watch! Tepidity is a germ to which none
of us is immune. Let us stifle the germ before it can bring
an unholy brood into existence. Small negligences continue
to multiply. We no longer respond immediately to the call
of duty. We are no longer scrupulous in our actions. We
permit ourselves to become critical of those who surround
us.

What disorder follows in one's whole life! The holy
will of God is no longer the incentive of our thoughts,
words, and actions; rather, we obey nature's whims. One
is not now faithful to obligations as one would have been
in days of fervor. Duties are neglected. Tepidity is consti-
tuted of a certain softness, a dissipation of spirit that relaxes
us instead of inspiring to greater effort. We begin to avoid
all constraint—and so glide gently down the fatal incline.

The definite sign of tepidity, that which characterizes
it above all else, is the absence of the supernatural. We see
others faithful to their duties, their obligations, but we find
excuses for our own laxity. "That is for the perfect," we
decide, "but as for me . . . well . . . I hope to be saved,
of course, but, after all, one needs a little relaxation." Thus,
we judge everything from the natural point of view. We

give a purely natural meaning to the finest actions. There is a pointed lack of the supernatural in our affections. We become disgusted with God in our religious exercises, above all, in our examen of conscience. There is a secret but marked antipathy among tepid souls for the daily examen. "I can carry out all my exercises of devotion except the particular examen."

One well-known sign is a secret envy of fervent souls. Their courageous lives are the condemnation of our cowardice. Formerly, we loved and admired that fervent person; but after we have glided down the incline of tepidity, we have only a blind rancor for him or her. There is a lack of the supernatural in our words. We appraise all things from the standpoint of worldly wisdom. We say with the world: "Blessed are those who are coddled, honored, given consideration." We criticize the intentions, depreciate the examples of the fervent, and find ways to ascribe their fervor to natural motives.

We follow the daily routine of our lives, but at a distance, so to speak. A tepid soul avoids everything that bores it in order to follow the leadings of purely natural attractions. By instinct, such a soul tends toward all things that give pleasure. She seeks the society of the tepid because their tepidity seems to justify her own conduct. How excellent the devout life formerly appeared to her! What do we think now of charity and the delicacy of that holy virtue? Alas, everything in our poor life has changed.

The effects of tepidity are appalling. The Holy Spirit says to us: ". . . you are wretched and miserable and poor and blind and naked." Yes! Miserable in the face of God, who lets His maledictions fall upon the tepid. He withdraws His consolations; helpless before the enemy, the tepid experience bitterness upon bitterness.

Another effect of tepidity is a rancor against those who are conscientious and fervent. "You are wretched and miserable," said the Holy Spirit, and added, "you are poor and blind and naked."

The fervent soul has but one thought: to amass treasure for heaven. The tepid soul never thinks of spiritual riches; it sees only personal satisfactions that never satisfy it. Such a person has not formally renounced mortifications, but what does he or she actually do about them? Where are his fasts? His penances? Mortifications annoy him. When does he think of edifying his neighbor? How many acts of virtue are omitted? The little good that he does is tainted with self-interest, self-love, spoiled by vanity, impatience, and a hundred other defects.

St. Bernard said: "It is easier to find sinners who will be converted from crime to virtue than religious who will leave tepidity to re-embrace fervor in the service of God." God turns away from the tepid soul whether lay or religious. He rejects it. There is no intimacy between Him and a tepid soul. "Because you are neither hot nor cold, I will spew you out of my mouth."

Certain conditions are necessary to change from tepidity to fervor. The first is *prayer*. Tepid souls do not pray; they recite formulas. That is all. Second, *corresponding with grace*. The tepid soul continually resists grace. Third, the *particular examen*. This last is a very effective means, yet it is precisely this means that inspires the most repulsion in tepid souls. They do not dare to confront themselves, to feel their spiritual pulse. They resemble the unhappy man who avoids returning to his family for fear of meeting with reproaches. The fourth remedy is *mortification*: not only the mortifications which God imposes upon us, but also those we impose upon ourselves.

There is much more to be said regarding tepidity, but that remains the work of our Lord.

SPIRITUAL READING

The Imitation of Christ: Book I, Chapters 6, 21
Book II, Chapters 2, 3
Book III, Chapter 11

13. *"The Tepid Shall Become Fervent"*

W<small>E HAVE</small> three graces for which to ask:

(1) To know my sins, their number, their seriousness;

(2) The grace of recognizing the disorder in my life; and

(3) Knowledge of the world.

Blessed be the day when our Lord annulled the anathema against the tepid. "Because you are neither hot nor cold"—that is to say, because you are tepid—"I will spew you out of my mouth." Our Lord does not spew them from His Heart. "Tepid souls shall become fervent."

At first sight, tepidity would seem to be the obstacle most opposed to devotion to the Heart of Jesus. Is not the devotion to the Sacred Heart a devotion of love? Of heart speaking to Heart? Is it not a devotion all aflame with fervor? And tepidity is a kind of coldness which reigns between two hearts. Yet our Lord said: "Those who honor My Heart, though they be tepid, shall become fervent."

We thank you, oh God, that we still have the power to love You, that we are not excluded from this privileged devotion, that we are still able to invoke You, to throw ourselves headlong into Your divine Heart, and to depend upon its privileges.

Ask of God the grace to know your individual sins. Ask of God the grace to know the number of your sins and their gravity. They are more numerous, and, above all, more serious, than you could ever imagine. We ask the grace to recognize them and to have a horror of them so that we may be driven to avoid them instinctively, without making ourselves take recourse in an appeal to faith or in thoughts of divine justice.

Let us not, however, be discouraged if we find it painful to excite ourselves to this degree of horror for sin, and are obliged to recall the nature of sin and of the punishments that follow in its wake.

Even the saints were not naturally penetrated with horror for their sins. St. Stanislaus Kostka said: "It is a good sign when we feel a horror for sin increasing in our hearts." This is, indeed, the first grace, for which we asked at the beginning of our *Exercises*.

In a colloquy addressed to the Blessed Virgin, suggested in the *Exercises* of St. Ignatius, we ask her to obtain for us the grace to perceive the disorder that reigns in our lives. A frightful disorder fills our lives. This may not always be the result of sins which we find actively present, but of imperfections which have disastrous effects because they prepare the way and incline us to sin. Many souls do not even suspect this, do not even think it to be true. For this reason, St. Ignatius tells us to ask for the grace to recognize the enormity of our sins, venial and mortal. Everyone within the range of my acquaintance may see plainly that I have a certain defect. I alone may be completely blinded to it. Everyone sees, for instance, that I am vain, self-centered, overly sensitive; I alone fail to perceive it.

What disorder there is in our thoughts, our memories, our affections! Our actions are carried out with so much natural eagerness, or with a fostered repugnance. Those actions that please us naturally are done first and with more eagerness, more perfection. From the beginning of my life to the end—thoughts, words, actions, omissions— what do I find? Frightful disorder reigning everywhere! Above all, we must really feel this to be true. We must be affected by it, not merely accept it as an intellectually perceived fact.

In the Jesuit novitiate we found ourselves gathered together from the four corners of France. In consequence, we had exercises in the pronunciation of our common language, in order to smooth out the various regional dialects. Each novice pointed out the defects in his brothers' pronunciation. With some, these defects were so deeply rooted that the criticisms had to be repeated time and time again. How often the same criticisms had to be repeated in order to show those in default how to pronounce correctly the simplest words! Those criticized failed to understand, could not perceive their defective accent, had never even noticed their failings in that regard. It took months of study and of effort, after having had it brought to their attention, before they could correct their accents and speak the language correctly.

So, first, of all, the defects in our lives must be felt interiorly. The disorder might not be culpable, but it must be corrected before it leads to sin. Sin follows upon our indolence, our lightness of mind, our failure to exercise a close discipline over our tongue, our ears, our eyes. Our enemy plays upon our weaknesses; he attacks us through them, and we fall.

In other cases, this disorder is the result of sin. It becomes for the soul a kind of second nature. One must be well-versed in the spiritual life in order to understand these things. We ask, therefore, that we may be enabled to examine ourselves, to understand, to analyze this disorder, so that we can correct it. Everything in our lives must be related to God.

It remains for us to ask for a knowledge of the world.
The world! Our Lord astonishes us when He speaks of it.
The world! It is the environment in which Satan reigns,
where the spirit of domination prevails, where the wisdom
of the world is sovereign. It is a concerted movement of
ideas, of principles, of reasonings, of ways of looking at
things that are condemned by the Gospel. The world!
Even after we have fled from it, we cannot seclude ourselves from its spirit. The spirit of the world penetrates
everywhere. We breathe it in the very atmosphere that
surrounds us. It insinuates itself into the very pores of
our being.

The world esteems riches, exterior advantages. Does
not this spirit even penetrate into religious houses? One
day a penitent of St. Francis de Sales presented himself for
spiritual direction all upset. "Oh, my God," he cried, "I am
lost!"

"How is that?" asked the saint.

"Just now I took up the Gospel and there I read,
'Blessed are the poor.' I have always thought that the rich
were blessed. I read, 'Blessed are those who weep.' As for
me, I have always complained of such people. I read,
'Blessed are those who suffer.' But I have always thought
them to be unfortunate. You see, I am lost!"

How many words shall we have to retract at the tribunal of God! At almost every instant in our conversation,
there enter in purely human reasonings.

One of our missionaries wrote that he had converted
the king's favorite. The king was furious. He summoned
the man to appear before him and gave him the choice of
apostasy or death. At the designated hour the young convert entered the king's presence between two rows of
armed officials. "You have dared to renounce Buddha to
follow the Christ? I demand to know the reason," said

the king. "The reason," the youth replied, "is that Buddha lied."

My dear friends, we are constantly placed between Buddha and Jesus Christ. The ideas, the opinions of the world, are in favor of Buddha against Jesus Christ. Is it Jesus who has lied in recognizing so much deceit in worldly wisdom that He does not permit us to be influenced by the maxims of the world?

What damage this spirit does within communities as well as among devout persons living in the world! At first, it enters imperceptibly, microscopically; then it becomes rooted, and importance is attached to success, to enterprises considered great in the eyes of the world.

Oh, let us ask earnestly that we may recognize, root out, this spirit so contrary to the humble spirit of Jesus Christ, our Master and our Model.

14. *Peace of Mind*

St. RADEGONDA, at the moment of quitting her throne to enter a monastery which she had founded, heard our Lord say, "My daughter, long enough you have remained at My feet; come now to My Heart."

Our Lord likewise repeats to us those reassuring words, "Long enough you have kept yourselves at My feet; come now to My Heart." He invites you to a heart-to-heart communion.

When, following an interview, a spiritual director says, "Go in peace," it is not merely a wish, a pious desire; it is more than that. It is not even a counsel. It is an order.

"Go in peace!" He commands you in the name of God. You are to obey.

"Ah, Father," you reply, "I wish to obey, but Satan is not far away. I know that he awaits me at the door. He whispers in my ears a dozen things, a dozen inquietudes." Refuse to listen to him. All that troubles us unduly comes from the demon.

There are two fruits to gather from the sacrament of penance. The principal one is the grace of God. The second, likewise most precious, is peace. How many souls garner grace, but not peace, from their confessions.

Through the years one comes, unfortunately, to live in a continuous fever of activity. Do you understand what peace is? It is the health of our souls. One can be alive without possessing health, but life without health is a sorry gift.

Do you see this poor paralyzed person? She is helpless. She is unable to exploit the treasures of life. She passes her days languishing, enduring an enervating existence, gradually wasting away. How many souls are in an identical condition! Here is a soul that has not committed a mortal sin for many years; she possesses life, grace. But it is a sad sort of life. There is always an intimate uneasiness within her soul that incessantly gnaws at her heart and mind, paralyzing all spiritual effort. She is never at peace, but is always worried, always interiorly disturbed. Where am I, she asks herself, in regard to contrition, to my past confessions? Go in peace!

Some souls are accomplices of the demon against themselves. They entertain themselves with him, unknowingly. They converse with him, listen to his false counsels, and end by not beholding other than sins in themselves. Deluded souls! At the last great day when they appear before God, when they behold His love and mercy in all their compassion and grandeur, they will cry out: "Oh, had I

but known! Had I but known that God had generously
pardoned all, forgotten all; how I should have passed my
life on earth in peace! How generously disposed I would
have been to accept all sacrifices."

Had I only known? Why do you not believe it now?

Has not your confessor said to you innumerable times,
"Go in peace!"

But the seducer is always there with a hundred propo-
sitions, a hundred falsehoods, which fill the imagination
with a hundred phantoms. When I say to a soul, "Go in
peace," the demon says the opposite; and it is often he who
wins out.

"Sadness," said St. John Chrysostom, "is the devil's
bath."

I beg of you, do not allow yourselves to be enticed into
the devil's bath. The souls whom the devil drives to extremity arrive at that point through sadness. When the
devil finds he cannot bring death to a soul, he endeavors
to ruin its physical or mental health, to weaken its personality, to keep it in a feverish whirl, or to paralyze its energy. Such sickness of the personality is a first step on the
road to death. That is the reason St. Teresa of Avila has
such strictures against melancholy.

There are a multitude of devout souls who have but
one obstacle to their spiritual advancement, to their happiness. It is always that dismal, unhealthy state, the fever
that frets them: "If I but knew that God had pardoned
me." Go in peace. The most frequent temptation for devout souls is sadness, inquietude, anxiety. The danger is
that this is not recognized as a temptation. One believes
that one is listening to the voice of conscience, when it is
but the surly voice of the seducer, always ready to irritate,
to torment, to disquiet, to trouble. The real voice of your
conscience is that of God, but the demon imitates your
conscience in speaking to you. He is incapable of inventing

anything new, but he is adept at imitating. He employs pretexts. It is astonishing how much facility he displays in adapting snares and traps for his subtle purposes, and how souls permit themselves to be taken in by them. All that troubles us unduly comes from the demon.

In this kind of temptation, all becomes suspect which is not the voice of God. His counsel invariably bears within it an atmosphere of peace. And it is only in an atmosphere of peace that we can fully distinguish the tones of that "still, small voice."

I understand perfectly this objection, founded on reason: "It is not my fault if I am tempted." That is true; unfounded sadness is a temptation. But I have the right to say to you, "Do not listen to the tempter. Do not become his accomplice by dealing with him." The great misfortune lies in giving place to the demon by entering into negotiations with Satan. He possesses angelic intelligence and knows only too well how to indoctrinate you quickly. In the beginning of my ministry, in giving a report of my small beginnings to my venerated Father Superior, I said: "I have noted in souls desirous of perfection a strange ailment, which appears to be general and which results in destroying the energy, all the glow, from the service of God. It seems to be worry, sadness."

The holy religious, who had grown gray in the apostolate, gazed at me with close attention. He seemed to drink in my words. Then he replied: "Oh, how happy I am that you have recognized that condition. I beg of you to consecrate your apostolate to lightening and dilating souls, putting them at peace with themselves. I guarantee you, in the name of God, that your apostolate will be blessed and fruitful." I have obeyed him.

St. Teresa of Avila was forty when, in the confessional, she found herself at the feet of a Jesuit, Father Padranos, for the first time. She must have remained there a long time, and her Sisters probably made many acts of patience. Later, she wrote about this occurrence: "What a great thing it is to have the soul in peace and the heart at liberty." The demon has nothing so much at heart as to endanger the liberty of the children of God. St. Teresa's maxim was, "Let nothing trouble you," a maxim of the highest spirituality.

The demon knows well what it means to be discontented—and it is nothing good. Do not ask discontented persons to make a sacrifice for God. They do not know what it is to experience a generous impulse. They are trailing their conscience down a beaten path. "Lord," said David, "when Thou hast dilated my heart, I run in the way of Thy Commandments."

The time has arrived for us to follow the counsel of Père Coudren: "Love God at any cost. To escape His justice, hide yourself within His Heart." Let us go quickly to rest within His Heart. Too long have we trembled before Him.

If tomorrow, upon our awakening, God would find among us only His loving children, what happiness for His Father's loving Heart! Of servants, of slaves, He already has too many. It is not for them that He yearns. I beg of you, let us make an end to the vexations that torment us. The devil fights against peace, against calmness, against our well-being. The devil is a sad, miserable spirit; he cannot endure witnessing our happiness.

St. Teresa of Avila, writing about melancholy people, said, "We take great care not to admit them within our monasteries." Those with sad dispositions are not meant for the religious life. They should be content to walk in the way of the commandments. To run, to fly, in the way of the counsels, we must needs have wings.

St. Philip Neri had a particular affection for happy temperaments. He was averse to sad, morose, narrow, self-centered people. St. Margaret Mary said: "God does everything peacefully. If an inspiration is not marked with His seal of peace, reject it. It comes from the demon."

I admit that when I have a vocation to decide upon, I take extreme care to specify this point. I ask this question seriously, decisively, "Have you an open, joyous temperament? Or do you tend to sadness, to somber thoughts and feelings?"

"Yes, Father, I am often sad. Everything looks black to me."

Think no more of the religious life. It is not for you. However, if the depths of your personality are not sad, you may have a vocation. In order to be fully disposed for sacrifices, for renunciations, it is necessary to have a certain uplift of heart which joy alone can give. The soul is paralyzed by sadness. It drags itself along painfully. I should like very much to preach a modern crusade against sadness.

Our Lord said to St. Margaret Mary: "Know that the demon can never bestow peace upon a soul." Peace is the seal of God. All other virtues can be imitated by the demon. He can even inspire a certain love of God, zeal, humility, all the virtues, in order to deceive in the end and bring the soul to destruction through pride. Only one virtue is excepted: peace.

When we examine ourselves to determine the spirit that animates us, there is one sure sign: are we in peace? Peace is the criterion of our relationship with God. When a thought depresses me, saddens me, makes me feel "on edge," it is more than probable that it proceeds from the demon.

St. Ignatius says to us: "When you are in sadness, in desolation of heart, never make a resolution, not even a good one." You then run great risk of deceiving yourself, for you are then subject to the whims of Satan. You have not the grace to occupy yourself with past happenings. That is a snare in which the demon traps many souls. They

occupy themselves with the past when they should be
preparing themselves for the present or the future. From
January first until December thirty-first, I behold souls
always looking backward, always wrangling with their
past. Take care! You know the fate of the unhappy woman
who left Sodom, but looked back. Many souls are similarly
petrified, though they know it not. Always looking backward! During those moments, grace passes them by. They
fail to profit from the graces made available to them.

15. The Community

M<small>Y</small> <small>DEAR SISTERS</small>, in the Gospels
there is the story of a privileged soul who responded to the
advances of our Lord with amazing ingratitude. We shall
now examine how our Lord conducted Himself toward
this apostle, how He treated him. I speak of St. Thomas.

Had St. Thomas died within the seven days following
the Resurrection, he might have gone straight to hell. He
was not in the community with the other apostles when
our Lord appeared on the evening of the first Easter day;
therein lies his great misfortune. What a misfortune it is
for us to separate ourselves from our community! There,
in the bosom of the community, the graces of God rain
down. If we flee from them, they will not follow us. St.
Thomas wept bitter tears over his absence.

There are religious who desert their community. They
may be present in body, but not in spirit; they retain the
religious habit, but are no longer members of their religious
family. Their affections are elsewhere. For a long time
they have not really lived under their Rule, under obedi-

ence. They live under the same roof, attend the same exercises, but are no longer members of the religious family.

There is a mysterious patrimony of graces that pertain to your community. As long as you are united to your community, you participate in these graces. Do you participate? Have you these rights? Have you turned your back upon your community in spirit? Do you behave with a kind of rancor toward your superiors? Take care. Your Sisters will behold our Lord, and you will not see Him. He will pass by, and you will not even recognize His presence.

Poor, disconsolate Thomas! After the Crucifixion he had not enough tears with which to weep over his grief. He finally returned to the Cenacle. He walked along slowly, sullen, discontented. The other apostles surrounded him, crying out in an outburst of joy: "We have seen the Master! He is risen!" But Thomas could only reply: "I will not believe it. It is all an hallucination." What a contrast! Look at the apostles, how happy, how expansive, they were. One feels the happiness in their hearts even after nineteen hundred years. But Thomas? He was sad, gloomy, discontented. He would not even admit that he was wrong in absenting himself from the Cenacle, from his community. Why? Oh, Thomas, had you not deserted, had our Lord found you among them, you, also, would have seen Him. But now you are offended by the joy of your companions; their fervor gets on your nerves. "No, I do not believe it. You will never get me to accept that," he reiterated. The apostles insisted, pleaded with Thomas not to plunge himself further into the mist of incredulity.

"Do you not recall that the Master promised to arise from the dead? He has never deceived us. He multiplied miracle upon miracle among us. The seals of His tomb were broken; the tomb is empty; the stone was rolled away. He appeared to Magdalen, to Peter, to the disciples at Emmaus, to us all."

"I shall not believe unless I can place my hand in His side, and in the wounds of His hands and His feet. Otherwise I shall not believe." How could this stubborn man impose conditions upon our Lord?

We meet with souls who persist in their incredulity. When they have once taken a step out of their community, they do not want to acknowledge that they were in the wrong. Like Thomas, they become intoxicated by their own obstinacy. I understand why St. Ignatius lists an attachment to one's own opinion as an obstacle to the religious life. It was this that led St. Thomas into doubt. It is this that blinds certain souls. Lower their banner? Give in? Never. They prefer to maintain their personal point of view against all comers.

The unhappy apostle left the community, sad, brokenhearted. During the days that followed, I can see the great-hearted St. John going to visit St. Thomas secretly. I hear him say, "My dearest friend, listen to me, I will tell you everything. He made Himself known to us. He ate in our presence."

"Let me in peace. I do not believe it." The headstrong man!

St. John made no headway. There are those who have no other motive for continuing in their sins than obstinacy in not being willing to acknowledge that they are in the wrong.

I see St. Peter, head of the apostolic college, going to find Thomas: "Listen to me, believe my testimony. I saw Him this morning. He spoke to me. I beg of you not to persist in your stubbornness." Thomas threw Peter an expressive glance. Even Peter was unable to convert this man. Remonstrances fell thick and fast. The Blessed Virgin herself, Queen of the Apostles, spoke to Thomas with all the eloquence of a mother's heart. She exhausted all the resources of her zeal, but remained powerless against his stubborn incredulity. How sad, how unhappy, he was! What a contrast between his gloom and the happiness of the other apostles!

There are souls who imitate St. Thomas. Once they start out on the wrong road, they will not change paths. "I have been given that charge, placed in that House. As long as this continues, I shall not correct myself, I shall not change." There are souls who stand before God in a state of dull and opinionated resistance. "No, I shall not go to Communion as long as I do not obtain a certain grace, or this or that thing." What a pity to see little earthworms setting themselves up against God! There are other souls who appear to have heads of iron, breasts of steel. They base their pride, their "honor," on never giving way; they harden themselves even against God. They dare to withstand everyone; and if our Lord through His adorable graces does not draw them out of their foolishness, they will, one day, become a savory prey for the demons.

Where would Thomas have been, had our Lord treated him according to his deserts? Our Lord humored him with admirable condescension. But we must point out that our Lord did not appear to him until he had returned to his community. Woe to him, had he never returned! Eight days passed. At the end of this time, weary of warring, Thomas returned to the Cenacle. The apostles received him, full of bitterness as he was, and, doubtless, in a sullen mood. And it was within his community that God awaited him.

The apostles were talking among themselves about the Resurrection of the Master, when, behold, He appeared to them! "Peace be to you," came the familiar refrain. He spoke to Thomas: "Come, examine My wounds, and be not unbelieving but believing." Thomas was completely upset, beside himself, overcome by shame and confusion: "My Lord and my God!"

Realistically, what right had he to call Jesus his "Lord and his God"? Rather, he deserved to remain plunged in fear and terror, he who had all week long regarded Jesus as an impostor. "My Lord and my God" indeed! Yes, prostrate yourself, blush, strike your breast, flood the earth with your tears. But our Lord acted toward this wayward apostle with a goodness, a condescension, that confounds us. He advanced toward him and said: "Thomas, give Me your hand: place it in the wound in My side, the wounds in My hands and My feet. You have made your own conditions, Thomas; I comply with them. But, I beg of you, doubt no longer, but believe."

What a complete revolution of thought and feeling in the heart of the poor apostle! He felt himself crushed under so much charity, such great tenderness. Not one of the others had had the privilege of placing his hand in the wounds of the Saviour, against the Heart of our Lord. Thomas alone, and at the lowest point of his unbelief, had this right. Down the ages the saints have envied him this privilege.

Such are the rigors of the Divine Master. He revenges Himself by bestowing more and ever greater love. Review the memories of your life. Was there not a day in your life when you proposed certain conditions to our Lord? And was it not He who made the concessions? He who accepted your conditions? He it was who took your hand and placed it within His Heart. Yes, our Lord performed miracles for you. When you were following the path of tepidity, our Lord intervened at precisely the moment when you least deserved His help. He opened His Divine Heart to you, despite your resistance.

Oh, I have known souls who rebelled against God— souls who refused to give themselves to Him—and it was just those retreats, made at that exact time, that were most filled with His graces. It was then that they felt most profoundly His Heart, His love. It is just then that souls come to understand that the power, the omnipotence, of God resides, not in menaces, in threats, but in goodness, that they are not at His feet, not even in His arms, but enclosed within His Heart.

So Thomas learned for all time the depth of the Heart of the Master. Now, oh apostle, you can travel the world over; you can endure martyrdom; you are ready for all heroism; at last, you comprehend truly the Heart of your Master.

A soul which has not learned to know the Heart of God profoundly, which is moved only by fear, has neither strength nor vigor; but once it has plunged its regard into the Heart of God, once it enters into the way of love, that soul is conquered. Oh, the happy conquests of the Heart of Jesus!

We have but this one thing to do: study to comprehend His adorable Heart, to penetrate the mysteries of His tenderness, and to unite our poor hearts with His Heart. In that will consist our happiness for life and for eternity.

16. "This Is My Commandment"

MY DEAR FRIENDS, our Lord came down from heaven to beg the loyalty of all Christians to His Divine Heart. He addresses Himself especially to those souls who are consecrated to Him—His spouses. St. Margaret Mary was careful to tell us that our Lord counts very especially upon the fidelity of religious to console His Heart. Confidence! We have a special and sacred right to count on the support of His adorable Heart. Let us profit by it.

Our next conference will deal with charity. Fraternal charity is of major importance in religious communities. Our Lord said, "This is My commandment, that you love one another as I have loved you." That is, "Cherish one another tenderly." This is not a cold or neutral tolerance, but a tender love, a love of preference. Our Lord said: "This is *My commandment*." What? Are not all the commandments of the Gospel those of our Lord? Ah, through these words we are taught a great lesson. This is "*My commandment*," the commandment closest to My Heart, the law *par excellence* of My Heart.

St. Francis de Sales said: "I recognize but one perfection—to love God with all our hearts and our neighbor as ourselves."

Our Lord abrogated the ancient law to proclaim the law of love. "It has been said, you shall hate your enemy. I give you a new commandment. I say unto you, love your enemies. Pray for those who persecute you and calumniate you." Here you see our Lord offering an innovation. This new commandment is the seal of His mission. "They will know that you are My disciples by the love that you bear one another." The early Christians had but one heart and one soul. The pagans could not resist crying out in admiration, "See how the Christians love one another!" It has been said, "If you love one another, you are of God. If you hate one another, you are of Satan." The demon said to St. Teresa of Avila: "I am he who cannot love." Miserable creature!

St. Jane Frances de Chantal said: "She who does not have charity for others is a religious in name and habit only, not in spirit."

Doctors of the law, wishing to ensnare our Lord, asked Him, "Master, which is the greatest commandment?" He answered, "You shall love the Lord God with all your heart, with all your mind, with all your strength." Without giving them a chance to interpose a word, He continued: "And the second commandment is similar to the first; 'Love your neighbor as yourself, for the love of God.'" "This is charity: neighbor beloved in God, God loved in our neighbor. Progress in the love of God is measured in direct proportion to our progress in the love of our neighbor. These principles are inseparable. "If any one says, 'I love God,' and does not love his neighbor, he is a liar."

Here is a mother of a family, to whom a friend says: "I love you with all my heart. I love you tenderly, but I detest your children and I shall persecute, hate them." That mother would quickly reply: "No, no, you do not love me, or you would also love my children, my family."

"If there is one person in the whole world whom you do not love," said Père de la Columbière, "do not flatter yourself that you love God. It is an illusion." Do not resemble those false devotees who believe themselves filled with the love of God, while all the time they nourish within their hearts noxious growths of hatred, aversion, and jealousy for their brother. Our Lord does not wish that the two elements be separated. "To love God and to love our brothers is to love the same object," said Père de la Columbière. If, at the moment of presenting your offering, you remember that your brother has some grievance against you, leave your offering and go first to be reconciled to your brother, then bring your offering to the Lord.

"Oh my God," said St. Teresa of Avila, "what great love You bear for the children of men. How is it that they do not love You for Your love alone?"

St. Mary Magdalen de Pazzi declared that she was happier in relieving the necessities of her neighbor than in the highest contemplation. St. Ignatius took pains to assert: "Know how to leave God for your neighbor."

Our Lord, in order to bring us to love our neighbor, adopted a divine strategem: He personified Himself in our neighbor. "What you do for the least of these, My brethren, you do unto Me." Each Christian is another Christ.

Doñoso Cortes was asked how be became converted. "Did you make great sacrifices?" "No," he replied, "my conversion was due purely to gratuitous graces. However, if anything contributed to draw down upon me the mercy of God, it was some acts of charity that I had occasion to perform. I have never seen a poor person pass by without saying, 'There goes my brother,' and trying to relieve his distress, if possible." St. Francis de Sales had a holy practice. Each time he heard steps approach the door of his room, he would say to himself, "Christ is coming."

Our Lord even arms Himself with reprisals lest we fail in the practice of charity. "Forgive and you shall be forgiven. The secrets that you keep concerning the faults of others, I shall guard on your behalf. Give to your neighbor, and I shall render it to you again." Each day we repeat, "Forgive us our trespasses as we forgive those who trespass against us." What would happen if God should take us at our word?

How few dare to say each evening: "Lord, act toward me as I have acted toward this or that one of my neighbors this day." Especially that neighbor to whom, on account of the sharpness of his temper, I refuse to speak. Or that other one whom I cannot pardon, or the one to whom I cannot bring myself to be obliging. Yet, I dare not forget: God will do unto me as I do unto others, and at my own prayer.

Our Lord gave Himself to us as our model. He wishes to establish between Himself and us a kind of parallel, a source of emulation. "This is My commandment, that you love one another *as I have loved you*." We must, therefore,

re-evaluate our love for our neighbor against that of our
Lord. Let us not be harder to please than the good God
who loves our neighbor just as he is.

It is true that this precept of charity can present a particular difficulty in a religious community. In the world,
those persons who are antipathetic, or who have trouble-
some temperaments, can isolate themselves from their
fellows, retire into their room, and close the door with a
double lock if necessary. But we must follow the common
life where our patience is often tested. Those moments
when we long for solitude, for peace, are often the very
times when we must appear in the community and face
contrarieties of various kinds. In the world, a person with
a small store of charity can refuse to be bothered with the
importunate, but in community life there is no choice. We
are forced to live daily alongside temperaments that may
be, to us, uncongenial. Lacking the constant exercise of
charity, we would offend God at every step. God has all
kinds of models for the infinite number of personalities
that He creates. He loves variety.

"Give me a religious who never offends in charity,"
observed St. Mary Magdalen de Pazzi, "and I shall canonize
her immediately."

In a General Chapter of Jesuit Fathers, the following
question was proposed for consideration: "In what way
are the members of our Society most likely to sin mortally?" The seventy senior professed members of the
Society present, all virtuous men, answered unanimously,
"In charity."

St. Alphonsus Liguori, writing of certain communities in
Italy (and note that he is speaking of Italian convents), said,
"One meets people there who cannot open their mouths
without slandering their neighbor. Evil tongues," he cried,
"you are the ruin of convents!" How horrible it is to see
religious meditating, communicating every day, yet nour-

ishing aversions for their fellows, always seeking to depreciate them, refusing to speak to them, turning their backs upon them. Woe to those who behave in this manner, with the hatred in their hearts that God abhors!

Our Lord said that we must love our neighbor, love him tenderly, with a sincere love, not through a purely natural sympathy, and not only when we experience a natural sympathy for him. We should not show him an exterior charity, merely humoring him under the mask of politeness. No, no. No such comedy.

We hear people of the world say, "How happy I am to see you, Mrs. S.; what pleasure it gives me." But listen, as soon as the visitor is on her way: "How unbearable she is, how glad I am to be rid of her." No, let us not have such an exterior polish of affability. That is to enact a farce. We must love with a true love, not through form or rule, must have the habitual disposition in the heart, in the will, to wish well to all the world.

We must not imagine that we can love God without loving our fellows. We must love our neighbors for love of God. One day a priest was accosted by a man who said, with upraised fist: "Priest, if you only knew how I hate you!" The priest responded, "If you only knew how much I love you." St. Francis de Sales said, "If, through hatred, you destroy one of my eyes, with the other I shall regard you with the same love." The perfection of the law is the love of neighbor. He who does not offend God in words is perfect, says St. James in his Epistles.

Let us bear one another's burdens. On the day of judgment something mysterious will come to pass. Our Lord foretold that, turning to the right, to the elect, He will say: "Come, blessed of My Father, I was hungry and you gave Me to eat; I was naked and you clothed Me; I was a stranger and you took Me in. Come, take possession of the throne prepared for you from all eternity." The verdict in our judgment, then, will depend upon the charity that we have exercised in His name.

Let us come down to details. Let us examine charity in our sentiments, our words, and our acts.

Charity in our thoughts, that is to say, charity in our spirit: our Lord asks us not to judge our neighbor and He will not judge us. Admirable promise! See yourself arriving at the tribunal of God and saying to Him, "I have never judged anyone. I accept Your word as my authority; You have not the right to judge me." "The measure with which you judge your brother will be the measure with which I shall judge you." There are those who have an abnormally keen eye for discovering the faults of others. When it comes to recognizing their own faults, they have the eyes of a mole, that is, none. They see nothing but good in themselves. Ordinarily, the keener one is in discerning the faults of others, the more negligent he is in discovering his own imperfections.

We even advertise the faults of our neighbors. Why harp on the faults of such and such a person? Listen, I believe that you have faults that are no better, no more agreeable; but you carry them on your back, where everyone can see them except yourself. I am of the opinion that they are found equally insupportable.

Think first of the defects that you carry for others to see, and you will endure with more patience those of your neighbors. You find that a certain person has a defect of character. Well, I would like to observe you if you had his work, his tasks. The business of reproving is easy; that of doing better is decidedly more difficult. "What a painful occupation is that of examining the lives of others," said Père de la Columbière. "He who is truly humble never thinks that others treat him badly," said St. Francis de Sales.

When the defects of others are visible, when they

strike the eye, we must learn how to interpret them. A certain action appears to you to be a marked imperfection, but the motive which prompted your neighbor to act may have acquired for her great merit in the sight of God. Yet you insist that her motive was faulty. Have you actual proof to substantiate your charges? "Yes," you say. Take care! He who is dizzy thinks the world is revolving around him. There are some dispositions that are predisposed to judge everything from the least favorable point of view. They see everything as black. There are, on the contrary, fine persons with excellent hearts, who invariably see the most favorable side of things, the good side of the medal. I beg of you, look at things around you on the good side. Do not imagine bad intentions. We must do unto others as we would wish them to do unto us.

But suppose our neighbor falls into a sin that is visible to all. It is an open and condemnable action; I judge it to be wrong. Here I am not guilty of rash judgment. My reasons have a sound foundation. Rash judgment is based upon probable proof. There are suspicious natures naturally prone to making these accusations. In vain do they repress these suspicious thoughts that constantly assail them. But do they really desire them to vanish from their imaginations? The fact of having thoughts against charity does not constitute a sin, but the act of voluntarily dwelling upon them, of judging rashly, does. Never think of the defects of your neighbor; think, rather, of your own imperfections and of his virtues.

"Father, it is not my fault if I possess an unusual talent for observation. I quickly perceive intentions. I immediately discover reasons for and against both weaknesses and strengths." Perhaps, but rather the weaknesses, I imagine. All is not imperfection with your neighbor. He, too, has his virtues, his excellent qualities.

St. Catherine of Bologna said: "I have never had aught

but good thoughts about my Sisters, because I realize that those who appear to me to be the most blameworthy, are, perhaps, the most beloved of God, while those who appear the most perfect, may be less acceptable to Him." It is remarkable that great virtues may exist side by side with great defects, and *vice versa*.

An attempt was made upon the life of St. Francis de Sales by placing poison in his food. His sole retaliation was the prayer: "My God, be Thou blessed that I find myself incapable of a similar action."

Charity in our sentiments: let us study our antipathies, learn how to recognize truth. Here in your community is a disposition entirely different from your own. What would you? God has chosen a pattern absolutely different from the masterpiece that we believe ourselves to be. There are dispositions of myriad types. The variety of personalities in a religious community is a great blessing and can be turned into great merit. We do not choose our companions. We are obliged to accept those who are bestowed upon us by our superiors. Unite in the same community all the canonized saints, recalling them to life for this experiment. Turn the key upon them when once assembled, and I can tell you they would suffer. Yes, even canonized saints do not all have identical viewpoints.

Monsignor Dupanloup was asked one day how he expected to live amicably in heaven with Lieutenant Veuillot, with whom he had never been able to agree. "Oh," he replied, "after we shall have passed centuries in purgatory, we shall come to love one another."

Antipathies are not incompatible with charity. On the contrary, through antipathies we can practice true charity. Our Lord said to St. Margaret Mary: "My daughter, I shall multiply your repugnances." The good saint trembled, but replied: "My repugnances are, therefore, not faults, for the good Lord would not increase my faults."

"Charity," said St. Francis de Sales, "does not consist in supporting the defects of those who are agreeable to us, but of those whom we find disagreeable. God polishes one diamond with another diamond."

What shall we do then? Suppress our antipathies? Impossible! If our Lord is pleased to multiply them, what shall we do then? Master them, dominate them. Do not permit them to betray us into sin. I advise you to master them. However, it is not always within our power. It suffices that neither by word, act, nor expression do we betray our repugnance. This is the work of the most intense charity. It is not, however, sufficient to fight against an antipathy. We are obliged to go further and to wish well to our neighbor; that extends to our enemy, if such we possess. We must learn to pardon, to pardon sincerely. It took a God to say, "Love your enemies."

To pardon means to renounce all thoughts of vengeance. This is a delicate point. We often meet with those who hope that God will some day make those who have offended them realize their offenses. But this is infamous! You do not wish to be guilty of revenging yourself, but you wish to be revenged by another; that other is God. Are you obliged to renew with that person who has offended you all the privileges of friendship which he or she enjoyed with you before the offense? You are not obliged to extend to them the same intimacy, the same congenial companionship that you formerly showed them. To do this would be heroic, and you are not under obligation to practice this high degree of charity. It might even be indiscreet to do so. God wills that we render good for evil. It is not always easy. We must have recourse to prayer.

My dear friends, we are always between two extremes, two dangers. There are those who exaggerate everything. Others minimize everything.

The spiritual director hears this: "Father, I have a great hatred for one of my companions." Do you wish evil to befall him? Do you refuse to pray for him or to render him a service?

"Oh, no, no, Father." You say that you hate him, but you do not know what you are saying. It is simply a natural antipathy. You must fight it, but do not therefore conclude that you have hatred in your heart.

"Father, I have desired the death of one of my fellow workers." Well, you are sanguinary!

"But, Father, he is an impossible person. I cannot work with him." Let us reason together a moment. If he were fifteen hundred miles from here, swimming in happiness, would you be content?

"Yes, Father, for then I would be rid of him." You do not, then, desire his death.

"Oh, yes, for then I should be rid of him." But you say that if he were living happily some distance from you, you would be satisfied. Therefore, what you really desire is not his death, but an end to the petty annoyances to which his presence subjects you. You wish an end to the annoyances, not the death of your fellow man.

"Father, I am subject to having grudges against others." Is that true? Are you positive?

"Yes, I cannot forget the things they do." That is not within our power. Some one has broken my leg. I take a step, and recall that this person has caused me to become crippled, at least temporarily. Or, someone has caused me to lose an eye. Certainly, I cannot forget it. Some one has wounded your heart. It is not yet healed. The pain is still active. That is not a grudge, not even rancor. Some people are too demanding; we are annoyed and find it impossible to forget our annoyance.

"Father, I refuse to speak to him. I avoid meeting him."

To cause him pain? To make him feel your displeasure? That is bad, evil.

"Father, I act adroitly toward those who offend me so that they will not perceive it. I know myself. If I speak to them, I shall wound them, offend God." If you are aware of your weakness, do not expose yourself.

"As for me, Father, I avoid speaking to the person who has offended me because it causes me suffering." That is permissible, providing you do it in such a way as not to cause pain. But it is not the most perfect way.

There is much to be said on the subject of charity. Let us beg our Lord to inspire us with a great love of this virtue. St. John, in his old age, repeated the same words over and over: "Little children, love one another." To those of his disciples who inquired the reason, he replied: "Because it is the precept of the Lord. He who fulfills it, fulfills all the law."

An estrangement the size of a grain of powder between two hearts is contrary to this law of love. It undermines charity and brings a shadow between our heart and that of Jesus. The least indelicacy touches the Heart of our Lord. The least negligence may separate us from Him.

SPIRITUAL READING

The Imitation of Christ: BOOK II, Chapters 7, 8
BOOK III, Chapters 6, 25

17. At Bethlehem

PREPARATION: The same—I will to procure the glory of God, His greater glory. I wish to procure His glory in a supereminent way, cost what it may, because He has called me to walk in the way of the perfect.

I see the Holy Family at Bethlehem; my imagination penetrates into their intimate family life. Had I been there, how my eyes would have opened wide, how all things would have spoken to my heart! I should have beheld great lessons—practical ones—upon poverty, in gazing upon the poverty of God. How many things would have entered my soul through my eyes!

I shall employ the sense of hearing in meditating upon this mystery. I hear the songs of the angels announcing the birth of the Messiah. I hear the Blessed Virgin and St. Joseph discussing the mystery that has come to pass. I hear the feeble cries of the divine Infant. I hear the usual sounds of the city of Bethlehem: the riotous songs of the taverns telling of a senseless world. All there are sharing in the tumult, never dreaming of the great mystery of the ages being accomplished at their very doors.

I enjoy with the Blessed Virgin the happiness of possessing Jesus, a happiness mingled with the bitterness of extreme poverty. I touch the crib, the damp straw. I speak to the Blessed Virgin asking permission to take her Infant in my arms. I press Him against my heart. Tomorrow morning I shall also be happy as I receive Him, not only in my arms, but in my innermost heart.

I meditate upon the Gospel. I see the persons; I hear the words; I see what happens. I am present; I strive to meditate upon the scene exactly as if I were there. How I should have been touched! What emotions! I should have been transported. How many momentous lessons I should have learned for the remainder of my life.

In meditating, it is necessary to employ the three faculties of the soul: memory, will, and understanding. This does not mean that it is necessary to commence upon one point by means of the understanding, and another through memory. No, the faculties are exercised simultaneously. As required, one turns to the memory, the understanding, the will; and if a word touches me, I shall not say to it, "Wait a moment. Be silent, I must not consider that point now!" No, the only order to follow is that of your natural attraction.

St. Ignatius adds a prelude: the first point is the historical element in the mystery. St. Ignatius is a precise man. He does not like the words "almost" or "nearly." Before all else he asks, "Of what does the meditation treat? With what am I to occupy myself?"

Joseph and Mary are on the road to Bethlehem. They are poorly attired; the rich regard them with disdain. Traveling along, they entertain themselves with holy thoughts and conversation. Because night is falling rapidly, they must seek shelter; they are penniless. St. Joseph addresses himself to innkeepers: he asks shelter for himself and his young spouse. "We have no room here." Oh, had they been rich, all doors would have been opened to them. Finally, St. Joseph, fatigued and at the end of his strength, must enter a deserted stable.

Let us observe the road leading to Bethlehem. There are hills, ravines. Then I see Bethlehem, all illuminated. I arrive at the stable, open to the four winds.

I ask for the grace I wish to obtain, a perfect understanding of this mystery, not in order to satisfy my curiosity, but that I may love our Lord more and more, that I may cleave to Him more closely, prove my love for Him through my works, and follow Him ever more closely.

I shall explain some points briefly. Let us take ourselves, in spirit, to a poor little town, the most scorned in a despised province, Nazareth in Galilee. Behold on the outskirts of the village, a poor little carpenter shop. It is there that the Queen of Heaven lives with St. Joseph. It is there that my God is about to reside. I take permission to inspect the interior of this humble dwelling—breathing, as it does, the most rigorous poverty. I wish to follow our Lord more closely, to be lodged, garbed, like Him. I sit in at a meal. I see the coarse food and few dishes. I admire the frugality of the table. Were I fed so poorly, I should complain. Ah, when shall I learn to be truly poor with the God of Bethlehem?

During a mission or a retreat, one seeks carefully to find what one can sacrifice to God. I shall inspect my living quarters, to see if all is conformable to the poverty that I encounter in Bethlehem. When one finds nothing that one can spare, that is to say, when one has only what is strictly necessary, it is well and good. Yes, now I understand the strange ambition of the saints who sought the poorest cell, the most disagreeable, feeling themselves well provided for if they were assigned a closet under the stairs as their dwelling place. And I? I seek comfort. Was it with true sincerity that I prayed that I might resemble Jesus? To be poorer and to be well-treated are incompatible.

At Nazareth I see the perfect order in the little household—all speaks of cleanliness. Cleanliness is a religious virtue. When one is condemned to live with people who lack this virtue, one can be miserable. Yes, there will be souls at the tribunal of God who will learn with surprise how much suffering they have caused on this point. Uncleanliness, never! Poverty and cleanliness—well and good!

Let us return to Nazareth. The order has been given. The little family must undertake a long journey in the most rigorous season, the month of December. They must travel many miles in order to have their names inscribed at the native city of their family, Bethlehem. And all in order to satisfy the pride of a pagan prince, the Emperor Augustus.

The Blessed Virgin was but sixteen. Should she have remained tranquilly in her humble retreat at Nazareth? Human wisdom would have advised her to forego the trip, to hide, to disobey the edict. The young girl, "full of grace," elected to fulfill the prescriptions of the law in all its details. Could not our Lord have dispensed her from the journey, from exposing herself to all the privations of a journey at such a critical time? She was even penniless. No, He willed that His holy Mother and He fulfill all the words of the prophets and of the law to the least and last point, cost them what it might.

Let us follow the travelers. We see them on their way in a small and modest caravan. Worldly travelers in their sumptuous equipages have glances of disdain for the poor young woman mounted upon a donkey, but heaven regards her with love. This caravan is escorted by an angelic host; serenity and peace shine upon the faces of the modest couple. I try to render them some service, to lighten their burdens. I imagine myself to be their servant, offering them my small services. When their caravan halts for a rest, I gather dry branches for a fire so that the Blessed Virgin can warm herself for a few moments. I study how to make myself useful.

At last they arrive at Bethlehem. What do I see? The spouse of the Queen of Heaven begging for shelter. It is well known that he is of royal lineage, but now he is forced to join the indigent, to be a mendicant begging for a roof to shelter his young spouse. It is the first time they have had to submit to the humiliation of being shelterless. Now he is but another poor man in the royal city of his fathers, going from door to door asking for shelter from the elements, the cold, the rough crowds, noisy and unsympathetic. Behold the humiliations to which the two are subjected! They find themselves rebuffed on all sides. It grows late; only a stable is offered them. They are obilged to accept, and Mary must bear her royal Infant in the dwelling place of beasts. Has not God abandoned them? Has not St. Joseph the right to complain?

"It is enough for me, oh my God, to be what You will me to be!"

This couple, surrounded by the heavenly choir, this moment for which the ancient prophets longed, about which they prophesied, this central point in the world's history, all, all, are immersed in the deepest abasement, humiliation upon humiliation, that the power of God may issue forth with no admixture of human complacency.

"My God, I give You full permission to do with me what You will. Do not ask my consent. Do not consider my desires. It is true that I have often, before this moment, protested that I will only to accomplish Your Will, but I have never said it with as much sincerity as I do today. I accept all the trials that may come to me, freely and with all my heart."

Joseph and Mary retire into the stable. The wind whistles through the crudely thrown–together hut. Mary is trembling with the cold. Already she realizes that her time has come. Behold in the midst of the night the divine Infant appears. St. Joseph adores the Child. He and Mary are the first adorers of Jesus. I prostrate myself before Him, tiny Infant as He is. I profit by the lesson taught me by this humble family: to despise riches, ostentation, all that activates the passions of the worldly-minded.

How uncomfortable would the great of this world be if they were to find themselves in the condition of this poor family! How humiliated they would be if reduced to take shelter at such a critical time under this poor roof, where I see, where I find heaven. Blessed are those who suffer! Blessed are those who weep! Blessed are those who are persecuted!

On this blessed night marvelous things happen. There are dazzling lights, but only shepherds behold them. Mary and Joseph see only the darkness. Celestial harmonies flood the heavens as angels announce peace upon earth—only shepherds hear the heavenly melodies. Mary and Joseph hear but the wind sighing through their dark stable, hear but the cries of their Infant.

When Jesus enters a heart, He comes with His cross and His crown of thorns. See His mother and Him reduced to extremest poverty. Hardly had Jesus made His long-awaited advent upon earth than the trials of Mary and Joseph were multiplied. Behold them now, cast upon the high roads, homeless wanderers. At Bethlehem, they are condemned to beg for lodgings—tomorrow they will depart hastily, exiled to a distant, pagan country, with no provisions for their support.

My dear friends, if you will but make room, our Lord will share His cross with you. He will ask you, too, to share His exile. He will reduce you to penury until, in all the world, you will have but Him alone as your Companion and your Guide.

Examine yourself at the foot of the crib. Up to the present how have you practiced the exigencies of your state of life? In a fervent colloquy, offer yourself to fulfill His divine desires, that you may follow Him in the obscurity, the contempt, the poverty, that He may expect from you.

18. The Child Jesus Lost in the Temple

DURING this week let us speak heart to Heart with Jesus—and then do what we will. The saints, who knew so well the Heart of Jesus, will not refuse, if we pray with fervor, to obtain for us the grace to penetrate more intimately into the secret of the love of the Heart of Jesus.

We shall meditate upon the mystery of Jesus lost in the Temple at the age of twelve.

Preparation: To the greater glory of God, through aridity, tedium, distaste, bodily discomfort, unwanted movements of the memory, the intelligence, the emotions. I ask but for the greater glory of God, and not for exaltations or for the absence of distractions or temptations. If others glorify Him more than I, I not only consent but rejoice.

I see the road leading from Nazareth to Jerusalem. I see the Temple: Jesus prostrates Himself between Mary and Joseph. I see the great hall in which the doctors of the Law study the Scriptures, discussing the meaning of various passages.

I ask for the grace that I wish to obtain. In the mysteries in the life of our Lord, I always ask for the same grace: that of knowing Him more intimately that I may love Him more ardently. And not solely with a love of sympathy for His sufferings, but with a practical, efficacious affection that will inspire me to follow Him more closely, so that in knowing Him as He passed His life among men I may the better comprehend the lessons He wishes to give me.

Jesus goes to the Temple at the age of twelve. He came into the world to give it the new Law, yet He wills before all to accomplish perfectly the law of Moses. Could not Jesus have exempted Mary and Joseph from the exactions of this Law? "Every year they went to Jerusalem," says the Gospel, "according to the prescriptions of the Law," leaving their divine Child to the care of relatives. Oh, fidelity to our Holy Rule, to our holy prescriptions, more worthy of respect than the Law of Moses! Another evangelist points out that they went every year to Jerusalem, "according to custom." What delicacy! The customs form an ensemble of observances, a family patrimony, a certain way of doing things, that religious should respect. Joseph and Mary left their home in Nazareth every year according to custom. Had they but wished, they would have been dispensed from the journey. Jesus was with them; He had the right to exempt them. Jesus did not will to do so. Joseph and Mary did not ask for an exemption.

There are religious who are always demanding permissions, who lose the merit of obedience on the least pretext, who are skilled in discovering moot points of the Rule. These are not religious according to the Heart of God. The superior, in spite of her better judgment, against her wishes, even, sees herself obliged to grant dispensations in order to avoid murmuring, an even greater evil. What answer will be given her Judge at the great tribunal by that religious who, all of her religious life, has not done the will of God, but her own will? My dear Sisters, let us have no extorted permissions. Out of twenty-five permissions granted by a superior, twenty will be granted against her own wishes.

During His early years, Jesus was unable to accompany His parents to Jerusalem. Hardly was He old enough, strong enough, when He undertook the journey "according to custom," the tradition of Israel. It had cost His parents dearly to leave Him behind in Nazareth. Obedience always costs something. When shall I sincerely immolate my whims, my caprices, my exemptions, to follow the common life? What does not belong to the common life is not blessed of God. Exemptions often foster self-love.

I see the devout caravan proceeding toward the Temple of Israel in Jerusalem. For three days they are on the march, on the highway, exposed to the burning rays of the sun, to the rigor of the weather. They become weary; sweat covers their faces. Jesus was still but a child. It took effort, much energy, to make such a trip. And I? I recoil before the least fatigue. I fear to disturb myself, to deprive myself. What humiliation if at each failure I should be condemned to repeat: "My God, I love Thee! I love Thee above all things. I love Thee so much that for love of Thee I have not the courage to carry out this point of the Rule!" Oh, how we would blush!

I admire the modesty of Mary and Joseph traveling along the dusty road. Something of reserve, of recollection, envelops them. My dear Sisters, those of you who are not hidden behind cloisters, behind grills, have a more than ordinary obligation to be more serious, more strict in observing an irreproachable exterior. Your life is passed in the full light of day, so to speak. The world sees and spies upon you; its scrutinizing eyes are fixed upon religious persons. People of the world, when they enter your parlor, observe everything. Sometimes they may seem to applaud easy manners, but they are really severe, easily scandalized. Wait until they leave your presence, get off by themselves. Listen to their more truthful opinions and see how they criticize easy manners so lacking in religious modesty. Before the tribunal of God I shall be astonished at all the thoughts and impressions I have occasioned unknown to me at the time. Take care! Modesty—this is the religious habit *par excellence*. It is easy to scandalize. It is easy to edify and thereby to do much good. In observing us, people of the world should be able to say: "There are people who are really consecrated to God."

I see Joseph, Mary, and Jesus entering the Temple of Jerusalem. Their entire attitude speaks of veneration. The smallest of our chapels is a hundred times more worthy of reverence than the Temple of Jerusalem. What are our thoughts as we enter with the Holy Family? I consider the attitude of Jesus. He prays silently, but His entire person procures the glory of God. Is there nothing that needs reforming in my attitude? Often one is unable to pray readily, one's thoughts refuse to flow smoothly, but we can at least pray through an attitude seasoned by mortification. Our Lord has not only ears, He has eyes, also. There is the story of the soldier who, having forgotten his evening prayer, donned his uniform as an act of mortification and made his prayer.

The child Jesus remained in the Temple. Following their visit to the Temple, Joseph and Mary, with their relatives and friends, started on their return journey to Nazareth without the least suspicion that the child Jesus was not in the caravan. This indicates that Jesus behaved like all children in sometimes leaving his parents and seeking companionship among relatives and acquaintances.

Hence it was that on the return journey from Jerusalem, Joseph and Mary took for granted that their Child was traveling with another group in the long caravan from Nazareth. When evening arrived, they went from group to group seeking Him, interrogating all members of the caravan. No one had seen Him since leaving Jerusalem. What reproaches the young parents must have received. Their hearts were heavy. Such poignant pain! Had some misfortune befallen their Son in the city filled with Roman

soldiers? Why had Jesus not taken the precaution to advise
them in advance? One word from Him would have spared
them the keen pain of loss. His silence imposed a real martyrdom upon his parents. Did He not foresee their suffering when they found Him missing? Yes, He knew that a
sword would be plunged into the hearts of Joseph and
Mary, but He willed through their suffering to bequeath
to us a great lesson. Mary and Joseph found Jesus the
object of heart-breaking desolation, as He was also their
greatest glory. They were stricken in their most sensitive
affections. Why did God permit it? Had they merited
this pain?

I wonder why we always think our trials are merited?
"I have merited this. . . . God is punishing me." Stop
reproaching your poor soul. How sad it is to see souls
so misunderstand the ways of God in dealing with them.
Instead of beholding in their afflictions a mark of God's
love, they persist in seeing only chastisement. Was it this
that the child Jesus designed for His parents? A trial is a
gift from the hand of Jesus. If we understood His intentions aright, we would kiss His hand in gratitude. Joseph
and Mary submitted themselves to all the designs of Providence. Thrown back upon themselves, they would have
said, "So be it! Jesus willed to leave us. We shall await
His return."

There are stoic souls who say, "I do not find God in
my meditations. He can do as He wills. He will return
when it pleases Him." No, God loves to be sought for.
When Joseph and Mary found Jesus was missing, they instantly took to the road to find Him. They traveled all
day. What matter if they had no rest? In trials, doubtless,
we must exercise resignation, but a fervent and generous
resignation. What shall I do in my aridities, my dryness
of heart? God does not require of us success in overcoming
them, but only that we struggle against them. The saints

knew how to be ingenious in their efforts to recover fervor of heart.

The Blessed Mother and St. Joseph went straight to the Temple in their search for Jesus. Do you desire, in your moments of pain and anguish, to find consolation? Then go to the Temple. Go straight to Jesus. The more that you need prayer, the less will you feel the need of prayer. I know well that in such moments it becomes painful to go to chapel. Instead, you will want to seek human consolations. But no, not that! Human hearts and minds are too fragile, too unstable, ever to answer our deepest needs.

St. Ignatius tells us that in dryness of heart, in desolation, we must not seek to dam up the pain within our hearts by distracting ourselves with study or work. We must triumph over this temptation by prolonging the period of prayer. Thus we prove that we have not succumbed to our emotions, but have triumphed over them.

When the Blessed Virgin found Jesus in the Temple, in her privileged position of Mother, she went straight to Jesus and reproached Him. "My Son, why did You do this to us?" Why? "There must always be something that we do not understand, something that we do not will, in order to leave room for generosity, a generosity to be followed by joy," said Père Pouleroye.

"Why have You treated us thus? Behold Your father and I have sought You sorrowing." We have to bear the reproaches of relatives when we refuse to permit them to infringe upon our Rule. They have not the higher light that illuminates our path, tempers our sacrifices. Our relatives do not understand our vocation; it rends their hearts. "Why do you do this to us? Why desert us in the midst of our trials, of our solicitudes? Why?"

"Do you not know that I am where the interests and the glory of God call me to be? I excuse you for not knowing, but my duty is to recall it to you each time that you assail my vocation, each time that you ask me to take up again what I had renounced forever at the call of Jesus." Joseph and Mary did not understand either. Clouds enveloped their hearts.

Lord, I promise to respect your laws. "Woe to that religious through whom relaxation enters into the community," said St. Francis de Sales. Some religious leave their native lands that they may more completely belong to God. They are fortunate; they belong wholly to our Lord.

"Lord, if Thy glory and my salvation require that I become greater and more powerful than I now am, raise me up, and I shall glorify Thee. If it be to Thy glory and my salvation that I remain in the state in which I now am, preserve me therein, and I shall glorify Thee. But if through humiliations I can contribute to Thy praise and my own spiritual well-being, abase me and I shall glorify Thee."

PRAYER OF THE
EMPEROR FERDINAND II

19. *The Two Standards*

Part I

My DEAR FRIENDS, it should be well understood that we do not have the grace of state to occupy ourselves with the past. The demon knows that he can cause us great loss through inquietudes, worries, and ordinarily it is in this way that he prevents us from benefiting by the precious fruits of a season of meditation and prayer. No, we must turn our thoughts toward the future. The future alone should occupy our thoughts.

The moment for making our resolutions for the future has not yet come. From now on, the purpose of our meditations will be to learn to recognize our weaknesses, to see more clearly the designs of God in our respect, and to draw up a plan of reform. It will be necessary to note the light that God gives us. However, the moment has not yet arrived to broach the matter fully. That will be the work of tomorrow. Today, under the eye of God, we shall study our soul in the full light of grace, to see the disorder in our lives, the strange confusion within our souls. At this decisive moment, we have need of order in our procedure.

Before all, we must distinguish two parts in our lives— the part of God—our spiritual exercises—and our own part. It is from our spiritual exercises that our spiritual vitality comes, our devotion, our effectiveness. It is here, therefore, that our reform must begin. Where our spiritual exercises are concerned, we must ask ourselves two questions: First, do I carry out all my spiritual exercises? Secondly, how do I perform them?

We must, first of all, perform our spiritual exercises integrally. Nothing must be omitted, nothing cut short. How many times have I not heard my venerated Father novice master repeat "You are good religious if you are always faithful to all your spiritual exercises"? Do you wish to merit a diploma as a good religious? Then perform with devotion all of your exercises of piety. Do not omit or cut short a single one through your own fault.

"But, Father, do you know how much I have to do?" I have no need to know that.

"But the greater part of the time, I feel myself far from meditation." Nor do I need to know that.

Here, too, I must be on my guard against those poor souls who calumniate themselves, who seem to take pleasure in putting themselves in the wrong. Have you failed to follow your exercises? I ask.

"Father, I am ashamed. Yes, I have missed them, often cut them short." Was it your fault?

"It seems to me that it was. I would rather answer 'Yes.' " I am not asking for an "It seems to me" or an "I would like." I want the truth.

"Well, the truth, strictly speaking, is that I think it was my fault."

"Strictly speaking!" That means to say, then, that our Lord demands that everything we do is to be done in an exact fashion, "strictly speaking." Oh, how I pity the good God who has to deal with you. What a hard reputation you give Him. Tell me, my dear Sisters, if you were superior, would you exact of your Sisters that they do everything with a minute exactitude? If our Lord were to meet you in the corridor on some day of overwork, would you say to Him, "Lord, this morning I was much interfered with, but it was not my fault; and I do not see how I can return to my meditation. However, strictly speaking, perhaps I could." Do you think our Lord would reply, "Strictly speaking, I shall see that you do so"? But our good Master is the best of all superiors. *Strictly speaking!* A bar of iron that never bends. Ah, if you were to omit your spiritual exercises through repugnance, whim, or laziness, that would be a different matter.

"Father, when evening arrives, I see that I could have better arranged my time and could have found the means of performing the exercises that I omitted." That only proves, my dear Sister, that you have not an angelic intelligence. An angel would have known better at the appropriate time. But if you were lacking in such high intelligence, why take it out on your poor soul? How I pity your poor soul with so hard a taskmaster! With what tyranny you weigh it down!

When our Lord appeared to St. Margaret Mary to reveal to her His Sacred Heart, He always appeared with the same symbols. God does nothing by chance. It would have seemed to us that the Sacred Heart would have appeared amid clouds of incense, surrounded by legions of angels. No, He did nothing of the kind. Each time that our divine Lord showed His Sacred Heart, it was surrounded by thorns that pressed their sharp points deeply into it, surmounted by a cross plunged into its depths, all surrounded by flames. Mysterious lessons!

Devotion to the Sacred Heart is not a devotion all tenderness, consolation, sympathy. No, it is a devotion of fidelity, of mortification, of immolation. Approach this Divine Heart. It is an established fact that those devoted to the Heart of Jesus have to endure contradictions and persecutions. Margaret Mary was the first to find this out. Her superiors treated her as a visionary, a dreamer, obliging her to act toward our Lord as if He were the demon in person. They even required her to throw water in His face.

Devotion to the Sacred Heart is a devotion of generosity. The Heart of Jesus is a sign of contradiction. Thirty bishops, meeting at Pistoia in a synod, united against the devotion to the Sacred Heart. There are pious people today who oppose this devotion. We find souls suffering cruel trials on account of their devotion to the Sacred Heart of Jesus.

My dear friends, I have the honor of announcing to you that if you devote yourselves to the Sacred Heart, you will pay dearly. I have thought it fair to give you this advance notice before giving you our next meditation. It is one of the most serious and decisive meditations and one which will be the keystone of our conferences.

At this moment, I declare war. It is against, and concerns the overturn of, all human wisdom. It is a central meditation and so important that St. Ignatius ordered us to make it twice in each of our annual retreats, even though we might have behind us years of religious life.

It is the meditation of the Two Standards. In the *Spiritual Exercises* of St. Ignatius, those that precede it are but a preparation; all those that follow it, confirm it. It is truly mysterious in its exposition, and there are many who do not understand it easily. Even after grasping its main points, there remain many things to discern in its deeper aspects. For this, I pray our Lord to speak to you Himself.

The preparation is the same: I desire only the greater glory of God.

I represent to myself the camp of Satan, in the midst of which the standard of Lucifer is flying. Opposed to him is the camp of our Lord with the standard of Jesus Christ. In the thought of St. Ignatius, we are concerned to determine under which standard we wish to enroll ourselves. For a long time we have considered this question. To propose it anew seems to be little short of an insult to our intelligence. We have protested to our Lord that we love Him: better to die than to enroll ourselves under the banner of Satan. Altogether different is the purpose of this meditation. How many pretexts have I not met with from those who have not comprehended this mysterious teaching! The gospel texts concerning the Blessed Virgin at first sight contain nothing out of the ordinary, yet they hold a great secret of profound spirituality for those who can penetrate to their depths.

St. Ignatius, my blessed father, spreads out before our eyes the banners of the two chiefs, and invites us to read within their folds the maxims therein inscribed. He desires to initiate us into the intimate thoughts of our Lord and of His great enemy, Satan; to recall to us the strategy adopted by each to save or to corrupt our souls. Mystery! Consummate strategy! How many souls fail to understand it.

I ask the grace fully to understand the desires of Jesus Christ and of Satan.

Transport yourself to the vast plain of Babylon—Babylon, city of trouble, city of confusion. That is the etymological meaning of the word—confusion. We recognize the headquarters of Satan by the inquietude, vague and anxious, that permeates the city. All that troubles, confuses, or saddens, arises from the machinations of the demon. All thoughts that bring with them true joy, a veritable expansion of the heart, of well-being, come from God. Trouble of soul is the unique sign by which we can recognize the work of the demon. The thought that makes us downhearted, that grips us as in a vise, that upsets us and throws our soul into discouragement, into worry, into anguish, infallibly comes from the demon.

Upon this immense plain, I see a multitude gathered, a disorderly mob. These are the sinners. Upon their foreheads is written: TROUBLE, WORRY. In their eyes one reads of passions of every kind. How sinners are to be pitied! Continually gnawed by remorse and pain, they never enjoy a moment of true peace of heart. They know nothing of interior consolations. In the center of this smiling mob, I see Satan—that horrible, repulsive being, the mere sight of whom inspires terror and disgust. Behold, then, the god of sinners, the tyrant to whom I belonged in the past. Jesus Christ freed me from that horrible slavery. What immeasurable gratitude I owe Him!

Satan, the personification of pride, is seated upon a throne outlined in fire and smoke, but of no material substance. Nevertheless, it lends him a deceptive pomp. The demons, with horrible faces, surround their chief. Satan holds in his coarse hands strong chains, nets, traps. Oh, he can well boast of liberty, independence! The hypocrite, the perfidious creature! His whole scheme is designed to entrap souls into eternal slavery and tyranny.

At first, Satan takes great care not to propose odious or revolting sins. No, he opens his attack by holding the soul by a silken thread, before he entangles it in chains of iron. He opens his campaign by proposing small things. That soul that accepts the yoke of Satan can look forward, one day, to a descent down the abyss. It will be in spite of himself that he will fall. No person in his right mind chooses unhappiness or slavery.

Toward all points of the compass Satan sends out his satellites. They traverse all shores of all the seas, under all skies, searching out souls, his prospective dupes. They penetrate into the most angelic company, into convents, even into the sanctuary, even to the foot of the holy altar—everywhere, day and night, his emissaries spread their vile infection to soil souls. They are as avid for their prey as the eagle. These evil spirits are legion. They surround, envelop us. The air is vitiated by, infested with their multitudes. They resemble devouring animals circulating around us, planning our destruction.

Satan is not content with sending his myrmidons throughout the world. He schemes to entrap unwary souls through sinners, who, unwillingly enough, nevertheless act as his accomplices.

Oh, my dear friends, how happy, how fortunate we are, not to be living under the roof of sinners, in the pestiferous atmosphere of sin, in daily contact with evil! How we should love our beautiful vocation! In the world one breathes a demoralizing atmosphere. Those living in a worldly atmosphere absorb evil through the eyes, the ears, all the senses. Evil boldly parades before them. Scandalous sinners are not the sole emissaries of the demon. He counts upon accomplices even more dangerous in the worldly-minded, who, under the cloak of hypocrisy, labor against the maxims of the Gospel. They are saturated with a wholly human wisdom that gives the lie to Jesus Christ. Through words or actions, they say, "Happy are those who possess wealth, honor from men, pomp and pride of life." Satellites of Satan they are, organs of Lucifer, who go about repeating: "Blessed are those who are rich; blessed, those who enjoy the pleasures of the world. Blessed, those who never know the bitterness of tears."

Alas, even in the most fervent religious communities, Satan recruits his accomplices. They are those who, animated by purely human wisdom, and human ambition, have esteem for worldly knowledge, for pomp, for influence, and in the same degree as do worldly seculars. Their conversation reveals their too natural spirit. They are ambitious for human respect. It is not the spirit of God that rules their principles, but the spirit of the world. They raise up man against man. Our Lord said, "Blessed are the poor. Blessed are those who weep. Blessed are those who are persecuted." These worldly religious praise a free and easy, comfortable, pleasant life. What a contrast with the life of Christ!

Satan possesses, even within ourselves, his secret agents. The schemes and plans that he develops with his satellites for our destruction reveal a deeply strategic intent. He studies each soul in its most complex aspects. What he strives to do is to cultivate the Natural Man, the Self, the Ego, Nature, Self-love—these are the great obstacles to divine grace. Grace builds upon nature, it is true, but nature must first be brought to terms, its undue pretensions unmasked.

Our Lord can only triumph upon the ruins of our inordinate ego. A saintly religious said: "We must devastate and plunder nature." We must die to ourselves. This is the indispensable element of our supernatural life.

But the demon speaks another language. He finds within nature his point of contact. "The human ego? Oh, no, it must not be destroyed! On the contrary, furnish nature with all that it seeks. Give nature all that will develop it, cause it to mature, to flourish. I, why I strengthen nature, I render it exuberant." Satan thus schemes to cause our ego to develop while grace declines. In his book of rules, nature must extinguish grace.

That he may succeed in his covert designs, Satan whispers to his accomplices: "You must cultivate the love of riches in these souls, the desire for possessions, for pleasures. You must cause them to thirst for wealth, for enjoyment." Behold here the point of departure. Farther along, he will cause them to thirst for honors. "When you will have become wealthy," he will whisper, "you can lift your head above the common herd, you can demand consideration." One then thirsts to sit in the councils of the great. The ego becomes inflated, and finally pride dominates the individual. Pride! It is the triumph of nature. Pride! It is the triumph of self-love. Our Ego then crucifies our Lord anew. Self must rule until it vanquishes the humble Christ. It becomes a fierce duel to the death between our Ego and Christ. Pride stands between man and his Creator.

God, obeying His own laws, resists pride. He retires from the proud and gives His grace to the humble. We ourselves experience an inner resistance to the proud. It has been said that there is no poison that kills the body so quickly as pride slays the soul.

"A proud century is a corrupt century," said Joseph Le Maistre, the great historian. A righteous man lacking humility already totters on the brink of disaster. He is not far from sinning against purity. How many falls are initiated through the empty pleasures of a proud enjoyment of success! He who yields to such dazzlement leans over the abyss; the vertigo that ensues is a fall begun.

"Chastity," said a holy Father, "is a recompense to the humble." "Out of fifty souls lost through impurity," said another saint, "only three did not fall through pride."

The demon's strategy proceeds in this wise: he advances toward his goal at a forced march. He must first inspire in the soul which he has determined to capture a love of riches. What are the riches most seductive to a religious? Long ago we renounced the lure of gold and silver. There are riches more subtle than those earthly substances from which we have detached our hearts. I give the name of wealth to all that possesses the heart, and to all that the heart possesses, to all that by which the heart is captivated, to all that upon which it feeds.

But how, you ask, is the love of riches to be found in the cloister, when those living there have engaged themselves through a vow of poverty? Precisely, but let us understand the matter. Look, my Sisters, upon that religious who is naturally well-endowed. She has talents; she makes an important place for herself in the community. Others have recourse to her; others consult her. Soon she feels herself superior to her Sisters. She looks upon herself as one who cannot be ignored, set aside. Woe to the rich! Blessed are the poor!

There are riches of knowledge. Here is a religious who, over the years, has acquired a broad and varied store of knowledge. She is well-versed in her specialty. She is brilliant in her classes. She astonishes her Sisters and her pupils by her vast knowledge, and that brings her a revenue of eulogies, of esteem, of praise, of regard. Woe to the rich! Blessed are the poor!

Riches of understanding of human behavior! Here is a religious who possesses great natural ability, who succeeds marvelously in all that she undertakes, who knows how to solve the most complicated affairs. People consult her about their problems, for she has the ability to bring the most delicate matters to a happy conclusion. Little by little, this religious has arrived at a position of eminence in her order or congregation. She is surrounded by good will, by flattering attentions. Woe to the rich! Blessed are the poor!

Riches of influence! Another religious exercises influence upon all who surround her. She possesses qualities which attract. Others feel themselves obliged to give in to her judgment, to follow her advice. This brings her a revenue of delicate adulation, of regard on the part of those who surround her, or who know her. Woe to the rich! Blessed are the poor!

Riches of reputation! Another religious is well-thought of by everyone. She possesses general esteem. Her superiors repose confidence in her. She is a good religious without open faults. From all this esteem she derives an intimate and personal satisfaction. Woe to the rich! Blessed are the poor!

Do you not feel that the Ego is nourished by all these satisfactions? Such religious resemble a self-made man who has achieved a fortune. My dear Sisters, if you recognize yourself in one of these portraits, you are walking on the broad highway—and the broad highway is the road to perdition. We can only reach heaven by an entirely different route, a route that is precipitous, rugged, bare, denuded.

All that nourishes the Ego, that inflates it, all that causes nature to overrun and extinguish divine grace, I class as riches. In general, all natural gifts are "riches," upon which the heart feeds more avidly than upon any other goods less personal to the self.

There are riches of certain talents: one succeeds marvelously in art, music, painting, making of novelties. One has magic fingers. Others humbly solicit the services of such a religious. They ask with condescension to hear her beautiful voice, to see her exquisite paintings. Woe to the rich! Blessed are the poor!

Riches of success in one's employment! Here is a religious who "feathered her nest." She is not a newcomer. She resembles the man who has succeeded in making a fortune; everyone must bow to her. She exercises a certain independent charge. It is a little kingdom of which she is queen. Such a religious is not one of those of whom aid is requested by others. No, she has full liberty of action, full scope for her inclinations, plenty of leisure for her whims. Woe to the rich. Blessed are the poor!

There are riches of memories. One religious comes from a distinguished or wealthy family; it is important that none forget this fact. She takes care to refresh memories of her past grandeur. In conversation, she casually mentions her ancestors, or her former high standing. Oh, she does it adroitly, indirectly. Woe to the rich! Blessed are the poor!

"Having all been formed of the same slime," said St. Teresa of Avila, who was herself of noble birth, "to argue as to which one is of greater or lesser nobility of origin is the same as to dispute about what kind of earth makes the best brick or mud walls. For myself, it is enough for me to be a daughter of the Church. I would be far more ashamed of one single venial fault than of the lowliest origin."

"I was once your mother's servant," said a poor woman begging from St. Vincent de Paul, hoping thus to gain a larger alms. "You are mistaken," replied the saint gently; "my mother never had a servant in her life, having been but the wife and daughter of poor peasants."

And there are riches of work accomplished. One person carves out a fine career for herself, has high positions, fills important posts. People surround her with favors, consideration, regards. Such a religious believes that she does not belong to the class of mediocre people who never accomplish anything great for themselves. Woe to the rich! Blessed are the poor!

Behold the riches of the heart, the most seductive of all. Oh, how they hinder spiritual advancement. This religious draws everyone to her. She inspires general affection; she is petted, coddled, flattered. She possesses an admirable personality, is an agreeable conversationalist. Her days are gorged with attentions. She is the friend of all the Sisters, of all the seculars who frequent the convent. No one would ever wound her, cause her pain. She enjoys general esteem, finds it pleasant and stimulating. Woe to the rich! Blessed are the poor!

There are riches still more seductive: riches of the soul, spiritual consolations. We taste of them greedily, seek them eagerly. The proof that nature is still active is shown by the murmurs that arise when they are withdrawn.

"True poverty," said St. Teresa of Avila, "consists in this, that the soul does not seek consolations, that it supports patiently every pain, every suffering for love of Him who suffered so much for us. If we are imprudent, over-desirous of heavenly favors, if we abuse them by gathering from them only more confidence in ourselves, in our imagined merits, alas, we shall deserve the application to ourselves of those terrible words, 'Woe unto you, rich of the earth, you have had your consolations here below.'"

I have described many kinds of riches for your consideration. There is still another: the riches of desire. That poor man, that beggar, looks with contempt upon the well-fed, well-dressed man whom he passes in the street. Thus he may crave riches with more passion than the man who possesses them. His heart is full of the riches that he does not possess. His soul is devoured by the desire for possessions. He gazes about him with eyes full of jealousy, suffers from the envious desire to enjoy material possessions. He is rich in heart. Woe to the rich! Blessed are the poor!

"It is a great evil, " said St. Francis de Sales, "to have nothing to suffer. In prosperity, the soul runs great danger for its salvation." When everything is successful, when everyone exalts us, how is it possible not to walk with head in air? How is it possible not to desire honors? Not to overreach others when everyone is burning his grain of incense at our feet? Then comes pride, the forerunner of shameful falls. This is the time to think seriously of those words of St. Augustine: "I tremble when I think of the columns of the Church whom I have seen to fall."

Let us turn our eyes toward the Heart of Jesus, to the cross. My Jesus, how Your poverty attracts me! Give me a deep understanding and love of true poverty.

SPIRITUAL READING

The Imitation of Christ: Book I, Chapters 9, 16
Book II, Chapter 2
Book III, Chapter 3

Part II

LET us meditate upon the extent of our Lord's realm. It is exactly the opposite of Satan's. Our Lord stations Himself in the valley of Josaphat at Jerusalem: Jerusalem, City of Peace.

Peace is the seal of God, the unique, inimitable seal of the spirit of God. The demon never brings peace; he can never even imitate it. The demon is able to imitate every other sentiment: zeal, even love of God, when it suits his ulterior purposes. St. Ignatius says that the devil is able to inspire sentiments of contrition, even of contemplation, when it suits his dark purposes. The devil can inspire humility—a false humility that depresses the heart, enervates the will, lessens courage, throws the soul into confusion, and develops within us an anemic, pusillanimous temperament. The demon can inspire all the sentiments except one—that of interior peace. St. Margaret Mary prayed: "Cause me to recognize the snares of the devil. My Saviour, cause me to understand that the devil can never inspire peace of heart."

The work of Père Caussade, *Abandonment to Divine Providence*, is a masterpiece. His letters, above all, are admirable. There we read just what I am trying to explain.

"My Father, I experience a great peace of heart, but I fear it is an illusion, a snare." You are afraid, my dear friend? You suspect the gift of God, a gift *par excellence*, the most certain sign, the most infallible sign of the presence of God within you? Peace! Oh, enjoy it while you have it.

"Peace!" said Madame Louise of France after she had entered the Carmelites. "It is the only pleasure a religious can allow herself without remorse of conscience." Jerusalem, City of Peace! My dear friends, come, then, to Jerusalem. With your fears, your doubts, you are in Egypt, in Babylon. Père Surin wrote to St. Sophie Barat: "May God bless you with your sempiternal fears, your perpetual tremblings!"

I see Jerusalem, City of Peace, City of God! I see Jesus surrounded by angels, by the apostles. What intimate joy I experience near our Lord! What a contrast with the doomed city of Babylon! All the faces here are serene. They are radiant with the reflection of heavenly peace, of a sweet serenity, the privilege of the souls who love God and are beloved by Him. Their peace results from joy of conscience, a gentle joy, a calm joy. In the world, joy is superficial, however exciting it may seem. It is a dissipation of energies. The intimate joy bestowed upon those who love our Lord does not resemble worldly joy. It carries with it a certain warmth, an atmosphere of peace; it reveals that one is among those who are friends of God.

In this vast gathering, our Lord does not sit upon a throne. He comes to teach humility. He circulates among the ranks of His disciples. "I am not come to be served, but to serve. He that is greatest among you, let him be as the least."

I admire His royal beauty. Tradition claims that His beauty enthralled the crowds, fascinated them to the point that we behold five thousand people of every rank, age, and condition, following Him into the desert country, forgetting to eat and drink that they might listen to His words and behold His gracious presence. His beauty subjugated them; His goodness captivated them. I have the honor to belong to Him. He is my King. How fortunate, how happy, am I to belong to Him.

Near our Lord are the holy angels. The skies are full of them. At every instant they come to our aid. God placed a special angel at your side. This angel is attached to the person at infancy and accompanies him until death. He never abandons us for an instant. His solicitude is always alert. It is he who suggests good thoughts to us. Is it possible that a Christian could fail to profess devotion to his guardian angel? Could a Christian become so familiar with the good offices of his guardian angel as to forget or ignore them? If, for the first time, we were to learn that God had placed near us a prince of the heavenly court, invisible, active day and night to protect us, to surround us with delicate attentions, what would be our astonishment! What an explosion of gratitude! Alas, we become so familiar with the benefits showered upon us by our Heavenly Father that they come to mean little or nothing. In addition to our guardian angels, many other angels, heavenly visitants, celestial spirits, have converse with our souls. They come bringing graces, showering graces upon us. Myriads of angels thus surround us. They combat the demons; they protect us.

God sends to us not only angels, but His ministers on earth: pontiffs, bishops, priests, and messengers from every condition in life who may, even unknowingly, minister to our welfare. My dear friends, have you ever calculated the number of the ministers of God who are devoted to the salvation of souls—your soul? How many priests have administered the sacraments to you? How many others have contributed to the welfare of your soul in countless ways? Count all those who have taught you to love God through words or through books, all those whose gentle influence has led you toward God. A whole army of priests has thus been devoted to your service. How many poor souls only see one, two, three priests in a lifetime?

Our Lord chose, to serve you, not only His priests, but His friends. His friends are all those who propagate His doctrine, who spread abroad His Spirit, who cause His Kingdom to come, through the mysterious spiritual influence that they radiate about them. How many persons have contributed to your education when you were but a small child! How many devoted religious have contributed to form your attitude toward religion! Their modesty spoke to your eyes, to your soul; their gentle influence turned you toward the things of God. How many others, sent of God, have been placed along your path, enveloping you in the mysterious influence which, little by little, drew you into the way of perfection. It is, therefore, true that you have found yourself among the friends of God. Their words, their actions, have constantly brought you thousands of graces all impregnated with the spirit of our Lord. What happiness is ours!

Our Lord develops His plan for our salvation. Here the mystery commences. Our Lord knows that we must die to all else that He may reign within us. Nature and grace are engaged in a relentless duel. One or the other must succumb. Things of earth must give way to things of heaven.

"Empty your hearts," cries St. Teresa of Avila; "God will fill them." Our Lord is well aware that He has an enemy within the fortress of our hearts—an accomplice of His dire enemy, Satan—nature, Ego. We must be delivered from inordinate self-love that is attached to things of earth, those things that tyrannize over us. The roots must be severed that self-love will die of starvation. The death of self-love is humility. True humility—that is what destroys self-love, root and branch. Humility crushes nature. Humility reduces the Ego to its proper place: a zero, nothing. Humility, true, sincere, is the starting point of all grace. Without humility, nothing; with humility, everything.

"God enters into our hearts," said St. Vincent de Paul, "in the exact measure of our humility." Consequently, it is by the degree of our humility that we must measure our advancement. Do you want a sign as to how you stand in relation to perfection? What is your humility? "The stoutest weapon with which to conquer the devil," continued St. Vincent de Paul, "is humility."

"To attain to life," wrote St. Francis de Sales, "we must pass through death." "Humility is the chosen insignia of those who are dear to God," said St. Vincent Ferrer.

"You ask of me the way to perfection," wrote St. Augustine. "I reply that the first degree is humility. If you repeat the question, I reply that the second degree is humility, that the third is still humility. If you should ask me the same question a hundred times, you would have the same reply."

Our Lord said to St. Mechtilde: "In hell there are virgins. There are no truly humble souls." "I prefer that you have more humility and fewer other virtues, than more virtues and less humility," said another saint.

God does not augment His Love in us save as we annihilate our inordinate self-love. When our Lord sought St. John Baptist and asked to be baptized, St. John refused to baptize Him out of humility. Our Lord replied, "Let be, for so must justice be accomplished." What pregnant words! Yes, all justice is in humility. We shall find the perfection of all virtues in humility.

The demon said to St. Macarius, "Oh, Macarius, you cause me to suffer extraordinary violence. All my power against you is taken from me. But you must know that in many ways I practice perfection more exactly than do you. You fast sometimes. I never eat. You occasionally keep nightly vigils. Sleep never closes my powers of perception. There is one thing in which you excel—humility. It is this virtue that neutralizes my power over you."

What virtue rendered the Blessed Virgin worthy to become the Mother of Jesus? The saints unanimously attributed the divine maternity, not to her virginity, but to her humility. Lacking humility, she would not with all her virginity have become the Mother of the Messiah. She herself proclaimed this in her *Magnificat*, that sublime chant of humility: "Because He has regarded the humility of His handmaid, behold all nations shall call me blessed." This is humility, true and great. "The powerful He has cast down from their thrones, and exalted the humble."

We must, at all costs, attain humility. We understand this, intellectually, but it would be an illusion to desire to attain humility without passing through humiliations. It is vitally necessary to pass through all the stages inherent in that precious virtue.

Let us pay heed to our Lord. He explains His plan to His apostles, to His disciples, to His friends. Go through this world combatting the influence of Satan and all his accomplices. He inspires love of riches, of honors, in order to cause souls to fall into pride and avarice. "Those who love Me will follow the opposite path. I will inspire souls with a love of poverty. I will teach them to fight against love of riches and pleasures, and will persuade them to pursue these false allurements even into their most secret hiding places. I will cause hearts effectually to despoil themselves of every inordinate attachment, of sensual pleasures, of all that encumbers them, all that could slow down their progress. Then I will lead those souls into a realistic poverty, an effective despoiling of self-love. Through these measures they will pass into the highest degree of humility: the love of humiliations, the seeking out of humiliations. By these degrees faithfully followed, they will infallibly be led to true humility of heart and mind."

As we hear our Lord describing this mysterious ladder, we are inclined to fall upon our knees and pray for humility. But that would be an illusion. Then we hear the words: "I forbid you. To be loyal, you must pass through all the stages of the spiritual life." Fall upon your knees, yes, but ask for poverty of heart and, if possible, a real renouncement of all that is not God. Nature trembles with shame at the thought. But it is necessary to put nature to rout, reduce it to the last extremity. Ask for real humiliations, that you may be under the feet of all. Consent to lose your reputation, to be under suspicion. Ask that you may be content when others fail to understand you and impute intentions to you of which you are innocent. Ask to be plunged into the salutary bath of humiliations. And when you have asked for all these, do not add another word. Wait. Expect. You may be sure that the blessed hour will arrive, when, at the end of the way, you will find perfect humility.

Here we must be on our guard against illusion. We may fritter away our aspirations upon whims or impulses. Humiliate yourselves. Subdue nature. Sometimes the awakening can be terrible. Nature clings desperately to its natural rights and privileges, even through the wreck of itself. We must cut off the supplies that nourish the natural self.

How shall we obtain the desire of following this rigorous road, devoid of all that nurtures the ego, so insistent, so obstinate in seeking its own advantages? How come to experience an appetite for the things that are on high, as St. Paul counsels, while our hearts are saturated with the things here below? Does he who is satiated feel hungry? Does he who has drunk well feel thirst? The heart full of itself has no room for God.

Paul Fevel lost his fortune in a financial crisis. "God be thanked," cried his wife; "now there is nothing between you and God." "God must love me greatly, to have chastised me so harshly," replied Fevel.

"Lord, I cannot believe that You love me unless You give me great sufferings, and over a long time," was the prayer of Père de la Columbière. How we should pity that soul that has nothing to suffer! How we should pity the soul that travels on the broad way! That is not the path beloved of the friends of God.

Doubtless it is true that one can be poor of heart in the midst of wealth; one can detach one's heart, keep it free, even perfectly free, as we see in the lives of saints who filled exalted positions in the world. St. Henry, Emperor of Germany, and St. Louis, King of France, were poor of heart. This virtue is as admirable as it is rare among those surrounded by worldly seductions. How is it possible not to be attached to riches, when, every day, they seduce the heart? How is it possible to detach the heart of all that flatters nature, when one has everything that one could wish for? Our Lord said, "It is easier for a camel to pass through the eye of a needle than for a rich man to enter into the kingdom of heaven."

Oh, how hard it is for the rich to be detached, disengaged, their hearts wholly empty. Our Lord, who never loses sight of our true interests, arms Himself with a holy rigor upon beholding a soul attached to riches and, piece by piece, point by point, takes from him all those things in which he trusts, despoils him of all his wealth. Formerly, this person had known glorious days. He possessed great talents, a fine mind. Now this glory passes. No one appears to take any notice of him, to place any value upon his opinion. Thanks to his varied gifts, others formerly consulted him. His talents were often called upon, encouraged, used. Today he is completely set aside. Formerly this person excelled in all that he undertook. His practical knowledge was extraordinary. His employments—with what praise did he acquit himself of them! He had but to appear, it seemed, and difficulties vanished. He therefore became full of himself. He counted upon his own lights, his own ability. Our Lord took pity upon him. Today, he succeeds in nothing; he is put to one side. Others less experienced have replaced him. No matter. Blessed are the poor of heart!

Formerly, this person, thanks to his amiable personality, to his congenial exterior manners, enjoyed the friendship of all who made his acquaintance. Now he is surrounded by an atmosphere of indifference. How everything has changed! Then, everyone had confidence in his opinion; he was termed prudent; his advice was sought. Now he is set aside, his advice is no longer considered in the councils. Blessed are the poor!

Here is another individual. He has always enjoyed flourishing health. He has given himself unstintingly for the good of his fellows. He was happy in giving his labors, his toil, happy to devote himself for the good of souls.

Perhaps he might have been too complacent over his natural gifts. Perhaps his devotion was tinged by a too human self-seeking, by personal satisfaction. Today, look upon him confined to a hospital by a cruel malady, incurable perhaps. There he is, nailed, as it were, to his cross, no longer able even to render services to himself, much less to others. He is but a ruin of his former self. Blessed are the poor!

Here is a person who had created a favorable position for himself in his work. He was free: he could take time for things that he wanted to do. He could arrange his own leisure time. Today he is wholly at the mercy of others who impose upon him extra duties, even in his present state of helplessness. In other days, everyone smiled upon this favored person. Everyone sought to do him a service, to foresee his needs and forestall his desires. Everyone took pains to please him. Today all the world ignores him. He is forgotten. He is heartsick. Blessed are the poor!

Another person was noted for carrying important work to successful completion. Now no one seeks him out; no one tries to please him. All pass him by with indifference. He once had the confidence of all those associated with him; today all avoid him. He appears to be suspect. In those happy days, he received spiritual consolations: holy lights, consoling emotions. After Mass, during his thanksgivings, he experienced the presence of God. Now, all that is a closed book, finished, over with. He remains in a profound darkness, unrelieved by conscious ardor or zeal. He is plunged into a painful night. "God seems so distant," he says. "The Heart of Jesus is nearer to you when you suffer than when you are joyful." But he experiences no spiritual uplift; to all appearances he is abandoned by God and man. Blessed are the poor!

Some years ago, a true Christian, upon learning that his fortune had been lost, cried out, "Thanks be to God,

I have lost my fortune! Now I can serve God alone." At the tribunal of God, many will cry: "Thanks be to God that I have lost my fortune." How many will be forced to admit that, had they kept their fortune, continued to walk in the broad way, in the way of the purely natural man, there would have been little place for God in their lives, full as they were of natural satisfactions.

"Do you know," asks a spiritual writer, "how the original *Rule* of St. Francis went about making a saint? It took the man who presented himself as desirous of treading the path of perfection, stripped everything from him that he possessed. It put a sack upon his shoulders, a cord about his waist, and sent him out to beg his bread with the injunction, 'You will find yourself so unhappy upon earth that you will be forced to seek heaven.' "

God sometimes is forced to treat certain souls in the same way. They are well-endowed; life smiles upon them. They taste the exquisite joys of the heart. They find themselves upheld, encouraged, supported. Suddenly, the picture changes. They are under a cloud, suspect. They fall into imprudences; this increases the suspicion with which they are surrounded. Once universally beloved, now they perceive a void about them. They are set aside, not knowing where to find solace or repose for their hearts so full of anguish. Yesterday, their way was luminous, joyous; now behold them plunged into a sea of scruples. Those upon whom they had counted for support have now deserted them. They have not a ray of human happiness to support them, to comfort them. They exist as in a desert land. Who can describe the terrors, the frightful sense of loss, that torment them?

Coming to understand, at long last, that God alone can appease the profound hunger and thirst of the human heart—a thousand times more terrifying than all other torments—this soul finally says, "I shall arise and go to my

Father." And God, the loving and wise Father, who but awaits this moment, embraces that soul, and pressing it to His Heart, makes but one reproach: "How long it has taken you to come to Me!" And the soul, overwhelmed, cries out: "My God, is that Your only reproach for my wanderings, for my coldnesses, my weaknesses? How wonderfully loving and good You are!"

Ah, I beg of you, pray that you may come to a moment in your life when you will find yourself so unhappy, so abandoned, so neglected by men, so little loved, so little noticed, that you will be forced by the imperious needs of happiness and love to throw yourself, naked as it were, into the arms of God.

God, however, does not despoil all souls in equal manner. Occasionally we meet people who seem to have everything that heart could desire. But God knows well how to make them pay dearly for such purely natural satisfactions. He knows well how to cause them to make up for their riches by other means, how to disengage them from the sensible world, how to empty their hearts of all their treasures. When one penetrates into the intimate depth of such a soul, one discerns a mysterious martyrdom. Such souls carry, in their depths, an abyss of sorrow hidden from the world. That person, so well-endowed, who appears to have been created to excite envy, is in reality plunged into the most excruciating perplexities, often frightful temptations, or, it may be, tortured upon a bed of scruples. Praise appears to him to be derision. He carries within his heart an ever-present sense of his unworthiness. A strange sense of despair weighs upon him. He is ever conscious of the infinite chasm between his interior vision of holiness and his own unworthiness. A true martyrdom!

"Happy the soul whom God scourges," wrote Bossuet, "from whom He takes all strength, that it may rest in Him alone." It is thus that God bruises and bends nature to His purposes. When everything reveals to us more and more forcibly our intimate misery, our nothingness, when upon all sides we behold but ruins, the shambles of our pride, our conceits, our petty weaknesses, we are then forced as rational creatures to accept humiliations as our due.

How can we be proud when everything reveals to us our insufficiency, our incapacity for good, our nothingness? How naturally, then, do we come to give precedence to others, to lose all sense of exigency in regard to our personal interests, no longer to expect or desire attentions or praise? Thus, at last, we willingly accept obscurity. We are content to remain unknown, to accept humiliations, since we now regard them as our due. If there still remain within me repugnances of nature, I now know how to make use of them as precious steps to heaven. And then, not only do I resign myself, but I bless God for them. Even more, little by little, aided by divine grace, I am no longer content with casual humiliations—I seek them out. When they arrive, the soul sings out, jubilantly, "Thanks be to God! *Alleluia!*" It is by this double action that the soul attains a true humility, which, upon this solid foundation, increases and develops with the years, until it becomes a permanent attitude, an habitual grace.

Listen to the prayer of General de Sonis, which expresses so perfectly the virtue of humility: "My God, behold me before You, poor, insignificant, denuded of all things. I am nothing, I can do nothing, I have nothing. I am here before You, plunged in the depths of my own nothingness. Oh, I long to be able to offer You something, but I possess nothing of my own except my distress. You, You, are my all! You are my riches. My God, I give You thanks for having willed that I should be nothing before You. I love my nothingness, my humiliations. I thank You for having removed far from me the satisfaction of self-love, the consolations of the heart. I thank You for disappointments, anxieties, humiliations. I recognize that I have need of them for my own greater good and that to have been the recipient of consolations might well have alienated me from You. Oh my God, blessed are You when You try me. I desire to be bruised, wounded, consumed, for Your sake. Annihilate my self-love more and more. May I be, in Your Temple, not the stone polished and smoothed by the hand of the workman, but as a grain of sand lost in the dust of the roadway.

"My God, I thank You for having permitted me, at times, to experience the sweetness of Your consolations. I thank You equally for having deprived me of consolations. All that You do is just and good. I bless You for my poverty. I regret nothing, except not having loved You enough. I desire nothing except that Your will be done. You are my Master; I am Your possession. I long to be reduced to nothing for love of You.

"O Jesus, how wonderfully good is Your Hand, even in the midst of the fiery furnace. May I be crucified, but crucified for You!"

SPIRITUAL READING

The Imitation of Christ: Book I, Chapters 9, 16
Book II, Chapter 2
Book III, Chapter 3

20. Holy Communion

M<small>Y DEAR FRIENDS</small>, have you never experienced a certain envy at hearing the words repeated, "I will engrave upon My Heart forever the names of those who propagate this devotion"? But why be envious? You can all participate in this devotion. In your conversations it will be easy for you to allude to the Sacred Heart and tactfully to suggest the practice of the Nine First Fridays. In your conversations with people with whom you are sufficiently well acquainted, suggest the idea of a novena to the Sacred Heart. Mention the date of the First Friday in advance. During the month of the Sacred Heart seek to attract others to this devotion. Once engraven in the Heart of Jesus, your name will never be effaced.

It is now time to think about our resolutions. First of all, I must promise not to miss any devotional exercises of obligation according to my Rule of life, including Holy Communion. That is the most important of all practices, a hundred times more important than all the others. The Council of Trent expressed the desire that each Christian would communicate each time he assisted at Mass. "Above all things, I recommend Holy Communion," said Père de la Columbière; "the fathers of the Church, without a single exception, exhorted all Christians to communicate often."

It is far better to communicate through love than to abstain from respect. There is but one reason that should keep us from the Holy Table; that is mortal sin. Outside of that, go to Communion. The weaker we are, the more we need nourishment. The great need that you have for

Holy Communion should prevent you from missing a single one. Is it when we are most dangerously ill that we should abandon all remedies? I have been wounded; I have committed faults; therefore I shall not go to Communion. This amounts to saying, "I shall wait until I am cured before I seek that divine remedy." It is the same as concluding, "Today I do not know what dangers, what enemies, await me; but whatever they may be, I have no need of God's help. I shall meet them depending upon my own strength."

General de la Morcière had a young daughter known to be leading a worldly life, but permitted by her confessor, nevertheless, to go to Holy Communion twice weekly. The General was amazed. "What," he inquired, "you permit my daughter with her love of dress, of worldly pleasures, to go to Holy Communion so often?" Surely, he thought, her confessor cannot know this, and he felt it his duty to warn him. "My dear Father, doubtless you are not well enough acquainted with my daughter: she loves balls, the theater, fashions, and yet you permit her to communicate twice weekly. I feel in conscience bound to tell you that she does not deserve that great privilege."

"General," replied the priest gravely, "she does not merit the privilege of weekly Holy Communion, nor do we, but both she and we have constant need of the Bread of Life."

"Many thanks," replied the General; "now I understand. I have been given a hundred reasons for frequent Communion. Today you have given me the best reason of all." And turning to his daughter in whose presence the conversation had taken place, he said, "My daughter, communicate as often as your confessor will permit."

Among the early Christians, children of two and three years were permitted to approach the Holy Table. Had Christians more fervor in those days? More faith? Those favored children had but one preparation: absence of mortal sin. Were their Communions waste effort? No. A potential treasure reposed within their pure souls.

Be faithful, then, to your Communion. When you omit Communion without a sufficiently serious reason, you make Jesus do penance. You deprive Him of the greatest and most precious consolation—that of giving Himself to you. Have you ever had a great disillusionment, a serious disappointment in your life? You could never have one as great as that which our Lord experiences when you voluntarily omit one Communion. He comes to you loaded with graces, and He finds your place vacant. What pain for His Adorable Heart! The demon rejoices; he celebrates his triumph; he applauds himself.

Fidelity, then, to your Communions! Could you but realize the incalculable graces of one Communion, you would never again miss even one.

The saints have maxims that disconcert us and reverse our little ideas: "The Heart of Jesus is nearer to you when you suffer than when you are happy."

"Father, in my Communion this morning, God seemed so far away. I was in desolation, in anguish. My heart was stricken by trials, bitterness. I was bathed in pain." The Heart of Jesus is closer to you when you suffer than when you are full of joy. I cannot understand how it is that the cross, in our eyes, is always wrong. We always think that it comes at the wrong time, in the wrong place, for the wrong motive. Our motto seems to be: I suffer, therefore, I am guilty.

My dear friends, you are being schooled in the school of Job. In the midst of his grievous pains, his good wife could think of no better consolation to offer him than to say: "You must be very guilty in the sight of God for Him to punish you thus." What encouragement that was! We shall have very different ideas before the tribunal of

God. Yes, my dear friends, the Heart of Jesus is closer to us when we suffer than when we are joyful. We should, then, be faithful to frequent Holy Communion despite aridity and sufferings of body, mind, or soul. I beg our Lord to enlighten you upon this point.

21. *Three Stages of Humility*

WE ARE ABOUT to study the strange words of our Lord to St. Margaret Mary: "The heart that is the most despised, the most humble, will be first in My Heart." To love to be humble—I understand that up to a certain point—but to love to be despised, that is opposed to all of our human ideas.

The memory of a holy religious whom I once knew inspired me after twenty years. She was the most despised soul that I have ever known. She had offered her life for the salvation of her father, an outspoken sinner. She was taken at her word. God accepted her offer and required of her a price in exchange for his soul. Up to this time her charming personality had caused her to be favored by religious and superiors alike. Suddenly, she was accused of a serious fault. Her superior, through the permission of God, treated her with harshness.

The religious decided: "I must be greatly culpable to be treated so rigorously." She never fully understood the fault of which she was accused. She had but one consolation, Holy Communion. One day, being ill, she asked of me the favor to commence a novena with her for the intention that she might never be compelled to lose one Holy Communion before her death.

Following this novena, the superior, a good woman at heart, treated this religious with fresh severities, believing her illness to be feigned. One day the superior decided that, if she wished to go to Communion, she would have to present herself in the chapel. The physician and the chaplain both protested, but the superior overruled them. Every day thereafter the poor Sister rose from her bed to make her way, tremblingly, to the chapel, knowing that without Holy Communion to sustain her, life would be insupportable. One day she fainted in the corridor upon her return from chapel. Recovering consciousness, she said to herself: "Is it possible that God will not answer my prayer?" At four o'clock that afternoon, a complication developed; and within four and one-half hours after she had received her last Communion, she was dead.

At the moment she expired, the veil of blindness was torn from the eyes of the superior; she understood. Overcome with grief and repentance, she threw herself beside the body of her long misunderstood spiritual daughter. "O my poor Sister, how falsely have I suspected you! Forgive me!" For fifteen years the poor victim had been plunged into the most abject humiliations. I have never known a soul so content in her humility and her sufferings.

We will now attempt to pierce the mystery that makes saints: the three degrees of humility. There is a mysterious document bearing this name and dictated by St. Ignatius. At first sight, it is difficult to understand. Many think they have meditated upon it, when they are very far from the point. Let us ask for wisdom to understand this document which is destined to help us arrive at true saintliness.

If you read it, you may say, "I remain speechless, Father. I see three degrees of perfection, of holiness, but it is hardly more a question of humility than it is of the other virtues, for all the virtues are united here. Why do you call these three degrees of holiness, the 'three degrees of humility'? Ah, I understand. You showed me in the meditation upon the Two Standards, that all virtue is contained in humility. Humility is the base, the starting point of all saintliness. God enters within us in exactly the degree of our humility." Behold the mystery of this appellation: "The Three Degrees of Humility."

THE FIRST DEGREE OF HUMILITY

This is the state of a soul that has vowed mortal hatred to every grave sin. Such a soul would die rather than deliberately commit one mortal sin. This is the habitual disposition of the person who would enter the first degree of humility. This must not be the affair of a moment—the moment of going to confession, perhaps. No, it means to have such an habitual disposition, a permanent state of soul. One might fall, commit a mortal sin, or mortal sins, accidentally, so to speak; but one will return immediately to the habitual disposition of preferring death to mortal sin.

This is the lowest rung of perfection, but it is already true sanctity. We must attain this degree. It is an obligation of our state. I meet with devout persons who believe themselves to love God truly. "Ah, Father," they say, "the good God has given me the gift of tears. I have wept throughout my thanksgiving. I felt my heart all-burning with love for our Lord." Yet, within a few days they have committed several mortal sins. Is that devotion? It is something that happens often and is very deplorable. What an illusion! This fervor of a moment on going to Holy Communion, is it a reality?

There are those who refuse to partake of Holy Communion because they are wallowing in gloom, with no feeling for things of the spirit. They are plunged into a kind of obtuseness, believing themselves unworthy of Holy Communion. Let us examine this state. Would you, in cold blood, go to Holy Communion in a state of mortal sin?

"No, Father, it seems to me that I have an ever-increasing horror of mortal sin." You are, then, in the first degree of humility. This degree is that of the martyrs for the Faith. Martyrs are those who elect to endure any torture rather than commit a mortal sin. It is a perfect state and one in which we must be to receive absolution, even if the disposition be but temporary. A poor sinner, after fifty years of sins of all kinds, must have this disposition when he asks for absolution. The saints had this detestation of mortal sin. They fled from it as if it were a viper.

The safest guardian of humility is distrust of ourselves. Père Canisius asked this grace of God every day after his Communion: the grace of never apostatizing, of never becoming a nonbeliever, of never treading underfoot the cross of Christ. He believed himself to be capable even of that act, and pleaded with our Lord to keep him from it. Where is the person sufficiently humble who will say during his thanksgiving: "Even now, upon leaving this church, I am capable of becoming an apostate." St. Margaret Mary said to our Lord: "Place no trust in me, Lord, for if You do not watch over me, left to myself, I am bound to betray You." Ah, the entrance to our hearts! Here it is that we must thwart the designs of Satan. He works upon us as a seducer uses his wiles with a young girl. He commences by saying, "Now, say nothing about this to your mother. Let us keep quiet about it." When the demon seeks to entrap a soul, he desires nothing so much as for that soul to withdraw itself from all spiritual direction, in order that it will no longer give an account of temptations endured. In this secrecy in dealing with spiritual directors lies one of the greatest dangers for the welfare of a soul.

THE SECOND DEGREE OF HUMILITY

This is the state of the soul that bears an implacable hatred for all venial sin. This person would prefer to die rather than commit one venial sin. It is the reaction of the person who fully understands the nature of sin, in itself the greatest of misfortunes. The smallest sin ranks as the greatest calamity that can befall a soul. The person of whom we now speak understands that clearly. If it were suggested to this person to commit a sin, however light it might seem, consent would never be given. Nor would the promise of all terrestrial pleasures or the fear of all earthly disasters move that person to consent to even the lightest-appearing sin.

Divine love, delicate as it is, has ravished that heart. In the second degree of humility, we prefer death rather than be guilty of the least falsehood. Let us beg of God that we may have this detestation of venial sin. Such delicacy of soul is an excellent symptom. When a person can testify of himself: "It seems to me that I detest venial sins above all else, that I flee from them as I would from a dangerous reptile," this soul is advancing by giant strides in the way of perfection.

"Lord," said St. Alphonsus Rodriguez, "I would rather suffer the pains of hell than commit one venial sin." To be in this degree of humility, one must be perfectly established in Holy Indifference.

"But what connection is there between Holy Indifference and flight from venial sin? I cannot see the mysterious bond that unites these two dispositions." All sin arises from a lack of Holy Indifference. To be established in the second degree of humility, one must not be attached to anything. One must be in a state of perfect equilibrium in relation to everything. If I still have my little attachments, my whims, my preferences, it is evident that I am in the state where venial sin is possible. This second degree is more sublime than the first. Yet, it is not at the summit of perfection. There is another habitual disposition that is more admirable than Holy Indifference.

THE THIRD DEGREE OF HUMILITY

The third degree was revealed to us by the example of our Lord. It was He who revealed the third degree of humility when He appeared and so changed the aspect of all things. The third degree consists in giving preference to all that is humiliating, crucifying, to sufferings, to the cross. Even though I should find no more spiritual profit than from riches and honors, in which I would have as much merit as in the most profound abjection, nevertheless I would choose to walk, not in the broad way, but in the narrow way. Even though I could procure the same glory for God in a life of opulence, of grandeur, nevertheless I would choose poverty, humiliations. Thus speaks the heart in its profoundest depths. "The heart has reasons which reason can never know."

It was a difficult thing to be indifferent to all things before our Lord appeared in the world. At that time the high estate of poverty had not yet been revealed. But after our Lord had placed before us His own way, that of preferring suffering, the thorns, the cross, opprobrium, could I longer content myself with a cold indifference? Yes, if I knew only the religion of conscience, of duty. Oh, then, I could dwell at peace with Indifference. Conscience alone would not compel me to walk in painful paths. I would not be expected to, would not find any interior inspiration in following our Lord so closely. I would say to God: "If You desire it, send me sufferings; so be it! I shall accept them, but I shall not advance to meet them."

But when one deserts this religion of conscience alone, when one enters into the way of love, into the religion of the heart, how everything changes! Then one finds inspiration in His service. As for me, could I love our Lord, yet be disinterested as to His interests? Can I let Him be garbed in fool's garments while I drape myself in my dignity, all indifferent to His humiliations? Could I behold our Lord dwelling in a stable with beasts of burden, while I surround myself with the comforts of life? Would these considerations be all the same to me?

Had I been in Bethlehem that first Christmas night, could I have practiced a mere indifference? Would I not have preferred to have been as close to Him as possible in that poor stable, shivering with the cold? Would I not have longed for the high privilege of being treated just as He was? Had I been at Jerusalem when He was rigged out in the garb of a fool, could I have been indifferent? Could I have been satisfied to be dressed in sumptuous garments, loaded with honors, living in luxury?

When my divine King was crowned with thorns, covered with blood, would it have been all the same to me if I had walked in a rose garden while my Lord was tracing His lonely path to Calvary? Our human hearts demand that we try to resemble those whom we love, to be treated as they are treated.

My friends, here is a child living in a palace. She knows that her mother is but a few steps away, living in a dark dungeon with only bread for food. Could this child consent to dine luxuriously? Would it be a matter of indifference to her? If someone suggested that she visit her mother, would she reply: "It is all the same to me." If so, it would be evidence that she lacks a heart. If she had a human heart, would she not insist on sharing her mother's meager fare and straw pallet? She would, I am certain, choose to share her mother's sufferings.

There are those who think that they understand this because they accept poverty, humiliations, sufferings. But for the reason that by such acceptance they procure more glory for God and, as well, more merit for themselves throughout eternity, they expect to enjoy great recompense. They are at the second degree of humility, and not at the third.

Even though there were no spiritual advantages, no merits to be gained, no nearer approach to God to be looked for, still I would practice poverty because our Lord was poor. I would choose privations because my Lord lived a life of privation. He chose a stable for His birthplace. I would choose privations, suffering that I might receive the same treatment that was meted out to Him, and because I love my divine Master independently of all personal advantages. Even though I might be capable of meriting honors and through them be able to glorify God as much as through an obscure, unknown life, yet I would still prefer to resemble my King in His abnegation, His deprivations, His poverty.

I ask as a supreme favor to be bound with chains, to be thorn-crowned with Him, just as He was. Behold the third degree of humility! How admirable it is! It is the joy of the saints, the summit of their love. Now I understand why they thirsted for suffering. It was not because they naturally loved to suffer. Their nature was the same as mine; poverty, indigence, insults, sufferings revolted them as they revolt me. But into their ears love spoke words so entrancing that they left all, considered the goods and pleasures of this world as dust, that they might be worthy of the love of Christ. They willed to resemble our Lord, to be treated as He was treated. They suffered even more when they were without sufferings. The saints implored our Lord to fasten them to His cross. They were inspired by a holy enthusiasm. With St. Andrew, they cry: "O good cross, so long awaited, so ardently desired; it is you who are about to unite me to my Saviour."

One day our Lord said to St. John of the Cross: "My son, you have suffered much for Me; you have endured great labors on My account. What recompense would you wish?" The saint replied: "Lord, I desire but to suffer and to be despised with You."

St. Margaret Mary was once horribly calumniated, crushed beneath opprobrium of all kinds. Our Lord showed her a seraph in heaven all inflamed with love and asked her: "My daughter, would you prefer to rejoice in My love like this seraph or to remain on earth to suffer as you are doing?" "My Divine King," she replied, "I will suffer with You."

The watchword to the second degree of humility is "*Amen,* so be it! God wills it!" The watchword of the third degree is a cry of the heart: "Thanks, my God! *Deo Gratias! Alleluia!*"

Here are the two degrees in a face-to-face encounter:

Amen: the restrained cry of patience;

Alleluia: offers to suffer all with joy;

Amen: stifles complaints;

Alleluia: provokes enthusiasm;

Amen: accepts all that happens;

Alleluia: applauds all;

Amen: expresses fear;

Alleluia: expresses love;

Amen: is the response of reason;

Alleluia: is the response of the heart;

Amen: is the word of a servant;

Alleluia: is the cry of the child;

Amen: does not draw back before the cross;

Alleluia: advances to meet the cross;

Amen: prostrates in adoration;
   Alleluia: presses me against His Heart;
Amen: lives for Jesus to the advantage of self;
   Alleluia: lives for Jesus for His advantage;
Amen: confides itself into the hands of Jesus;
   Alleluia: delivers itself over to His Heart;
Amen: is the offering of a victim;
   Alleluia: is the consummation of the holocaust.

Happy the soul who, here below, has learned to say, *Amen,* and has gone on to sing, *Alleluia.* Between this soul and God there passes something mysterious. This soul becomes so intimately united to our Lord that God can say to His angels, "Behold how much I am loved."

22. Our Spiritual Exercises

IT IS TOLD of a certain ambitious politician that he ordered a servant to awaken him each morning with the words: "Sire, wake up! Today you have an appointment with His Majesty the King." We also have great things to do today. Let us remember our resolutions. Let us pray, asking for light. The success of our series of conferences depends upon perseverance in our spiritual exercises and our resolutions.

We can first make a general resolution. This will resemble an overall view, an impetus given to our will. Over and above this general resolution, it is necessary to make a particular resolution, precise and detailed. I ask you, then, to take two subjects for your particular examen. Why two subjects? Can a hunter chase two deer at the same time? Certainly not; but even the most zealous, always faced with the same subject, may become bored. It is good to have one subject to change off with. That does not mean that one should always change every week, or even each month, but at least every four or five months. When our good will slackens, it is well to leave that subject for awhile and exercise ourselves in another.

"Father, I intend to ask my spiritual director for a subject for my particular examen." I do not permit that. It is a poor habit. You are evidently one of those persons who do not want to do things for themselves. It is for you to sanctify yourself. Advancement in the spiritual life is an entirely personal work. You must work at it yourself in order to become expert. It is a good thing now and then to give ourselves a little penance as a part settlement for our failings.

If we are faithful in our spiritual exercises, if we take the part of God seriously, He will do His part. We must do all we can, apply ourselves to follow the methods recommended, start at the exact hour assigned, fight against distractions. When we do the best we humanly can, God will grant us lights, consolations, or, if He wills, He will bathe us in darkness. He will either give us sensible fervor, or abandon us to aridity and dryness. Any one of these results will be the work of God. He knows well what He is doing. As to us, we have but one thing to consider: how we do our part.

A multitude of souls delude themselves on this point. As for me, I have but one thing to do: take every possible precaution to pray well, to make good thanksgivings no matter whether my sky be dark or sunny. Once I have done my best, God will grant me, in His own good time, sensible fervor, though at other times I may experience none. From this variation in the spiritual climate may arise painful misunderstandings. I do not know if I can make this clear.

I ask, "My child, how are your spiritual exercises going?"

"Oh, Father, I have no consolations, no fervor." But your own part: how do you deport yourself?

"Oh, I do nothing. I have no desire for prayer." Again I am asking about your part. What are you doing?

"I am not succeeding in anything. All the time I am in a painful state of mind." God appears to be refusing you consolations. The reason for this you will learn on Judgment Day. But you, are you faithful in commencing your exercises on time? In ending them at the stated time? In following the methods that you have been taught? In recollecting yourself? At least do you make the effort?

"Father, I do all that I possibly can." Good. The good God does not demand of us success; that is for Him to bestow. My dear Sister, when you were in the world, if a dressmaker brought you a poorly made gown, you would have required her to remake it. "That is not properly made," you would have said; "it must be done perfectly." "But I have done the best I can," she might reply. "That means little to me," you would answer. "It must be perfectly made if you expect me to accept it." Little it would avail her to have had a good will. You demanded perfection.

The good God is not like that. When you bring Him the garment of your prayer, He asks but one question of you: "Have you done your best?" "Yes, my God." "Good," He replies, "I only require the effort, the struggle."

In order better to succeed in your spiritual exercises, seek to make use of certain little systems which will be of help at opportune moments.

"Father, I shall do as you say. How do I go about it?" You should decide upon a method that appeals to you.

"Father, I want to acquire purity of intention. Each

time I make a prayer, I desire to prostrate myself in spirit at the feet of our Lord, and protest to Him that I will only His greater glory." Good.

"Father, each time that I go to a spiritual exercise, I place myself in the presence of God, in taking an instant to recall that God sees me." That is very good.

"Father, I never commence to pray without having an intention decided upon in advance. I decide before I begin my prayer what I wish to ask for, what I desire to obtain." There you have an excellent system.

"Father, I demand of myself that I make all my exercises of devotion in a recollected as well as in a mortified manner." Good, but it is important that your attention is not concentrated upon these points so intently that it prevents you from praying.

"I, Father, say my prayers too rapidly. I shall impose upon myself the practice of stopping for the space of a breath between words." Very good.

The saints were not like us. They did not see sanctity in general, but in detail. The more they advanced in holiness, the more simple became the subjects of their prayer, their meditation, and their particular examen.

A little stratagem will complete what I said about exercises of piety. It is the pious practice of performing them under the patronage of a particular saint. I recite the rosary with my guardian angel. I make meditation with Saint Joseph. My communion is with the Blessed Mother; another prayer may be with my patron saint. There are souls for whom this practice is very effective. We know that the saints exercised their ingenuity to devise ways of stimulating their devotion.

"Father, I shall make this the subject of my particular examen." You, Sister, who fail so often in exactitude, who are so seldom punctual, who hardly ever respond to the first sound of the bell, examine yourself on this point of punctuality, and upon your tendency to delay the moment of going to bed. There are Sisters who react to this hour as if it were Satan himself; I have known religious who practically shed blood over this point.

Others will need to take for their examen their dislike to ask for permissions, even when necessary, and in the smallest matters. "Oh, Father, you do not know me. I am so naturally independent that to ask for permissions is the hardest thing in my life." So much the better. The more a thing costs, the higher its value. There are natures always ready to oppose others. No matter what is suggested, the sole fact that it is the hour for recreation is sufficient to inspire them to want to observe silence. They are always demanding exemptions from the task of the moment. I beg of you, let us live the common life, that of the community. How many times is it due solely to discretion that superiors feel themselves obliged to grant exemptions which otherwise they would feel obliged to refuse!

"As for me, Father, I propose to make my particular examen upon obedience." That is too vague. Make it more precise.

"And I, Father, propose never to betray any displeasure, either in my words or in my expression." This will demand great vigilance.

"As for me, Father, it often happens that I complain about the orders given us. I shall make that the subject of my examen." Well and good.

"Father, I shall make my examen upon charity." That is too vague. There are fifty subjects for that particular examen, all upon charity.

"I, Father, permit sharp words to escape me, even such as are humiliating to others. Too often I reveal little malicious things about my neighbor." Concentrate your attention upon this fault.

"As for me, I shall impose upon myself the obligation never to refuse a favor to others."

"And I, Father, each time that someone causes me pain, will say a prayer for that person."

The great value of the particular examen rests upon the effort made to concentrate upon some special point. We should not make the particular examen a universal self-examination.

"Father, I wish to make my particular examination upon humility." Admirable, but do not permit it to remain so vague. Particularize.

"A personal reference occurs in nearly all of my conversations. I shall watch over that point."

"For me, I constantly seek, adroitly and secretly, to attract attention to myself." There are persons whose conversation always starts with "I" and ends with "me."

"For all the humiliations that come to me, I shall say, 'Thank You, Lord.' I shall place my hand upon my heart to signify that I am happy to accept them for His sake."

"I, Father, have a special talent for excusing myself, justifying myself. It happens before I have time to realize it. I always have, upon my lips, a little phrase ready for my defense. In the future, I shall say nothing. If I must speak, it will always be after a little prayer." That is excellent.

"My great fault is that I am opinionated. I argue. I want to have the last word. In the future I shall try to accept the opinions of others."

"I, Father, am discouraged. I do not seem to have the spirit of mortification to any degree. I do not even try to be mortified. I think I understand its meaning, but I never put it into practice. I shall attempt to acquire this virtue, and to that end I promise to make three acts of mortification each morning in honor of the three persons of the Holy Family. And I shall offer five acts of mortification each afternoon and evening, one for each sense." That is very good.

"Father, you no longer speak of Holy Indifference. That would be a grand subject for the particular examen. It seems to me to be what I need. I am too soft, too delicate, too sensitive to the least contradiction. I want to see the will of God in even the most crucifying things, so that I can say from my heart: 'Thanks, Lord, *Amen.*' God alone! Let there be no secondary causes for me."

"I, Father, want to work for purity of intention. During these conferences, my eyes have been opened to the defects of my past life. I am too natural. God's part in my actions is very slender. For the future, I propose to offer Him my principal actions—to turn my heart toward Him in every change of employment during the day, or better still, at the beginning of each hour." That is a very good practice.

Here, my dear Sisters, I shall insert a parenthesis. A multitude of souls cover themselves with unmerited reproach. Many take temptations to self-love for sins and cry, "I am losing all my merits." It is false. Absolutely false! Each time that the principal intention is good and the person is in the state of grace, his work is good even if secondary, imperfect intentions enter in. It resembles money in which there is a certain alloy, but between that and counterfeit money there is a vast difference.

"I lose all my merits!" Who suggests that to you? Why, Satan, of course. He attempts to become your "little director of conscience." The dear little director! How amiable and encouraging he is! What fine compliments he pays you! How can you go about ridding yourself of his importunities?

"Father, I propose to keep constant watch over myself to see that I am not taken in by that liar." For myself I believe that it is better to forget him. The best way to forget yourself is not to think about yourself. Combat such temptations by positive acts of virtue. Offer to God your works and your hearts. Now, to make a start, what, and how many, acts do you propose?

"Father, I shall offer myself to God. I shall place myself in His sight every half hour." That is too much. Start with less, then advance as you form the habit. It is praiseworthy to take a certain number, for instance, three acts of the presence of God, morning and evening, in honor of the Holy Trinity and the Holy Family. Five mortifications in honor of the Five Wounds—that was the practice of St. Francis Xavier, who, at the Fifth Wound, made it his dwelling place, his retreat into the Heart of Jesus.

"I, Father, shall make those acts in honor of the dolors of the Blessed Virgin." Another might have the inspiration to make seven such acts in honor of the institution of the seven sacraments. Including the sacrament of matrimony? Most certainly. Why not thank God for having brought you into existence and for having preserved you until this hour?

"Father, I resolve in the morning to make twelve such acts in honor of the childhood of Jesus." Or, one can follow the fourteen Stations of the Cross. Or, go through the day in company with the fifteen mysteries of the Rosary. One sometimes finds souls who achieve thirty-three acts of the presence of God, in honor of the years of our Lord's life. You can observe that I think in rather exaggerated figures.

"I, Father, wish to say every day as many acts of contrition, accompanied by acts of thanksgiving, as I have spent years in religion." That is very good. These are all little stratagems that speak to your hearts, stimulate your fervor, concentrate your attention, and inspire courage. The important thing is to follow the advice of St.

Francis de Sales: "Follow the attraction of your heart, in all simplicity."

"There are those who, inspired by great love for the Holy Eucharist, offer in preparation the formula of their vows. It is the most beautiful offering, the most agreeable refrain, the sweetest to the ear of Jesus. The vows are for us the most beautiful prayer, after the Our Father. Our Lord is pleased when He sees a soul ingenious in trying to express its love for Him. In its efforts, awkward and stumbling as they may be, He beholds the vigor of love with which His own Heart is filled. They prove the good will of that soul.

Exterior modesty is a point upon which one could elaborate many points for the particular examen. We are not anchorites. Our exterior speaks to the eyes of all who observe us. Not to betray any too great carelessness, or too great freedom, demands great mortification and constant guard over oneself.

There are souls who find great help in spiritual communion.

"Father, it is precisely upon that point that I wish to renew my fervor." I congratulate you. A saint once saw angels presenting his sacramental communions in a golden ciborium, and his spiritual communions in one of silver. Spiritual communions are extremely precious.

Each one of you should choose for her particular examen a subject that has been well thought out. It is useful, then, to undertake some little penance, some small sanction, to impose upon yourself after each failure. St. John Berchmans was once asked how it would be possible to merit the good graces of the Blessed Virgin. "The smallest thing you can think of doing, provided you carry it out faithfully," replied the saint. I repeat the same thing to you: practice the smallest penance that appeals to you, provided you practice it faithfully. A little penance that is excellent for some dispositions consists in saying to our Lord: "My God, I love You with all my heart. I love you so much that, for Your sake, I have not the courage to ask for such a permission, to keep such a resolution." I can guarantee that, as little as your penance touches your heart, such a protestation will make you blush. After nine days of the practice, it will scorch your lips when you repeat it. Finally, it will rend your heart.

Whatever be your penance, the important thing is to select one that most appeals to you, and practice it faithfully.

Certain persons with energetic temperaments find asking for permissions painful. "I complain about obedience," they say. Very well, at the end of the week I shall denounce myself: "I have not had the courage to ask for such and such a necessary permission. Under these circumstances, this week, I complained five times."

I have called to your attention these practical matters because today we must draw up our little plan. I advise you to write in your spiritual note book (1) the general resolution that is to be the spiritual orientation of your life, (2) the resolution covering your particular examen, and (3) a little questionnaire that will serve as material for your monthly retreat.

The saints availed themselves of all kinds of ingenious means to arouse themselves to practice virtue and to animate their good will. They devised mottoes which served them as guides and stimulated them to perseverance. St. Ignatius had for his motto, "All for the greater honor and glory of God." This cry recurs three hundred times in his *Spiritual Exercises*. St. Francis Xavier repeated: "What does it serve a man to gain the whole world and lose his own soul?" The word of St. Aloysius Gonzaga was, "What does that mean for my eternity?" St. John Berchmans repeated, "Why make such a to-do over little things?" Father Olivaint: "Courage and confidence." The prophet Elias: "The Lord liveth before whom I stand."

23. The Baptism of Our Lord

PREPARATORY PRAYER: The same; ask earnestly the grace of working for the greater glory of God.

Our Lord left the Blessed Virgin and His home in Nazareth and went to the river Jordan. He asked of St. John a baptism similar to that of sinners. At first, John refused, astonished and confused by the humility of our Lord. The heavens opened. A voice proclaimed the divinity of Christ. The Eternal Father spoke: "This is My beloved Son, in whom I am well-pleased."

I ask for the grace to know my divine King better, His intention in each act of His gracious will, and to love Him with a love that inspires me to imitate Him more closely, especially in His humiliations.

The separation of our Lord and His Mother caused them great pain. It was an heroic sacrifice, exceeding all those that we may have made. How cold are our feelings toward our parents in comparison with those of our Lord for His Mother, and of our Lady for her divine Child! They were now to separate; afterward the Blessed Virgin could but behold Him from afar, through the crowds, at intervals. Our Lord would henceforth give Himself entirely to sinners, to us. He must now leave the humble home at Nazareth and His Mother.

The Blessed Virgin also made an heroic sacrifice. Our Lord abandoned her. There is a touching promise made to all those who leave their family or their possessions that they may follow our Lord more closely. "He who leaves father or mother, brothers or sisters, for My sake shall receive a hundredfold in this life and life eternal in the next."

Have you ever reflected seriously upon those words? This promise is not made solely for you; it is made equally for those whom you have left behind. Those parents who have given their children to God have also a right to count upon the hundredfold in this life and life eternal. They have in you a pledge of predestination. I cannot permit myself to doubt that the father, the mother, the brother, the sister, of a faithful consecrated soul will be saved. That is a dogma of my heart. The benedictions of God are showered upon your families. You will be astonished at the tribunal of God. Our Lord never lets Himself be outdone in generosity. Your dear ones have given to Him what was most precious to them. Our Lord will assist them in their necessities. They will lose nothing by their sacrifice.

The farewell between our Lord and His Blessed Mother was touching, heart-breaking. Like Jesus and His Mother, I also am permitted to experience the bitterness of separation. Our Lady shed tears. Her tears took nothing from the generosity of her sacrifice. She knew well that it was the beginning of the end. She would never again, in life, possess her Divine Son. Our Lord would nevermore be wholly hers, disengaged from the crowds. His Mother would be even more alone for the remaining years of her life. Then, after His sacrifice was consummated, she would have His apostle for support, and memories to sweeten her remaining years. Has not our Lord, who required such a sacrifice from His Mother, the right to ask a similar sacrifice from us?

Our Lord, in beginning His public life, began it by

humiliation. He made His entrance into the arena of public life by His circumcision. This Jewish rite attested to all that He had need to be purified from the sin of Adam —He, so pure, so immaculate. Should not He, for the glory of His Father, for His own dignity, have been exempted from so ignominious a ceremony? No, our Lord welcomed the humiliation. Now He is still seeking humiliation. St. John the Baptist is there on the banks of the Jordan; clustered about him are the sinners whom he has invited to come to the baptism of repentance. Jesus appears. He seeks to be lost in the crowds. Will He ever in the future be able to induce the crowds to recognize in Him the Son of God? Will the divinity of His mission be recognized? Pharisees will accuse Him to His face: "He frequents the society of sinners." That He might protect His divinity, would it not have been wise for Him not to descend into the ranks of sinners? How greatly in conflict with the wisdom of God are our worldly ideas! His divine wisdom is the opposite of all that we can imagine. Our Lord willed to be humiliated. He wills to surpass us in this glory, the glory of confounding human prejudices. What a pity to behold the self-styled friends of our Lord recoil before humiliations, reject them by strength of arms, so to speak.

When St. John the Baptist saw our Lord approaching, he was confounded. What! The Son of God! The Lamb of God, asking for the baptism of repentance? "Why, Lord, I am not worthy to unloose the strings of Your sandals, yet You come to me? It is I who should be baptized by You!" And again it is humility that speaks.

St. John the Baptist could well have said: "Behold, this is a fine time to exploit my ministry; to bring fame and success to my mission." Could he not have taken advantage of the occasion to say, "Now my words will have greater authority. This great prophet humiliates Himself before me. Hereafter, I shall address my words to the great of the world."

Ah, how easy it is to find a thousand reasons for seeking the esteem of the world! But St. John was moved by the spirit of God. He humiliated himself in his turn: "Lord, it is for me to be baptized by You." Our Lord responded: "So must all justice be accomplished." Yes, all perfection rests upon humility. Can humility exist without a love of humiliations? No! A humble soul wishes to be humiliated. To will to be humble without humiliations is an illusion.

I see our Lord enter the Jordan, bow His Head before the Baptist, pass under the waters of regeneration. Confronted with this scene, I feel deeply the vanity of all human glory. What a contrast between Jesus and me! I am always quick to hide my mistakes, my faults, quick to bring into the open my privileges, my good qualities. I seek to shine, to appear to dominate my surroundings.

Our Lord descended to the lowest degree of humiliation; He was accounted among sinners. God, His Father, could no longer resist this Son whose love for Him knew no limit: He was won by the humility of His Son. The heavens opened; the Holy Spirit descended upon our Lord and the voice of the Father was heard, "This is My beloved Son, in whom I am well pleased. Hear ye Him."

Yes, when you are humble, you are beloved of God. He casts upon you His regard of complacency and of love. Now He can point you out to His angels, to His saints, saying to them: "Behold My beloved child in whom I am well pleased." At that moment the Holy Spirit descends upon you; the heavens open above your head.

Let us demand of the Great Baptized One upon our altar a love of humility, the grace of entering generously upon the narrow way of humiliation, if His good pleasure grants that grace to us. Oh, what a grace it is! May Jesus make you understand this and draw you to follow after Him who is your model.

24. Martha, the Worried Virgin

My dear sisters, let us say with St. Francis de Sales, and with all our hearts, "I shall live and I shall die upon the adorable Heart of Jesus." To die upon that Heart, we must first learn to live there.

I recall what the Gospels relate about Martha, especially the scene when our Lord arrived unexpectedly. Martha was excited; she rushed around to get the dinner prepared for our Lord and, possibly, for several of His disciples. She fidgeted about excitedly. Magdalen remained at the feet of Jesus, absorbed in the sight of her good Master. Her calm got on the nerves of Martha, who was aggrieved that her sister had left the burden of the household work upon her shoulders.

"Lord," she said, "do you not see that my sister has left me to do all the work alone?" Our Lord responded, "Martha, Martha, you are troubled and anxious about many things. But one thing is necessary; Mary has chosen the better part that shall not be taken from her."

I see the guest room of this worthy family. I see Mary at the feet of our Lord while Martha comes and goes hurriedly within the house.

I see Martha all alone preparing the meal, not sparing herself. She knows how to work, to give herself to the task at hand. She is a woman devoted to her duty: duty above all things, always. "One ounce of execution is worth more than a hundred pounds of sermonizing," is her motto.

We, too, must apply ourselves to do little things with great perfection. A life that flows along, faithful to the duty of the moment even in the simplest things, is sure of meriting a great recompense. When one accomplishes work of a supposedly lower order, one is without pride of accomplishment. Nature finds it difficult to find sustenance there for self-love to grow fat upon.

"Let us do the smallest thing that God asks of us today. Tomorrow we shall see what else He will give us to do," is the advice of St. Francis de Sales. Another excellent piece of advice from the same saint is, "A little act accomplished with perfect love and a pure intention can carry with it more merit than a martyrdom endured with a weak and irresolute love."

The glory of Martha lies in her devotion to duty and in her virginity. On that score, Magdalen has the right to be envious. It will only be at the tribunal of God that we shall learn of all the privileges attending virginity. Our Lord has only virgins in his retinue, says St. John, the beloved, in the Apocalypse. It is with holy enthusiasm that we must thank our Lord for the great privilege of virginity.

But now for the defects of Martha. I hope St. Martha will pardon me if I here make her examination of conscience. Our Lord reproved her for her too great natural eagerness, but with an altogether divine delicacy, "Martha, Martha, why do you disquiet yourself? Why this anxiety? One thing alone is necessary."

"What our Lord reproved in Martha," said St. Teresa of Avila (how I love to see the great contemplative take the part of Martha!), "was not her work, but her natural eagerness, her febrile over-activity. The Blessed Virgin also did her own housework and took care of her own home. Had Martha not prepared the dinner, our Lord could not have eaten. Our Lord reproached her only for her too-great agitation. Haste is the plague of devotion."

St. Francis de Sales said, "It does not suffice to do

good; we must do it with discretion and in order. Virtue without discretion is no longer virtue."

There is nothing more beautiful than the quality of being always ready to lend a hand. Alas, that is not the general disposition of the majority of people. For the few who always know how to step into the breach, there are others who invariably step aside. How I congratulate those who always devote themselves to the service of others! Let us know how to help carry the burdens of others. To devote ourselves, however, is not to give unrestrictedly, but to lend our services. We must work with calm, with proportion, with perspective. We should not rush about like a whirlwind, a tornado.

St. Martha permits us to note another of her defects. The good saint is jealous. She complains of her own sister, "Do you not see that she permits me to work alone?" Often jealousy moves into a soul without our having the insight to detect it or the courage to admit it. How many thoughts it suggests, how many words, how many actions!

Here is a person given over to little things: jealousy gradually takes possession of him. He begins to think himself the object of a mysterious persecution. This happens sometimes even in Christian families. A young girl commences to practice virtue, piety, a retired life. This gets on the nerves of her sisters. "Why does she want to behave so peculiarly?" they ask. "Why does she attract attention?" The same thing happens in religious communities. One Sister may complain of the intentions of others, of which they may be wholly innocent.

Magdalen remained at the feet of Jesus; she had no desire to imitate Martha. Martha should not have envied her. "We must follow our individual leading in all simplicity of heart," says St. Francis de Sales.

Had Martha desired to share the aspirations of Magdalen, our Lord would not have approved. Ss. Peter and

John possessed different spiritual aspirations. When St. Peter inquired of our Lord, pointing to St. John, "What will happen to him? What will his end be?" Our Lord quickly replied, "What is that to you? Follow Me."

We shall close this conference with a request to St. Martha. We shall ask her to obtain for us double graces: first, that she shall obtain for us the love of duty, esteem for little things, her spirit of zeal and of devotedness; second, after having asked to share in her virtues, we shall ask to be granted the grace to avoid her faults.

25. *"Abide in My Love"*

OUR LORD, speaking of those devoted to His Divine Heart, said to St. Margaret Mary, "I will give them the gift of touching the most hardened hearts," another promise that arouses a holy emulation. Is not this promise for you also? Your vocation—is it not eminently apostolic? With this devotion you will be all-powerful over rebellious temperaments, hard characters. Honor the Sacred Heart; He will keep His word and will give you the gift of touching the hardest hearts.

There are various dissimilar types of spirituality in the Church. The saints do not resemble one another. Of each one, the Church chants: "He has no equal." Each saint has his own moral physiognomy, his own spiritual character.

St. Francis de Sales was visited from time to time by St. Vincent de Paul. Both were holy, but they differed greatly, nonetheless. The spirituality of the one was not that of the other. St. Jerome lived in the time of St. Augustine. They practically pulled one another around by the hair, as is revealed by their argumentative letters. They had no mutual understanding of one another. St. Jerome, who had lived a lifetime without soiling his baptismal robes, was stricken to the marrow of his bones when he thought of the Day of Judgment. St. Augustine, who, on the other hand, had led a sinful life, reposed upon the sentiments of love that filled his heart.

This is equally true of religious communities, of institutes, of orders. The spirituality of the Trappist is not that of the Carthusian. I learned this through visiting their monasteries. The spirituality of the Benedictines is not that of the Franciscans. That of the Dominicans is not that of the Redemptorists, and that of the Redemptorists is not that of the Jesuits. In each institute, I recognize divine love at work. It is the Holy Spirit that places the seal on each of the orders. In the garden of the Church, the flowers are varied: they can be recognized by their perfume.

There is a kind of family physiognomy common to all the saints of an order. The reason is that from their constitutions, from their Holy Rule, they receive similar spiritual directions. The saints are divided into tribes, so to speak. They belong to their race, to their century, even to their convent or monastery.

St. Bonaventure remarked that spiritual directors are divided into two categories. One is more attentive to bringing about the death of self, the other to fostering life and love. The first brings a man's thoughts back to himself; the second causes souls to repose upon the breast of Jesus.

Here is a saintly director to whose feet comes a soul just emerging from a life of sin. Before admitting him to frequent Holy Communion, the director requires his penitent to undergo a long and painful labor to correct his defects. This method does not touch the heart. The director says: "Later, we shall see. For the moment be attentive to correcting your faults."

The other director, wishing to draw a soul from habitual sin, introduces him to the Heart of Jesus. Once the sinner becomes enamored of the love of God, it is comparatively easy for him to conquer his faults. The latter was the system of St. Francis de Sales, who so insisted upon this method that he almost lost his reputation as a spiritual director. It was bruited about that he was not a safe director, that he understood nothing of the direction of souls, because he admitted to Holy Communion two or three times a week persons who were still addicted to vanities, who even brought their fashions and furbelows to the Holy Table.

This was remarked to the saint. "What of it?" he asked. "At the moment I am engaged in setting fire to the house. When it is well-lighted, then will be the time to throw the furnishings out of the window." Permit me to say that of the two systems, I give the preference to the one in which love predominates; love expands, dilates the heart. A holy religious had this to say: "As for me, I shall always desire that God be the God of my heart."

Some of you have been serving God long enough, with might and main, in a kind of nervous tension, calling upon your conscience in a spirit of fear. Begin now to serve Him with your heart, through generosity, through love. To serve God through love is far more in accord with the Heart of God as well as with our own. The good can never equal the excellence of the best—love. Love eclipses everything else.

Were I to say to a person, "I esteem you, I venerate you," I would be saying a great deal. But is there not something more that I could say? Have I exhausted the human language in those words? No. I can say, "I love you." There is no word that can be added to that. Human language has then exhausted its resources. It can go no further because the human heart can go no further.

"Love is the triumph of God in man," said Père Eymard. Even under the ancient law, the law of fear, do you know what God prescribed above all else? Love. "You shall love the Lord your God with all your soul, with all your strength, with all your heart." God is love—*Deus caritas est*. We can only respond to love with love. Since when is the heart content with respect? Love asks only to be loved. That was true under the old law, the law of fear that made Israel tremble. It is even more true under the law of grace.

"The goodness of God has appeared unto us; He has banished the strong by the strength of His arm." He knows only how to bless. He no longer employs thunder, nor even lightning, to express His majesty. But all that He has lost in majesty, He has gained in love. "My Saviour is little and amiable to excess." Is it to command our respect, extort our admiration? Oh, no, no, it is to win our hearts! That little Child I hold in my arms, I press Him to my heart. What? Do I see you trembling with fear, like a slave, even at Bethlehem? You are, then, of the ancient law.

Our Lord taught us only one prayer—one unique prayer. He did not commence it by saying, "God, all-powerful, infinite Majesty!" No, No. "Our Father," these words contain a whole revelation. At the moment when you say "Our Father," do you tremble, filled with fear and terror? Poor child. You, then, have had a cruel father. You are afraid of your Spouse? You have made a poor alliance? Ah, you have never, then, seen within the heart of your Spouse. You do not know Him. You have never penetrated the secrets of His love.

Our Lord, on the eve of His death, said to His apostles: "I no longer call you servants . . . but My friends." Be to Him, therefore, a friend, a spouse, a tender spouse. Bring to Him the homage of your hearts.

St. Paul cried out to the first Christians: "You have not received the spirit of servitude, but that of adopted children, who cry, *Abba*, Father." How happy would be the Heart of Jesus if He found among you not a single servant, but only His dear children! Up to now, you may have remained at His feet. For the future rest upon His Heart.

St. Teresa of Avila said, "He who receives Jesus in the Blessed Eucharist through fear and trembling is less welcomed than he who presents himself with confidence and love." How, then, can we pass our lives trembling at the feet of our Lord?

But our Lord wants no convicts in His service. He puts no one into a strait-jacket to force an unwilling compliance. If He asks a sacrifice, it is from a free and generous heart that He expects it to be made. Please, please, take off your strait-jackets and make a fire of love out of them! Our Lord will rejoice.

Do you know what is the distinctive mark of true religion? It is love! False religions betray themselves by jealousy of their rights. They arm themselves with brute force to make their laws obeyed. They seek to inspire fear through threats and chastisements. That is because all false religions come from the demon who said of himself: "I am he who never loves."

"The teachings of religion are nothing, if they do not tend to inspire love," said Abbé Perreyve. Here I could establish a parallel between Catholics and Protestants; I am struck when I study the question of contrasts. Protestants have an altogether official religion. They serve God with gloves on, so to speak. They respect Him; they fear Him; but they do not love Him. For this reason they marvel when they see a layman or woman rise from bed in the midst of winter to go to an early Mass. They are amazed. They ask, "Is that necessary in order to be saved?" "No," the layman will reply, "it is not necessary. I do it out of love." Love does not fear to go beyond the precept. Protestants are even more astonished when they see a young girl leave her family, sacrifice a promising future, and enclose herself within a cloister, to renounce her freedom of action. They cannot understand. "What does it signify?" they inquire. "Are you obliged to make such sacrifices to gain heaven?" they want to know. Ah, they know only the religion of fear, of conscience. Love does not count its gifts. It is never satisfied. Its ardor carries it to excess, to folly.

I do not absolutely condemn all fear; there is fear and fear. St. Francis de Sales had a word for it. "In order to love through fear, you must fear through love." "I well know," say certain souls, "that it is necessary to love God in order to enter into Heaven, but I fear He will send me to hell." And they try to force themselves to love God. The good God must be quite touched by such forced love. You love Him only through fear. How much better to fear through love! Ozanam was at the point of death. The priest who prayed beside him said, "My son, have confidence. God is good." Ozanam replied, "Why should I fear? I love Him too much."

"Father," you say, "I have misgivings. Is the religion of love really for me? Am I not condemned to remain in Egypt?" Mary Magdalen, at her first meeting with our Lord, was highly culpable. Instead of condemning her to fear, our Lord said, "My daughter, you have offended Me. Give Me your love. You have offended Me greatly, therefore love Me greatly. You have offended Me more than all others: love Me more than all others." Upon St. Peter, for his triple denial, our Lord only imposed a triple protestation of love: "Peter, lovest thou Me? Peter, lovest thou Me? Peter, lovest thou Me more than all the others?"

How cold is respect! The homage of our fears can

never respond adequately to the love of our Lord. When shall we give Him, at long last, all of our hearts? At the Last Supper our Lord said to His apostles, "Abide in My love." He was not unknowing of what enormous sins, of what strange ingratitude, they would be guilty, yet He repeated, "Abide in My love." What a magnanimous religion! Come, then, to the Promised Land. Leave the dark fears of Egypt. Our Lord appears to apply the law of like attracting like. "You adore Me, I am your God. You tremble before Me, I am your Judge. You offer Me your homage, I am your King. You love Me, I am your Spouse, your Father."

A good priest, a student with me at college, upon his arrival in a new parish met with a thousand difficulties from a certain eminent personage, difficulties that he seemed unable to resolve. After a while things changed for the better, and they became intimate friends. "How was it, Father," said this parishioner one day, "that upon your arrival here you always took me by the wrong side?"

"What else could I do," replied the priest; "that was the only side you showed me."

If you, my friends, only show your most difficult characteristics to our Lord, how can you expect Him to reveal to you His Heart? You leave your heart at the door of the church and enter with but your fears, your respect. Our Lord can only reach you by the side that you show Him.

Away with strait-jackets! We have within us a marvelous resource of incomparable energy—our hearts. It is love that gives impetus to our hearts; the heart and the emotions inspire the activities of the individual. Love is a lever superior to all others. The heart is a fulcrum by which God elevates the world of souls.

Thérèse of the Child Jesus said: "I am of such a disposition that fear makes me draw back. With love, I not only advance, I fly."

Love alone can command the heart; then the heart does all the rest. St. Teresa of Avila, toward the close of her life, said, "The more I learn, the more I see that everything should be done through love. I no longer govern with the same rigor as formerly." Had anyone attempted to take this saint by force, he would have wasted his time. She would have resisted. She would have rebelled. "That would have been natural for me," she wrote, "but with the least good will shown me, people can do with me what they will."

St. Augustine said, "Love, then do what you will." What a beautiful device is that of the Canadian Zouaves: "Love God and go on thy way." "All for love; nothing by constraint," said St. Teresa of Jesus.

The soul which hopes to attain the summit of love must be, from the beginning, well established in love. Love renders sweet all that it commands; light, all that it endures; precious, all that it touches. All is little without charity; with it all is great.

"A very little virtue practiced by a loving heart may possess more merit than a wavering martyrdom," said St. Francis de Sales. A soul confined within the narrow circle of an overactive conscience seems to say to God: "I love You; but when You want me to obey You, You must threaten me with hell." Is that the disinterestedness of love? No. You are then trembling for your own safety, for your own skin. You serve God for your own ends, to escape His justice.

Do I have to insist upon the truth that love makes all things easy? How many times have you not experienced this in your own lives? Something may be naturally repugnant to us. One day, moved by love, desiring to give pleasure to a beloved friend, we see all our repugnances vanish.

What appeared impossible before now becomes easy, even welcome. Nothing costs love too dearly when it seeks to give satisfaction to the beloved. Love faces all difficulties with courage.

"When I have succeeded in expanding a heart, I have gained it," said Père Poulevoye. "On the contrary, the demon constrains, narrows souls. When I have been able to release a heart that he has bound, I have gained that soul. Love is winged."

How is it possible to soar when the soul is compressed within the vise of fear? The capacity to love is the capacity to be happy. He who loves really lives. He who loves knows how to serve. He who loves is happy. "One atom of love placed in a balance against the universe will outweigh it as easily as a tempest carries away a straw," said Lacordaire. Love goes farther than fear. Love opens before us horizons of far distances. Love is limitless; its confines are the infinite. Love never says, "Enough." Love is the friend of "Too much."

"Am I obliged to do this?" Words of the cowardly. Go on dragging yourself in a rut if you must. "*Am I obliged?*" For myself, I love and I want to show my love. Poor souls, made anemic by a religion of fear, you live feebly, far from the sun of love! Have you never heard these words of your Lord: "Abide in My love"? Not through duty, not through respect, but "in My love." Establish there your dwelling place; raise there your tabernacle.

How many souls there are to whom but one thing is lacking to their perfection: confidence! "What would you do if the good God were to forbid you to love Him?" was once asked of a child. "I would love Him in secret," was the touching reply. Do you know what is the greatest obstacle to a religion of love? It is our ignorance. We are just not acquainted with the Heart of Jesus. We learn about His majesty, yes; His power, yes; His justice, yes; oh, above all, we learn about His justice. But His love? His Heart? No, we do not know His Heart.

St. Augustine said to God: "Too late have I loved Thee because too late have I come to know Thee." At the tribunal of God where it will be granted us to plunge our vision into the loving Heart of our Lord, what cries of astonishment will arise. "Oh, had I but known!"

A quite general malady is that of discouragement. A severe malady it is, a kind of spiritual anemia, arising from a lack of confidence. God permits us to call Him *Father*. We are, therefore, His children. Do you think a father would feel flattered to see his children constantly trembling before him? Falsity! Then you call God "the good God." Again falsity! I forbid such souls to use the words " the good God," in speaking of the hard Master whom they try to serve. Your God? Why, He is a tyrant, hard, intractable, unyielding, stern. Oh, how little do you know the Heart of God! St. John reposed upon the breast of Jesus. He penetrated into the secrets of that adorable Heart, and ever thereafter he could only speak of love. He never spoke one word of fear.

The way to reach this fruitful region, vivified by the great Sun of Love, is through devotion to the Heart of Jesus. This devotion is a divine remedy for the coldness of these times. Providentially, devotion to the Heart of Jesus was revealed to the modern world just at the time that the heresy of fear was making such ravages among souls of good will. The Sacred Heart is, *par excellence*, the devotion of love.

"The Heart of Jesus," said St. Margaret Mary, "is a good Master who will teach you to love with all your heart. The Heart of Jesus is an abyss of confidence and love. Abandon yourself to Him. He will teach you how to make fear give place to love."

26. The Kingdom of Christ

W<small>E SHALL</small> now make a meditation that is extremely important, a meditation which St. Ignatius proposes as a second foundation, a new basis, for the Christian and the religious life.

Preparatory prayer: the same, though made more seriously than before: "I ask sincerely that everything in me may be for the glory of God, *that God will glorify Himself at my expense.*"

I see, with the eyes of the imagination, the villages through which Jesus passed during His mortal life. I shall follow Him, step by step. I shall contemplate Him.

I ask for the grace to comprehend the divine appeal. It is addressed to each one of us. Jesus Christ calls upon each of us to walk, not in the ranks of the simple faithful, but of privileged souls. We ask for the grace to respond with all the enthusiasm and sincerity of our inmost hearts.

This meditation resembles a parable. To understand it properly, we must go back to the times of St. Ignatius. I shall represent to myself a great king who rules the universe. All recognize his authority. He has been chosen by God for this rulership; there is no doubt about this. He has given full proof of his divine election, and now wishes to undertake an expedition to subvert the plans of pagans who have gathered together formidable armies. He plans to ravage their countries. This king appeals to all those who wish to follow his banners, who wish to enroll under his standards. All those who accept and follow him will participate in his victory. No one will perish. Not one will fall victim to the enemy.

"Let all those who love freedom range themselves under my banner. Those who fail to follow me will go into slavery, servitude, death."

What should the subjects of this great king reply? Would not they who refuse such an offer be foolish? The king says to his subjects, "You are to live my life; you will have the same garments, the same living conditions as I. You will always find me to be first at the post of danger. You will never have to suffer anything that I have not first endured. Ultimate victory is assured." Certainly any sensible person would hasten to range himself under the standards of such a king to fight against the pagans who seek to destroy his realm and their own lives.

Application of this parable to our Lord: this King, chosen by God and descended from heaven, comes to make His appeal to all the earth. He comes to invite the children of Adam to range themselves on the side of His followers. He invites us to conquer His and our enemies: the world, the demons, the seductions of earth, of our own passions. He comes to declare war. He offers the sword to all his followers. He addresses each one in particular: "Will you follow Me? I am the Way, impossible for you to mistake it. I shall always lead you by the safest paths. I am the Truth. I promise you victory. I shall not deceive you. Will you follow Me? I am Life Eternal. Apart from Me is death eternal. I give endless life to those who, under my orders, have fought the good fight.

"Will you follow Me? You will always find Me in the lead. You will never be called upon to do anything that you have not known Me to be the first to do. I shall be beside you in weariness, in discouragement. I shall always precede you in combat and in danger. Will you accept My offer?"

In the parable, St. Ignatius shows us two classes of souls, two classes of persons. First of all, there are those who have good common sense; they accept these magnanimous proposals. One would truly have to be mad to refuse such an offer. On this expedition, one is sure of not perishing, but of triumphing, certain, even, of conquering. Then, to refuse and to go to certain destruction chained by passion, deliberately chained by the demon, chained by sin? To go, head bowed down in submission, to be precipitated into the horrible abyss of anguish and death? Such a decision would smack of folly, of madness. All of those who are not stricken by blindness would come to offer themselves and their services to God. "Here am I, Lord, ready to do all that You ask of me, ready to observe all of Your commandments."

But at the side of these persons of good common sense are those who long to render even more outstanding services to the King. These, says St. Ignatius, bring a more generous offering. They accept not only all the commandments of their chieftain, but they ask permission to renounce all that they possess to follow Him wholeheartedly. "I could serve my King in retaining my wealth, but I renounce it that I may serve Him with no ulterior thought, no backward look. I could keep my liberty, but I renounce it so I can be at His service every minute of every day. I could allow myself permitted pleasures, but I renounce them that I may find joy only in His service. He endured sufferings, privations; I embrace them also, in His example. I could follow Him in beautiful clothing, with a fine wardrobe. But no, he was poorly clothed, poorly lodged; I wish to resemble Him. Let Him place me at His most difficult post. That is my earnest desire. That is what I hope for."

Those who speak thus have not only good common sense, but also generous hearts.

Our Lord appeals to our hearts. He does not threaten us if we refuse this more unselfish offer. But those who add love to their loyalty will follow Him more closely, will be always at His side, always at the mercy of His least desires, of His plans, of His projects for themselves and for others. They will be ambitious to serve in the more difficult charges, the harder tasks, the more dangerous, there by His side, where He confronts the enemy. He will see their love and their courage. His heart will approach their hearts in love and gratitude and understanding. What a sublime ambition!

At the close of this meditation, we find St. Ignatius dictating this colloquy: "Oh, eternal King of worlds without end: the kings of earth have but a day for their glory. We see them, even upon the very day of their coronation, extended upon a bed of pain. Our King is immortal. It is to Him that I belong. With Him there is no deception, no bitter awakening. Oh eternal King of worlds without end, behold me in the presence of all the celestial court, under the eyes of Your angels, of Your saints, of the glorious Virgin, Your Mother. Here I affirm my most resolute intention to follow You as closely as it is possible for me to do so. And as You have deigned to choose me to share in Your privileges, I desire first to follow You in Your humiliations, in poverty, in chastity, in death to pleasures of the world. Long live the Lord! Long live the King, my Master! In whatever state it may please You to place me, Your servant will be there in life and in death."

My dear friends, you have been freely chosen to be among those souls of whom our Lord asks more generosity, more renunciation, more fidelity. Close up your ranks about your Prince, as did those resolute holy women

who followed Jesus about Judea, braving the sarcasms of
the Jews, risking the loss of their reputations, placing
themselves above all the opinions of the world, above all
earthly wisdom. They left all to follow our Lord.

Like them you have been chosen. Perhaps your heart
is rent at the realization that, so far, you have corresponded
but poorly to the hopes and expectations of your King.
He knows your sad past, but He reads the future. He sees
all the graces you have abused, the resistances you have
offered to His mercy, your ingratitudes, your pettiness,
your ignoble acts.

Today is a new day. Your King is not repelled by
you. He still regards you with a divine predilection. Your
miseries and your mishaps draw a larger measure of His
divine tenderness. Give yourself to Him with more love
than ever before, but also with more humility, with less
presumption.

Oh, King eternal, of a world without end!

27. Facing Oneself

MY DEAR FRIENDS, the vocation to
which we are called is truly sublime, yet we feel ourselves
to be so paltry, so weak. Do you wish to learn an excellent
means of corresponding to our divine vocation? It is devotion to the Heart of Jesus. "I shall raise them quickly
to the highest perfection," so our Lord said to St. Margaret
Mary. I do not know of any means more certain, more
efficacious, better suited to bring us to a high state of
perfection than devotion to the Sacred Heart.

Days succeed one another without resembling one another. Often there are changes in the physical atmosphere. Interiorly, these changes are even more frequent. In the moral world one can observe seasons succeeding one another in the same day. The warmth of summer—the movements of sensible devotion—is succeeded by the chill of winter—all good sentiments seemingly turned to a dull inanity. Then comes the beauty, the freshness, of springtime, or the winds and drooping flowers and falling leaves of autumn. Such phenomena are not necessarily a bad sign. Oh, I know well that we would prefer to be immobilized in good sentiments, not ever to feel impressions of weakness, of temptations. That would flatter our self-love, but that is not, ordinarily, the way by which God leads His saints.

"Father, everything goes well for me. I receive lights, consolations." That is well, St. Ignatius said, but do not be led away by enthusiasm. God is treating you as a favored child. He gives you sweets because He sees that you love such delicacies. He treats you like a child from whom one can get no cooperation without first giving some gift.

If God is treating you like that, it is because you are not yet a truly generous person. Wait a little and all that gorgeous sky will change. When you will have made true progress, God will feed you upon dry bread. Bread without sugar is of more value than sugar without bread. Bread alone will sustain us. Sugar alone will not. It is not that I do not wish you to have consolations, but I wish you to realize that, in bestowing them, God is treating you as if you were still a weak child.

Adroitly, without your knowing it, our Lord places His Hand under your cross and carries it for you. You go on your way happily, calling yourself joyful with a light heart: "The cross of Christ does not weigh me down!" I believe it—because it is He who carries it for you.

Some day He will say, "This dear soul has become more generous, stronger; she is making progress; we shall begin to let her bear the weight of the cross alone." So, slowly, without warning—that is the difficulty, there is no warning—our Lord withdraws His hand; and behold this soul is all alarmed, not knowing to what to attribute the change. "What does this mean?" she asks. "Other days, the cross of our Lord appeared lovable, light; today I find it heavy, even crushing." That is not a bad sign. It only signifies that sometimes our Lord does all the work; today you are doing it yourself.

I am not the friend of consolations. Doubtless, it may be permissible to ask for them, but not too many too often. My praise goes to that person who abandons herself to the divine good pleasure, learning how to say *Amen* to all that presents itself.

Another person comes to me to say, "Father, during this retreat I have not received any light. I have felt no devotion and am plunged into darkness. My state is painful; my conscience disturbed. I am suffering agony."

"Very well," says St. Ignatius, "it is worth all that it costs." Confidence! God is causing you to have to purchase His graces. It is an excellent retreat for you. Such a retreat may not be according to your tastes, but it is according to the Will of God. You can stand fearlessly before our Lord and say to Him, "Do with me what You will. It is not for my own sake or for my own consolation that I labor, but for Your glory. Do with me what You will, not what I might mistakenly desire."

But why, after accepting, in principle, everything that befalls us, do we immediately proceed to pester our poor souls when darkness falls and we find ourselves immersed in trials? "Ah, it is my fault. God is punishing me." It is forbidden to think or say such a thing. In this you resemble the wife of Job, who, seeing him plunged into afflictions, said, "You must be very culpable before God for Him so to try you." Why are so many thus inclined instantly to suspect their own souls when they suffer?

St. Margaret Mary, on the day of her religious profession, was filled with great devotion and spiritual joy. She said to our Lord, "I beg of You, keep these consolations for others who will make better use of them." Our Lord answered her: "Be content. You will lose nothing by waiting." Ordinarily, our Lord gives us a little farewell before sending us on to the field of battle. "At first I received consolations; then I found myself immersed in bitterness. Then consolations returned. I was thus torn between consolations and bitterness." "Very well," replies St. Ignatius. "Perfection!" The general rule is the best symptom in a retreat. Two spirits are working within you. Through spiritual joy, God is working within you. The next instant, the devil leaps at you, to plague your spirit and your heart. This action of the two contrary spirits is useful in the formation of souls, to strip them of their self-love. These are the two elements of success in a retreat.

Finally, a fourth soul says: "Father, this retreat is not going so badly. I have not suffered. I have not passed through any crises." But that is not a good sign either. This is the ordinary state throughout the year. "Ah," says St. Ignatius, "you are in the ordinary state. I am fearful for you. What? Nothing more than during the year? I tremble for you. An ineffectual retreat is an unsuccessful retreat. Ah, the demon is pleased. He has not judged you worthy of a serious temptation. A bad sign!" When the demon sees that a soul is going to misuse a retreat, he says to himself, "Take care! Do not awaken this soul. Make no noise! I shall lull it softly asleep." But when the demon sees a soul is making a good retreat, he enters into a rage and starts upon a campaign, taking strong measures. This is a good sign. "It is a bad sign," says St. Ignatius, "when a soul is agitated neither by God nor by the devil." This might be a state that would last, perhaps, for a few days, but, in general, it is not a good sign. Of that person, St. Ignatius asks, "Have you been faithful in little things?"

"Yes, in general," you reply. In particular? "Well, it has happened that I have failed in certain details. I have let fall curious, distracting glances. There has been a little going easy about things; I have not been very exact about answering the bell, and in the morning I have been slow to arise." "Ah," replies St. Ignatius, "there you are. You have not been willing to accept the sole means of making your retreat a success: fidelity in little things."

There are strong-minded persons who disdain little things. They cast a glance of pity upon those who are exact in leaving at the first sound of the bell, seeking to keep themselves in the spirit of the retreat. Such persons are not making a good retreat in which the secret of success lies in fidelity to little things.

"But, Father, I am not conscious of having failed in little things. I have done everything possible." As long as you are in that frame of mind, your retreat will be good. On that point I must watch my counsel carefully in order not to bring trouble to careful persons.

> "Heaven cannot be won at a discount. Let us be generous in the service of God. It is we, ourselves, who fashion our own heaven."
>
> PERE MARQUETTE

> "We must not bargain with our Lord. If He asks of you a sample, give Him the whole piece."
>
> ST. SOPHIE BARAT

28. The Vocation of the Holy Women

WE SHALL meditate upon the vocation of the Holy Women. According to the Gospel, there were seven. There was, perhaps, an even greater number who followed our Lord, and who, in order to attach themselves to His steps, abandoned their homes and their families. We shall take time to consider the seven mentioned in the Gospel.

Preparatory Prayer: the same, but with ever-increasing sincerity, "All for Thy glory, oh God; nothing purely for my own sake."

I see our Lord wandering over the Judean hills, and with Him I see these women: Magdalen, the sinner; the mother of James and John; and the others. I think about them. They are happy; the joy that lights their faces floods their hearts.

I ask for the grace to esteem my vocation more highly than ever, to love it, to attach myself to it with all the fibers of my heart.

215

Oh, my friends, how sad it is! I recall that while in the novitiate, one day we learned of the defection of an old religious, author of numerous works of sincere devotion, who had lived more than thirty years in his vocation, but who had deserted the Society of Jesus. We were ashamed. Our venerable master of novices said to us: "My dear Brothers, where is the religious who can say, 'As for me, I am certain that I shall die in the religious state'?"

We all must tremble, all must fear; all must remain on guard and attach ourselves more firmly than ever to our vocation. I know a Jesuit Father who bore upon his heart, written in his blood, a prayer in which he asked the grace of being torn to pieces rather than abandon his vocation. He died, crushed under a falling wall. His prayer was answered to the letter.

Our Lord has chosen us. Our Lord said to His apostles, "You have not chosen Me; it is I who have chosen you." My dear friends, you also can hear in the depth of your hearts these words of our Lord, "It is I who have chosen you. During your youth, in boarding school, in the world, everywhere, I turned upon you a gaze of tenderness. At last one day I placed you in My Heart forever, asking you to give Me your affections and your devotion. Even now you have not ceased to be the object of my predilection. I chose you from your tenderest years, from your infancy, from your cradle, from all eternity. Thousands of years before your birth, I thought of you. My thoughts dwelt upon you with love."

What an incomparable grace is that of the religious vocation! As long as I am in mortal life, agitated among the shadows and ignorance of this world, I shall not be able fully to comprehend this tremendous privilege. Before the tribunal of God, with what joy shall I be transported when I comprehend the goodness of our Lord! What folly of love He has shown toward me! Oh, if we could but comprehend the full meaning of this marvelous privilege, we would be penetrated with gratitude and with love for God. We would no longer see in our Lord a rigorous master, a harsh master, a judge, a tyrant, but a tender Friend, a beloved Spouse.

In His presence, we should be at our ease, happy. We can always depend upon His Heart without ever being deceived. He gave full proof of His affection before we even commenced to love Him. Our Lord said: "I have loved you with an eternal love." This divine appeal, how precious it is! How beautiful, how touching, to study the delicate ways of our Lord in attracting a soul, in attaching it to Himself, in ravishing its love. Do you recall the first time you heard our Lord's voice? It was, perhaps, during your thanksgiving, when you had our Lord within your heart, whispering to you, "My child, if you but knew how precious your soul is to Me! Will you renounce, for my sake, your father, your mother, your brothers and sisters? I dare to ask even this of you. Will you renounce the most legitimate affections that you may give Me your un-divided heart? It is an exchange that I ask of you—My Heart for your heart."

At these softly spoken words, we experienced an inspiration of holy delight, aided by supernatural love, and we responded quickly: "Yes, my God, You have chosen me. What a beautiful grace for a creature, so poor, so weak! Yes, I desire to be wholly Thine."

Perhaps there followed days of tepidity, when, weary of God, we sought to convince ourselves that it was not the divine appeal, but a decision lightly made. Perhaps we even turned a longing gaze upon the world. Perhaps we wished to enjoy its pleasures, its intoxications. We sought to disengage ourselves, to separate ourselves from the arms of God. But He followed us. He knocked at the door of our hearts. Instead of tearing us away from the affections of our family, He gently brought us to the foot of the altar, and there, still begging for our love, He said to us: "My child, give Me your heart. Will you be poor, chaste, with Me? Will you abandon yourself to My love?"

When St. Bernard left his family, he took with him all of his brothers except the youngest. Bernard took this one by the hand and led him out upon the terrace of their paternal chateau, where he said to him, "My brother, this whole domain now belongs to you. We leave all our possessions to you." The young brother, touched by supernatural grace, replied, "The apportionment is not fair. You are choosing heaven and leaving to me only earth." Some years later he, too, became a religious.

How much have those to complain of who remain in the world, surrounded by snares and dangers, carried along by the torrent; how difficult not to abandon themselves to the drift of their passions! I never return from a mission or retreat without feeling myself penetrated by gratitude that fairly transports me. "How good You are, my God, to have drawn me out of that frightful whirlpool, that mire that engulfs so many souls. Why am I not in their place?"

If we could but envision how much misery God has spared us in calling us to Himself, we should appreciate at its true worth the happiness of the religious life.

St. Bernard, transported with joy in his monastery, went and prostrated himself before the altar, crying out: "My God, from now on, You are my father, my mother, my brother. You are to me all things." We, too, can repeat those loving words. They intoxicate our hearts with joy and happiness.

Why has He chosen us? Why did our Lord choose the Holy Women? Were there not in all Israel others more worthy of the privilege? There were those more chaste than Mary Magdalen, who had dishonored herself; yet Magdalen was chosen. In Israel there were women for whom our Lord had performed miracles: He had raised the son of the widow of Naim; He had cured the mother-in-law of Peter; He had raised the daughter of Jairus. The neighbors of these women, the women themselves, should they not have attached themselves to our Lord? But they were not chosen. Mystery of love! At your side in the world were souls more innocent than you, more fervent. God passed them by. He did not choose them. How many young girls knock at convent doors, enter, then are obligated to leave! Our Lord has not chosen them.

From eternity our Lord has chosen us through a rare privilege. In the Society of Jesus, it is estimated that at least one half of the young men entering the novitiate leave, returning to the world. Why did God choose me? It is a mystery of love. God chooses one and leaves another.

In the same family there may be several daughters, only one of whom is chosen. The others may merit it just as much, even more. Martha merited as well as did Mary. Martha was perfectly chaste; the Church numbers her among the virgins, yet Martha remained tranquilly in the house, with her housework. It was Mary who was chosen to accompany Him.

This appeal of the Master to the Holy Women, how was it answered? Many refused His invitation. There were but seven who followed our Lord, yet many more must have been called. Other souls heard His appeal. Proof lies in the incident of the "rich young man" in the Gospel. There is a vocation clearly rejected even though we are told that Christ loved him. Our Lord spoke clearly to him: "If thou wilt be perfect, go, sell what thou hast, give to the poor. Then come, follow Me." The young man was fearful of sacrifice; he was saddened. He had hoped there was some new and easy way to perfection, to eternal life. Those women who refused to respond to the appeal of our Lord must have become likewise saddened, must have felt they had set up an obstinate resistance to our Lord that would compromise them for the remainder of their lives. Mysterious resistance to salvation! They returned to the world. Were they lost?

How many today refuse an alliance with our Lord? He offers them His hand to convey them to the espousals, but they will not. If our Lord abandons me to myself, it is not only a temporary refusal that I make to His divine proposals, but one that will bear a Dead Sea for a lifetime— even, perhaps, for all eternity. But our Lord pities us in our fragility. He never becomes discouraged. He watches us as we examine His divine appeals, seeking to convince ourselves that the invitation does truly come from God, and He does not grow weary. He follows us. He returns to the charge. Oh, the good Master!

My dear friends, am I rash in saying that many of these Holy Women were less obstinate than many religious? Had our Lord spoken as often to their hearts as He speaks to such and such a religious, they would have consented to follow Him, even unto Calvary. Many of these women attached themselves to Jesus for a time—for some weeks, some months; then they became discouraged: the itinerant life was too hard, and they returned to the warm security of their homes and family life.

How they are to be pitied! How unfortunate they were! It is said that Adam was more tortured by the re-membrance of the earthly Paradise than by all his other ills. Those intimate visits with God in the cool of the evening, the harmony of all creation, the absorbing happiness that he had tasted—all pierced him with a thousand swords. The greatest torture of those religious who abandon their vocation is the remembrance of the terrestrial paradise where they caught a glimpse of experiences so beautiful, and which they have lost forever. What kind of a malediction it is that attaches to their foosteps I know not, but everything seems to be against them. They become filled with fear and terror over their salvation. To reassure them is impossible.

However, of the Holy Women who attached themselves to our Lord and His mission of redemption, there were those who remained faithful to Him to the end: the blessed seven who aided and comforted Him in His trials, and who remained faithful, giving themselves without reserve. They left their homes, their friends, their most intimate affections. Doubtless their sacrifices caused suffering, but they redoubled their zeal. Once they heard the voice of Jesus, they were faithful. Happy seven! They went forth to embrace the cross, to solicit the privilege of being poor, of being chained to obedience, vowed to chastity with Christ.

Behold our happiness! May it always be so! May it be that not one person listening to these words will ever disengage himself or herself from the divine embrace to plunge into a deluge of pain and despair. Let us pray that we may all reach heaven. Let us close ranks about our Lord, supplicating Him to grant us the grace to die rather than to be unfaithful to our holy vocation.

SPIRITUAL READING

The Imitation of Christ: BOOK I, Chapters 1, 19
BOOK III, Chapters 18, 50

"Watch over me today for You well know that I am a traitor. Only too well You know how evil I am. If You leave me but an instant to myself, I fear I shall betray You. I am such a nothing that even when I go out to do a good work, I say to myself: You leave a Christian; perhaps you will return having betrayed God."

ST. PHILIP NERI

29. The Way of Confidence, Joy, and Love

How unspeakably happy I should be if these conferences would have the effect of causing you to enter in earnest upon the way of confidence and love.

"Father, I have come to understand what the religion of love is. For the future I shall reject everything that brings me back to fear." Very good.

"Father, I now understand that the demon has but one goal: to cause me to become troubled. He plunges me into a thousand difficulties. He knows but one thing—to stamp around and frighten souls. For the future I shall consider all that troubles me as emanating from the demon. I shall not reply; I shall not discuss anything with him. I know now that everything bearing the seal of the demon bears the seal of trouble." Perfect.

"As for me, Father, I feel as if I were plunged into a kind of spiritual anemia. My spiritual temperature is below normal. What causes this?" It is due to your lack of confidence. In proportion as one falls back upon himself, his spiritual constitution becomes enfeebled, rachitic. He finds his spiritual health undermined. Do not examine the imitation so seriously. Examine your original model, Jesus Christ.

There are persons, and they are numerous, who feel that Divine Providence should act according to their own desires. If something painful is presented to them, if the yoke of our Lord becomes heavy, they become totally disconcerted. They cast looks of astonishment toward heaven and raise their eyebrows in dismay, unable to understand how the good God could dare to conduct them by that thorny path, cause them to pass through such a trial. Accept the decrees of Divine Providence. Believe that the plans of God are at least as wise as your own. Permit God the liberty of making His ideas prevail. You can be certain they will be superior, in the long run, to your own.

There are others who find it necessary to reconcile themselves to the exigencies of the spiritual life. "I did not think it would be like this. I was far from expecting these difficulties." My child, you have formed a certain ideal of the spiritual life, an ideal of your own, that will never be adapted to life on earth. Many are victims of these preconceived notions.

Others have need to be reconciled to their employment. "In everything that is given me to do, I am good-for-nothing. It is, therefore, impossible to work at my perfection in such employment." How do you know but that the thing you long for would be, for you, a spiritual danger? Or, are you positive that you could carry it on with any greater satisfaction than your present work?

Still others need to become reconciled to their superiors. "As long as I am under that person, it is useless. May God change my circumstances and give me another superior." What do you really know about such a change? You would merely find yourself in another set of circumstances with other and perhaps greater difficulties. Trust yourself to God.

There are souls that are constantly quibbling within themselves. They seem to seek to crush themselves, always examining their consciences with a microscope. Such tormented souls live in a constant state of uneasiness about God and about themselves. Their vexations, their repugnances, arise out of self-love. *Spiritual poverty, well accepted, is one of the greatest treasures of the spiritual life.* Be at peace with yourself then. Have pity upon your poor soul. Oh, how much would your soul rather deal with God than with you! You are unforgiving, inexorable. If you treated a child as severely as you treat your soul, its disposition would be ruined.

There are many souls who practically require private revelations before they will believe that God has truly forgiven everything. Multitudes of pious souls will be seized with astonishment at the tribunal of God. "Had I but known that all was pardoned and forgotten, how my heart would have expanded! How generous I would have been, had I but known!" Why do you not know it now? Confessors and directors have exhausted themselves in repeating to you: "Go in peace."

Do you believe what your director tells you?

"Yes, Father." That is not sufficient. You must *do* as he tells you—"Go in peace."

"I am always afraid that I have not made myself clear. If I could only know that I had made myself fully understood." You will never know that. It is for your director to decide that, and to question you if necessary. He possesses the grace of state by which he directs you.

However rare spiritual directors may be, they are still

more numerous than the directed—that is, those who actually submit to direction. The reason? The latter become involved with their "little director," that dear little Satan. He is chased out by the door, to return by the window. When windows are shut in his face, he crawls in through the keyhole. The devil still has his angelic intelligence; he has never lost that. The most learned persons who have tried to enter into arguments with him have lost their peace. The devil's chief aim is to cause you to lose your peace of mind and soul, to deliver you over to sadness and distress. Sadness is the devil's bath. Sadness is the eighth capital sin. Never, with full advertence, would I linger upon a sad thought. Joy lends wings to the soul.

I have delayed speaking to you of charity in judgment and in sentiments. I must, however, say something about charity in words. This is the point upon which we are most likely to betray the confidence and love that we owe our neighbor. Let us distinguish between words spoken to others and those said in their absence. The former come under the class of disrespect, rudeness, or insults, and, generally speaking, are less serious because they are usually of less consequence. The spirit of contradiction inspires a great number of them.

St. Ignatius said: "Every time that the glory of God and the good of the neighbor do not require it, I do not argue." Agree with your neighbor then.

There are some people who appear naturally to have an acid tongue. It is a small instrument, very supple; but they use it as an arrow to wound others by means of sharp words that pierce deeply. With what eyes must our Lord look upon you when your neighbor brings to the altar his wounded heart—wounded through your fault. Oh, doubtless it is not forbidden to tease one another occasionally. Such humorous sallies season conversation. It is a good sign when one sees that hearts and minds are fully at ease, and that friends can sometimes address little teasing remarks to one another.

St. Francis de Sales excelled in this art. He had a brother priest who was pious, but of a difficult disposition, always moody and discontented. One day the good saint said to him, by way of fraternal correction: "My brother, I know a person whom you have made very happy."

"Truly? Who could that be?" asked the priest.

"The woman whom you would have married had you embraced the marriage state."

It is also related that a worldly man coming to visit the saint expressed contempt for certain popular devotions, among them that to St. Anthony of Padua for the recovery of lost articles. The saint had this to say, "My dear friend, you would not do so badly, in my opinion, if you would address a petition to St. Anthony for the recovery of the simplicity which you seem to have lost."

In words against charity, we distinguish between slander and calumny. To repair a calumny, it is necessary to retract the charge. To repair slander is more difficult. You have tarnished the good name of that person. You must restore it by praising him, by bringing out his good qualities. In slander, if I reveal a secret mortal sin, I commit a mortal sin. If I reveal a venial sin, I commit a venial sin.

As to public faults, sins committed by persons in authority fall into the public domain. Even if 100,000 persons are still ignorant of them, I can speak of them without wounding charity, but I would expose myself to the disedification of my neighbor. Now I must add that in revealing a venial sin I can commit a mortal sin, according to the wrong that I do. Here is a person who is successful in his work. Through the revelation of a small fault I might cause him grave harm. His authority will be diminished for years. His prestige may be injured. In the world such indiscretions have gone so far as to wreck marriages. The slope is slippery.

In conversations, there are certain reticences, certain gestures, a single shrug of the shoulders, that may fall upon certain natures like drops of gall. Words, perhaps insignificant in themselves, but emphasized by the tone of voice—even, it may be, by the praise that accompanies them—can be given overtones of exceptional malice.

Someone praises another: "Do you believe that?" "If I could only speak!" "It is better to be silent." "They say!" "Poor young girl!" "So much the better!" "I have heard so many bad things!" "Too bad, but she is no longer well thought of." "A little imprudence is permitted to the young." Add to these vague words, full of reticences, a tone of pity, a honeyed voice, a semblance of hesitation, of pain in speaking them, and behold, those who listen carry away certain suspicions, often false. The person under discussion will suffer from diminished esteem. Friendships will be paralyzed. How dangerous the consequences of such a manner of speaking. It is nearly always envy that prompts such utterances. Jealousy, perhaps, of the beauty that the speaker does not possess in the same degree. Envy of a reputation more widely known than our own, and the difference of which makes us appear to be of less consequence. Envy of talents, of acquired knowledge, of a higher standing than our own, of greater amiability, of the many advantages that another may possess.

It is rare to find pious persons dealing out calumnies wholesale, but of how many exaggerations are they guilty? Of how many falsities of all kinds, not invented, but gathered up and carried about? There are those who seem to possess a marvelous talent for amplification. With a mere grain of sand they build a hill, a mountain.

SPIRITUAL READING

The Imitation of Christ: BOOK II, Chapters, 7, 8
BOOK III, Chapters 6, 25

30. Duties of Our State in Life

To APPEAL to our Lord through His Heart means not only to adore Him, to respect Him, to fear Him. All of that is cold. To appeal to our Lord through His Heart, we must love Him, have confidence in Him. To go to Him through His Heart, I would wish to make of each of you a third St. Peter. The first St. Peter knew only how to tremble; the second was a little better, but still not perfect; but the third St. Peter! What a wonderful saint he was! And note how Christ solemnly confirmed His predilection for the love of the third St. Peter. With what delicacy He alluded to Peter's triple denial by imposing for each denial an act of love! Our Lord condemned him to love, to love more than the others because he had sinned more than the others. Our Lord never imposed any other penance upon a sinner, and He repeated this one without ceasing.

Now it will be appropriate to consider seriously how we discharge our duties. Many of you are occupied with children. This is a priesthood, an apostolate. Do you long to save souls? Honor the Sacred Heart.

General de Sonis said: "After all, we are the saved, and at the price of the Blood of God. That is what we must never forget. The souls confided to us have been redeemed by our Lord. Patience! The task is often thorny, rude. Our Lord was first to pass this way. Had we been abandoned to this life without a model, our lack of success might be excused; but we have had a Leader. Not only did He endure all possible humiliations, but even an ignominious death, something that will probably never be asked of us."

To correct children is a never-ending task. Teachers will never, in this life, see all the good they have done. Good is done silently; it germinates little by little in the hearts of pupils; it develops as they mature. The seed has nonetheless been sown. The sun of intelligence, which, with the dew of grace, develops the germs, will one day or another cause the fruit of your labors and your sacrifices to mature.

However, take care! Your mission is blessed, but at the same time it is a formidable one. Children are perspicacious; they observe everything; they concentrate their attention on their teachers and continually question their deeds and their motives. If they perceive something in your conduct that is reprehensible, they will be disedified. Their lively imaginations and their subtle observations will soon perceive that this teacher is not altogether of the same mind as that director. It need not be said in so many words—the fact betrays itself—and behold the word of God is nullified in their minds, rendered sterile; the apostolate is hindered, arrested. Doubtless your director is not perfect, but you also have defects. It is for each one of you to seek to hide the defects of your neighbors, to take care not to reveal them to others. In this resides fraternal charity.

So, when your superiors are in the wrong, cover them with the mantle of your charity. It is not necessary to let it be seen by your pupils. Learn how to be so adroit that nothing unseemly comes to their attention. Let there be no partialities shown before your pupils. The sense of justice is unusually well developed at that age. Children possess an integrity of heart and spirit more perfect than is usually believed. They never pardon certain partialities. They know well whether a teacher is just or not. There will inevitably be some children who are dearer to us than others. It may be impossible to avoid secret preferences, but I beg of you, never let them become observable to others. Our Lord has furnished us with an example. Among the apostles, St. John was His favorite, His best beloved, but our Lord acted with so much tact, so much discretion, that His preference never cast even a shadow upon the other apostles.

There are favorites, sometimes, in boarding schools, who completely undermine the authority of the teachers. It is a misfortune. Often these favorite children, praised and flattered, form habits that make them so demanding in their families and in ordinary social life that they become disliked. They seek all the attention, all the preferences.

There is a germ of sensuality in the depths of every human being, but with some it has a more rapid growth. Let us take care never to help develop this germ through particular friendships. Such friendships open the way to serious faults. A teacher might be good, pure of heart, even innocent, yet she might awaken in the heart of a child a sensual friendship that would encourage, through original sin, this noxious germ. The teacher who should have labored to extinguish it has, unconsciously, helped to develop it. What responsibility! And what a sad handicap it is for the child to carry into the world upon leaving school.

A friendship can be ardent, burning as a flame within the heart, as long as the body does not enter into it. The danger commences the day when this friendship passes from the domain of the spirit into the inferior regions of familiarity. This is the start of deplorable falls. Danger lies in the over-emotional friendship which is not combatted, not repressed.

There are sometimes, among the pupils, relatives of the teachers. This relationship often gives rise to certain injustices that are highly detrimental to the other children. Teachers who have relatives among their pupils should be even more severe with them than with the other students. I pray you, do not interfere with the supervision of such children to prevent their correction by those in charge of them. I believe that I render you a service when I point out these vexations that are encountered in operating schools, and by indicating how they can be avoided.

31. Three Stages in the Life of St. Peter

St. PETER started from the region of fear: the rigorous religion of slaves, that of duty, of conscience alone. He did not commence his career as an apostle out of perfect love. It was only after he had passed through three entirely distinct stages that we may behold him perfectly disciplined, elevated even unto perfect love.

The first stage started with the miraculous catch of fish; the second, with the apparition of our Lord upon the water; and the third stage, after the Resurrection, following his triple denial of our Lord—his grave sin. Let us study the three stages through which he advanced.

The first stage: this was the day on which our Lord had spoken to the multitudes on the shores of the Lake

Genesareth. When His sermon was finished, He said to His apostles: "Launch out into the deep and let down your nets for a draught." The apostles were poor; they depended upon their catch of fish for their livelihood. Our Lord Himself lived upon charity.

The apostles launched their nets over the side of their fishing boat. Oh, marvel! Fish swam from all directions of the lake into their net. The net was so filled with fish that it seemed it would be rent. Peter was transported with joy and threw himself at the feet of our Lord, "Depart from me, Lord, for I am a sinful man!" Do you get the point? He begged his Lord *to depart from him*. Ah, I admire the humility of St. Peter. But where is his love, in such words?

"Depart from me!" But love asks for union. Love seeks to reduce distance. It was not his heart that spoke. Rigid religion! A religion of respect. Do you think our Lord's heart was touched at hearing his apostle implore Him to depart? Beg Him to leave? "Depart from me, I am not worthy."

I know persons who, at the Holy Table, make the same prayer as did St. Peter. "Depart from me, Lord, I am not worthy to receive You. I am too poor, too weak, too contemptible. I only come to you through fear, through force. Were I free, I would not come." Here we have a religion of respect, of fear, of cold, glacial religion.

Later on, St. Peter will make progress, will even come to penetrate into the secrets of the Heart of Jesus.

One evening our Lord asked His apostles to enter their boat and sail to the opposite shore of Lake Genesareth. He remained on the far side to pray. He promised them that He would join them on the following day. The apostles obeyed. Suddenly, as they were sailing across the lake, which is seven and one half miles wide, the sky became overcast, dark clouds loomed above, the wind blew a gale. The tempest, as occurs often on Lake Genesareth, became more menacing every moment. Enormous waves threw the little bark up to their frothy summit, then dropped it down into the abyss of churning green water. The winds seemed to the frightened fishermen to be unloosed furies. At every moment the dark abyss over which the boat was battered threatened to engulf them. They were far from shore and exhausted. They had used up their strength and were, physically, at the end of their resources.

Suddenly, by the lightning's flash, they perceived a figure walking over the waves near their boat. The frightened men thought they saw a spirit, a phantom of the night and the storm. Worry, fear, and sadness are veils that hide our Lord's presence. It was He, and He spoke to them, "It is I, be not afraid." They were even more disturbed, frightened. Could a phantom speak? "It is I, be not afraid. Peace be with you." Our Lord had, so many times, brought them peace. He always expressed the same desire: "Peace be with you." Always the same hope rose in His Heart. On this day, likewise, beholding their fright, He again said to them: "Peace be with you." Peace? This salutation from the figure walking over the waves left them even more troubled.

How many souls, when I say to them in spiritual direction, "Do not fear. Go in peace," reply to me, "Oh, Father, I am more upset than before." Our Lord did not succeed any better than I. He performed a miracle in order to rejoin his followers and assuage their fright; but the apostles did not even recognize Him, and thought Him to be a phantom.

Then St. Peter, he of the ever ardent nature, cried out: "Lord, if it be You . . ." What insolence! If it be You! Our Lord overlooked St. Peter's lack of faith and replied: "It is I, be not afraid!" Peter doubted the word of our Lord. "If it be You!"

Even at that, Peter had made progress. Gone are the

days when he said, "Depart from me, for I am a sinner."
Now he sought to rejoin his Lord even if it meant walking
over the still raging sea. He longed to approach Jesus, but
he did not yet possess a heart fully abandoned to his Lord.
He did not dare, of his own accord, to throw himself upon
the waters and advance to meet his Master. His heart was
still the seat of two contrary desires: love drew him toward
Christ; fear held him back.

"Lord, bid me come to Thee!" Yes, I long to approach
You, but I dare not take the initiative: a religion divided
between fear and love, a religion in which the conscience
and the heart are, in a sense, opposed.

Alas, many devout persons believe themselves arrived at
great perfection when they say, "I wish to go to Holy
Communion more often, but I dare not ask my confessor
for more communions than are permitted me now. How
happy I should be if God, through the voice of my confessor, would direct me to come to Him more frequently.
But I dare not express this desire to Him." This is a religion
divided between love and fear. Conscience and heart dispute within that soul.

Later, St. Peter came to understand the Heart of his
Master far better. Then he listened but to his heart. He
broke away entirely from the stern bonds of conscience
and delivered himself over, wholly, entirely, to love.

Astonishing thing! At this moment he was most culpable, after his triple denial, his triple apostasy. Just then,
according to our way of looking at things, he should have
said: "Lord, depart from me!" Well, now we are going to
see how well he came to understand the Heart of Jesus.

Eight days after the Resurrection, the apostles were
again upon Lake Genesareth. They had fished all night,
but had caught nothing. They were fatigued, weary,
exhausted. Toward morning our Lord appeared upon the
shore and called to them: "Children, have you any food?"

The apostles looked toward the shore; they believed that they saw a stranger. Their sadness clouded their view; sadness always prevents us from getting a clear vision of our Saviour. The apostles failed to recognize Him. Even His voice, His accents, seemed strange. Often we, too, while under the cloud of sadness, take our Lord for a complete stranger. We cannot recognize Him through the mist that gloom creates about us.

The apostles answered the question by calling out, "No, we have taken nothing." Then Jesus said to them, "Cast your net on the right side of the ship and you shall receive." What are you saying, Oh Stranger? Why try again? What is the use of expecting success? Why make a new attempt? Would it be more fruitful? Is it wholly by accident that we always seem to cast our nets on the wrong side?

Happily, none of these objections rose in their minds. With perfect docility, in simple confidence, they followed the counsel of this seeming stranger. They cast their nets over the right side of the vessel. And lo, the net was so full of fish that it threatened to be torn asunder! In face of the miracle a ray of light struck the spirit of St. John. He examined more closely the supposed Stranger. *Dominus est!* Hardly had he spoken these words than St. Peter, beside himself with joy, cast himself over the side of the boat. There he is, throwing himself into the waves that he might be first to reach our Lord, the first to have a smile, a word from Him. What? How dare he hope for this privilege? Ought he not to hide himself, crouch behind the others? He who was the most guilty of all the apostles, should he not tremble to confront the Master whom he had betrayed? Had St. Peter been governed solely by conscience, I know what he would have done. Covered with confusion, he would not have dared lift his eyes to Jesus. He would have lingered behind the others, hesitated to approach our Lord. But do you think Jesus would have been pleased, touched, to have beheld His apostle afraid to approach Him? Drawing back through fear and fright? Oh, the good Master, how happy He was, how His Heart must have rejoiced at the sight of His poor apostle braving all in order to approach Him!

No longer does St. Peter say, as on the former occasion, "Lord, depart from me," even though the words would now have seemed appropriate. The time is now past when St. Peter, restrained by the cold, rigid law of the conscience, of fear, said to His Master, "If it be You, Lord, bid me come to You." Now he asks no permission, but throws himself upon the waves. How his heart speaks! How beautiful it is—Peter, so guilty, so culpable, but no longer doubting the love of Jesus! It is scarcely ten days after his triple denial, but he no longer hesitates to approach our Lord. Now he understands the love of his Master. He has learned to know the Heart full of love that beats within His breast.

But Peter deserves a penance. At the close of this scene, after our Lord had served a meal to His apostles, He took Peter to one side. Sitting by his side upon the rough turf, Christ turned upon His apostle a penetrating gaze, which at the same time was filled with love, as He asked, "Peter, lovest thou Me?" "Oh yes, good Master, You know that I love You." Truly? How had he proved it on that fateful day when he had denied, deserted Him, after so many protestations of fidelity? "Even if all the others desert You, I shall be faithful." How dares he to say that he loves our Lord when scarcely ten days have elasped since he apostatized three times at the questioning of a simple maid servant? Truly this man has a bold front.

Our Lord, answering, said to him: "Feed My sheep." Peter did not know what this meant. Was Jesus seeking to entrap him? After a moment's silence, Christ's gaze plunged deep into the eyes of Peter: "Peter, lovest thou Me?" "Lord, You know that I love You!" "Feed My lambs!" A longer silence ensued; then Christ turned upon Peter a look of inexpressible tenderness: "Peter, lovest thou Me more than these?" Oh, poor Peter! Now he understands. This he did not expect. How far he was from imagining what Christ had in mind! But he is no longer presumptuous. He no longer seeks a place superior to that of the other apostles. "Lord," he replies, "You know all things; You know that I love You." "Feed My sheep."

St. Peter would truly have been wounded had Jesus never made any allusion to his sin. Adorable penance! "Peter, you have sinned against Me. Tell Me that you love Me! Peter, you denied Me even unto the third time. Make a triple protestation of your love. Make reparation to Me from your heart." Our Lord did not condemn Peter to tremble in fear for the remainder of his life. He did not keep him prostrate before Himself in diffidence, in fear.

"Peter," He said in effect, "now you understand My Heart. I restore to you all your former privileges. I confide to you My lambs, My sheep. I grant you all your former familiarities with Me. I bestow upon you even more. Because I have pardoned you so very much, I have greater rights to your love, to your gratitude. He to whom much is forgiven, loves much.

"You sinned against Me, oh friend of Mine, you sinned greatly; then love Me greatly. You sinned against Me, more than all the others; then love Me more than all the others. Yes, I not only permit it; I direct you to do so. Rise from your sins and show to souls innocent of sin how you will surpass them in love."

Behold this, the true religion of love, taught by Christ Himself. On this poor apostle, the most culpable, the most ungrateful—on him who, on the very day of his ordination, not content with desertion, became a triple renegade, behold the penance imposed by Christ. He could give no other. It was the same penance imposed upon Mary Magdalen: more ardent love.

"You have sinned against Me? Then love Me. You have sinned greatly? Then love Me greatly. You have sinned more than all others? Then love Me more than all others."

Go throw yourself at the feet of our Lord. Go, offer Him your heart, as many times as you have deserted Him through sin.

I beg of you, let there be no more question of confusion, of fear; but if you feel yourself more guilty than all others, by that very fact you have the right to love Him more than all others.

32. *The Last Supper*

Do you see how our Lord seeks to draw us through our affections when He wishes to obtain our surrender to His Adorable Heart? He makes us a magnificent promise: I will make peace in your family. He knows well that family affection is the strongest, the most intense, the best affection in the world. Do you wish to draw down upon your parents, brothers, sisters, relatives, the benedictions of heaven? Honor His Heart. He will reciprocate. He will take care to give you pleasure, to bless your family, make it happy, establish it in peace. Peace! According to Holy Scriptures, peace is the embodiment of all the good that contributes to the happiness of mankind.

In the first two series of our conferences, we looked toward the past. In the second two, we prepare for the future. In the third series, our work will, above all, consist in consolidating our resolutions, in seeking to discover the designs that God has for us.

St. Ignatius throws us, all compassionate, upon the slopes of Calvary: "See what our Lord has done for you. Do you dare refuse Him anything? Witness His sufferings. Consider to what an extremity this Holy Victim has been reduced for your sake, then dare to break your resolutions in the future."

In the third week of the *Exercises*, St. Ignatius presses us to meditate upon the mysteries of the Passion. This is intended to confirm our good resolutions, render them unshakable. All the saints have had a special devotion to the Way of the Cross, in which they meditate upon the Passion. In certain states in which we find ourselves, these mysteries contain all the spiritual nourishment of which we may have need at the moment—all the lessons, new and mysterious, through which our Lord desires to teach us generosity.

Preparatory prayer: always the same, but with increasing fervor and more heartfelt ardor than ever before. "I desire only the greater glory of God. If I will only His greater glory, if I serve Him, not through fear, but through love, how glorious life will become! What heights will stretch out before me! I desire that such glory of God as may be procured through my humble services will surpass itself on each tomorrow. I desire, therefore, that each day His glory may be increased."

Let us consider the Last Supper. The historical setting of the mystery is the supper of the paschal lamb according to the prescribed Jewish rite. Our Lord washed the feet of His disciples, then returned to the table and instituted the Holy Eucharist.

Let us represent to ourselves the Cenacle: a large room

suitably prepared for the occasion. Peter and John had been charged with its arrangement.

I ask the grace to understand in these three scenes, in which I observe so many lessons to be learned: the goodness, the love of our Lord for men, and the grace to imitate Him in this love of my fellow men. I ask the grace to love Him every day more and more, but in an effective way, a fruitful way. I ask for the grace to prove my love for Him through acts, through generous sacrifices for others.

There are three points in this meditation: (1) the eating of the paschal lamb, (2) the washing of the feet, (3) the institution of the sacrament.

The Eating of the Paschal Lamb. Our Lord, even to the end of His life, was faithful to all the prescriptions of the Jewish Law.

The Washing of the Feet. After the eating of the paschal lamb, following the two rites, there ensued a strange scene. Our Lord arose, girded Himself with a towel, and had a basin of water brought to Him. He fell upon His knees before His apostles, before St. Peter. Our Lord undertook to wash their feet. Humiliating task!

Peter was astonished; he refused: "What, Lord, You to wash my feet? Never." Our Lord knew that humility is a difficult lesson to learn; He wished to mark this last act of His life by an example of humility. He placed Himself at the feet of His apostles, who, three hours later, would all abandon Him—even John, who boasted of having rested on the breast of Jesus at this Last Supper. All would betray Him upon the very day of their First Holy Communion— their ordination to the priesthood—all would thrust a knife into that gentle Heart. Jesus is there at their feet.

And I, who never want to hear of humility? I, who will not even consent to render certain services to my brothers in religion? I find all that beneath my dignity. I refuse to place myself at the feet of those who are my sisters and brothers in Christ. Behold the example that Jesus gives me! What a contrast! Jesus upon His knees before Judas—and I? When I consider myself betrayed with what anger do I look upon those who have offended me! Do I consent to fall at their feet? Jesus kissed the feet of Judas! What a lesson! Behold the vengeance of Jesus: love and service.

The Institution of the Sacrament of the Eucharist. I hear His words to His apostles: "I have desired with great desire

with you." Yes, it has arrived—the most

is life, the object of His ambitions and

well; tomorrow our Lord will repeat

"My child, for twenty centuries I have

eat desire to eat this Passover with you.

, do not deprive Me of this hour. Do not

our with you. It is My hour, the hour for

to your heart. Do not deprive Me of it. Do

My delight in coming to you."

When you fail to receive a Communion allowed by your confessor, you make our Lord do penance. What harm has He done to you, that you treat Him so casually? I forbid you to make our Lord do penance.

Our Lord takes wine. He lifts the cup toward heaven, raises His eyes to His Father, blesses the chalice, consecrates it into His Blood, so soon to flow for the redemption of men. He takes the bread and consecrates it into His Body. This scene is renewed every day before your eyes at the holy altar, when you have the great joy of assisting at the adorable sacrifice of the Mass.

The Curé of Ars said, "If a priest really comprehended the Holy Mass, he would die, overcome by the grandeur of the miracle as he pronounced the words of transubstantiation."

Our Lord gave Himself to His apostles, so miserable, so imperfect. He knew well that they were about to betray

Him. "Lord, come to me because I am weak! Protect me from sin during this day. Lift me up if I fail."

We shall close with colloquies according to our individual devotion: colloquies with St. John, who had the joy of reposing upon the Heart of Jesus; colloquies with St. Peter; and above all, with our Lord. We shall ask for great fidelity to our holy exercises, and the desire for, the love of, humiliations. We shall ask for the grace to apply ourselves to receiving Holy Communion with an ever-increasing fervor and devotion.

33. In the Garden of Olives

LET US consider the Passion of our Lord, His supreme Passion, which took place in the Garden of Olives. There He endured a Passion of the Heart, of Love spurned, rejected, betrayed. All the tortures that He endured after that—the outrages, the brutality of which He was the object when He was delivered over to the executioners—all of that was little compared to what He suffered in Gethsemane.

It seems that our Lord willed to pass through all the phases of suffering. Through His martyrdom, He willed to take to Himself all the sharpest elements in suffering, and thus in some mystic way to alleviate our sufferings. The soul experiences, in suffering, three bitter griefs, swords that pierce the heart through and through. We feel that we suffer alone; that our sufferings are valueless, without merit; and finally, that they are, in some way, culpable. These are the three maryrdoms that render our sufferings doubly painful.

First, it seems to us that we suffer alone. "If only I could know that I do not suffer alone." "I feel myself so isolated in my anguish." "It seems to me that I am the only one to taste such bitterness." "Alas, my sorrow must not spring from a good source."

The enemy of our soul, jealous of the glory we render to God through suffering, tries to render it insupportable to us by making us believe that our sufferings are sterile, that we suffer without merit. It is this aspect that causes us to feel our pain so intensely that it throws us into a profound bitterness, a kind of despair. "If I knew that through these pangs I were purchasing at least one soul, I should bless my anguish. I should be content to suffer. But what breaks my heart is that I can perceive no fruit to be gathered from my trials. They appear to be sterile."

There is a third pain, even more bitter than the two preceding ones. Not only do we believe ourselves to be suffering alone and without merit, but it appears to us that, instead of meriting, we are actually offending God. Our sufferings appear to have resulted from our defects and are, therefore, culpable. There arises within our hearts an accumulation of things that trouble our peace, our security as God's dear children.

But we never suffer alone. Our sufferings are never sterile. Above all, our sufferings are never culpable.

I do not want to exaggerate. Is it that in our sufferings we may not offend God by a lack of resignation, of patience, or by some other venial faults of that kind, arising from the very excess of our pain? I claim that there is very much less of this than is commonly thought. It may even be that we lose some merits, but how far does the indubitable gain compensate for the loss? How many good persons cover themselves with reproaches, distressing themselves unduly, over having felt a certain repugnance to their trials?

Oh, how I love these words of a saint: "The cross never appears in a life without leaving there some good." He did not say, "The cross, well-accepted, carried joyously by a generous heart." No, every cross leaves benign traces in a life, even—and I shall go so far as to say, above all—a cross meagerly, miserably accepted.

Our Lord, who gives individual care to each soul, says to Himself: "From every possible consideration, this soul is about to acquire more merits, make more progress, glorify Me more, if I send him this trial. It will be profitable to him." The hour, then, for suffering has arrived. It is the hour of salvation.

Let us ask of the Holy Spirit that we may fully understand this page—admirable, sublime, incomparable—in which He Himself dictates all the passages. Wonderful page, capable of furnishing a balm for all wounds, a remedy and a consolation for all who suffer! I admit that before I came to understand this, suffering was, for me, a mystery.

Jesus then went toward the Garden of Olives. On the way He felt Himself invaded by a profound, heart-breaking sadness which enveloped His whole being. It was a sadness that all His courage could not throw off and that wrested from Him this plaint: "My soul is sorrowful unto death." This was not a vain expression, a rhetorical exaggeration.

How strangely did I once misunderstand this scene! I should have imagined that, like the first martyrs, He would have gone into the midst of tortures singing, that He would have been joyous in the midst of His trials, of His incredible sufferings! Our Lord did not sing. He was not overwhelmed with joy. He was not full of happiness. On the contrary, He was overcome with sadness to the point that His terrible agony wrested from Him this cry: "My soul is sorrowful unto death, even to die of grief."

Ah, when I behold the martyrs throw themselves,

singing, upon the instruments of torture, kissing the instruments of their death; when I see them call their executioners, their benefactors, and express gratitude to those who persecute them, I can see clearly what they suffered in their bodies, but I do not see what they suffered in their souls. Their souls were in perfect serenity. Their souls already tasted heaven through anticipation. Their interior joy rendered them insensible to their physical torments.

The martyrs endured torture in their bodies. Jesus, King of Martyrs, willed to be martyred in His soul. My divine King did not sing in going to His martyrdom. His Heart was stricken. His soul was sad, sad unto death.

Oh, my soul, why then reproach me for my sorrow? Why are you so severe toward me? Why do you demand that I suffer with joy, when God permits suffering to invade me, to overwhelm me? Our Lord endured sorrow before I did, and more than I ever have, or ever shall, yet His sufferings were good, meritorious. Ah, then, in my grief I can present myself to Jesus, kneel beside Him in Gethsemane, unite my pain to that of His Heart. No, I am not alone when I suffer with overwhelming sorrow. Jesus suffers with me.

The Holy Spirit emphasizes another detail: our Lord commenced to be afraid. How is that? Our Lord afraid? Of what? Of His bitter chalice, of His Passion, of His cross, of the will of His Father? It was necessary that He drain His chalice to the last drop, yet He was afraid.

Do I still dare to believe that a generous soul must never quail before suffering? Do I believe that we must always look upon it with joy? Go out to meet it? Oh, my soul, why do you reproach me for my fears, my apprehensions? Even when I tremble before trials, even when the sight of the cross fills me with fear, I can still present myself at Gethsemane, can kneel beside Jesus and offer my sufferings to God for His glory and my salvation. His

Divine Son suffered even as I do. How good was our Lord in revealing to us the merits hidden even in sufferings that appear to us as paltry, unimportant!

But the Holy Spirit reveals to us a third suffering of Jesus, even more astonishing. Our Lord began to fear and to be troubled. "Troubled"? Is not trouble the emotion of a soul that is not entirely sure of itself, which is no longer master of itself? Is it not the emotion of a soul that is disturbed, disquieted? That no longer possesses itself in peace? A generous soul permits itself to be troubled? Should it not rather await, with a collected and firm mind, whatever the will of God provides? Oh, my soul, why reproach me for being troubled? Why represent it as a moral defection? Jesus was even more troubled than I.

Yes, even when I am worried, troubled, I can go to Gethsemane. I can prostrate myself at the side of Jesus and offer my troubles to God. He will accept them. I suffer, then, as did my divine Model.

A note even more surprising is added to this score: our Lord commenced to experience repugnance. He began to fear and to be heavy. Repugnance? Is not that the point at which we commence to abandon everything? Does not aversion amount to repulsion, and that to a high degree? Repugnance, and of what? Of His Passion. Of all that was most holy in the will of His Father. His repugnance was so profound that He was almost overcome by it. He could hardly control Himself.

Oh, my soul, why reproach me for my repugnances? Jesus suffered from repugnance of His sufferings before I did, and more than I ever have. You will that I love suffering? Jesus did not love it. He did not feel any attraction for suffering. On the contrary, it inspired him with fear, with sorrow, with repugnance. In the midst of my own repugnances of all kinds, I can still prostrate myself at

Gethsemane and offer to God those pains that devour my heart. It was thus that His Divine Son suffered.

The Gospel says then that He commenced to fear. Fear? Is not that a cowardly sentiment, small, miserable, despicable? Is not that the sentiment of a soul which feels itself to be weakening, which sees its courage evaporating? Fear? Is not that the feeling of a soul that asks itself a second later if it can still hold out, still consent to suffer? Our Lord was fearful, and of what? Of what was to Him most sacred and most holy: He feared His mission, His vocation of redemption.

Oh, my soul, why do you reproach me for being fearful? Jesus was fearful before ever I was, and even more than I, yet He is my model in suffering. Even then, in the midst of my fears, even while I feel myself to be so poor, so weak, in my discouragements, in my despairs, I can go to Gethsemane. I can kneel by the side of Jesus and offer my sufferings to God, who will receive them favorably for they resemble the sufferings of His Son.

To suffer generously, I once believed, was to suffer with a courage that never winces. I thought it meant to go to meet suffering, to hold out my arms to it. Now I understand that we can suffer just as generously, yet suffer with sorrow, fear, worry, repugnance, that we can suffer miserably.

When, in the midst of suffering, we feel our heart to be resigned, generous, it is to be feared that self-love is taking its toll. But to suffer without realizing that one is suffering well, to suffer with all the sorrow and discouragement which lead one to believe that all merit is lost, that we are even offending God with our lack of generosity, this is to suffer without any consolation. This is pure suffering. When a soul is conscious of its generosity, can testify that it is fully resigned to the will of God, its sorrows are softened. But to suffer in such an interior confusion that no luster issues from the suffering, when one fears one's pains are sterile—ah, that is suffering *par excellence*. It is that of our Lord in the Garden of Olives.

Let us accompany our Lord further in the Passion of His Heart, and we shall find more precious lessons. When our Lord arrived in the Garden of Olives, he knew that His agony was about to begin, and He took with Him three apostles, Peter, James, and John, the identical three who had accompanied Him to Thabor. He did not wish to be alone in His sorrow. He longed to have near Him hearts that would sympathize and console Him. He was begging, wordlessly, for a little consolation. "Watch ye, therefore, and pray with Me." I have encountered critics who declare that in order to merit, we should refuse all aid, all consolation. They forbid the seeking of a little support, a little spiritual comfort, lest all merit be lost. Was not our Lord a martyr to grief? Yet He sought consolation. It is true that our Lord's attempt was a failure. He came to His disciples and found them sleeping. He returned to His prayer, then came a second time to seek a little consolation from His apostles, whom, only an hour before, He had called His "friends." I have, therefore, the right to go to a friend in whom I can confide, or to a superior, that I might find some comfort in his sympathy, his counsel. I have the right to seek out my spiritual director. He will have precious words to offer me, words of life that will help me. I have the privilege of seeking to open my heart to those who have the right to console, to aid me. This does not mean that I lose the merit of suffering.

Our Lord fell to His knees; He began to pray. A strange prayer! Do I hear it aright? "My Father, if it be possible, remove this chalice from Me!" But, oh, my good Master, this chalice is the will of Your Father! This chalice, if You drain it, means our salvation. You came into the world to drink this chalice; it is Your vocation. And You refuse it? You ask that it be withdrawn from Your lips? "Father, if it be possible, remove this chalice from Me!" Our Lord is the model of all generosity. Yet, in spite of this, His poor human Heart refused to suffer.

Oh, my soul, why do you afflict me? Why do you reproach me because at the foot of the tabernacle I, too, have said, "Lord, if it be possible, remove this trial from me; let this suffering be softened. If it be possible, let the designs of Your providence be changed. If it be possible, remove this cup from my lips."

It is true that our Lord added: "Not My will, but Thine be done." But after having made this act of resignation, He seemed to retract it and to begin again His former prayer: "Father, if it be possible, remove this chalice from Me." And for two whole hours He was hard pressed to say: "Thy will be done."

My dear friends, you, too, have sometimes come to the foot of the altar to protest to the Lord that you accept a certain trial. An hour later, you are surprised to find yourself saying: "My God, if it be possible, remove this cup from me." There were within the Heart of Jesus identical motions of acceptance and refusal, of resignation and repugnance. Our Lord had His interior conflicts. We can well have our own.

The last prayer of Jesus, that which terminated these alternations of resignation and acceptance, was, "Father, not My will, but Thine be done." Do you grasp the full significance of these words? I do not know in all the Gospel any words so human, that so bring our Lord down to our own stature. Do you grasp their full meaning?

Our Lord did not say, "Father, I will what You will. My will is Your will." No, just the contrary was their significance. "Father, do not ask Me to will what You will. Everything within Me is repugnant to suffering. This is all that I can bring Myself to say, 'Our two wills are not in accord, but since one must be sacrificed, let it be Mine—let Your will be done, not Mine.'"

How good of our Lord to make of Himself a model for our weakness to copy, and to give us, in His Person, so many motives for encouragement, making it easy for us to imitate Him. He repeats the same lessons over and over, bringing them down to our measure. He permits us to read within His Heart so many lessons of the very essence of divine wisdom, of charity.

Thus it seems to me that I can present myself to Your will, Oh my God, and say in the simplicity of my heart, "My God, our two wills are not in accord, but carry out Your will. Close Your ears to my groans, to my complaints, to my reproaches."

Our Lord, after this prayer, after this resistance to suffering, felt His strength failing. He fell, His face to the earth. A bloody sweat poured from His Body, running down to the earth. He fell in an agony.

There are severe, austere directors, who say to a poor soul, "What? You think that your health is injured by your moral sufferings? You have become ill? Why, you lack moral strength, energy, generosity. Had you been more resigned to God's will, your health would have held up." Did our Lord act so? Is it that He was not generous? He, the model of all generosity? He finally became exhausted, threw Himself down upon the earth, sweated blood through all the pores of His sacred Body. If He experienced such weakness, so can I.

An angel came from heaven to comfort, to sustain Him. When God sends an angel to comfort me—an understanding friend, a confessor—I reproach myself for having accepted consolation, for not having rejected the aid of an angel. I believe myself to have lost all merit through having accepted such consolation. Did our Lord refuse the angel's aid? Was it by chance that the angel was sent from Paradise? Did Jesus refuse the help sent Him from His Father? Does perfection consist in refusing the help that comes to us from God? When He sends us an angel, let us know how to profit from the encounter.

Doubtless, there remains a certain balance to observe. But our Lord has furnished us with the example. "My God, when You send Your angel to me, I shall accept his help. I shall rejoice in his consolations."

SPIRITUAL READING

The Imitation of Christ: Book II, Chapters 11, 12
Book III, Chapter 19
Book IV, Chapter 8

"The Heart of Jesus is the source of all graces; a treasure house of graces, to which the key is confidence."

ST. MARGARET MARY

34. The Three Crosses

IT IS NOT conscience, then, that opens to us the Heart of Jesus. It is not fear. Both leave it tightly closed. It is confidence. It is love.

Do you recall this scene in the Gospel? Our Lord was asked for a miracle. The divine Master paused, prey to a mysterious emotion: "Have you faith?" Anything is possible to him who has confidence. If you could but visualize all the possibilities that lie before you! Horizons so sweeping that they are lost to view. Enter upon this way of love and confidence! There you will find all joy, all peace of heart and mind.

We shall meditate upon the three crosses: those of the two thieves and that of our Lord.

There is the cross that saves the world, the cross that saves the penitent sinner, and the cross that damns the impenitent. How many lessons are to be learned at the foot of these three crosses!

Preparatory prayer: the same, but spoken with more fervor, more sincerity, more purity of intention, than ever before, "I will only the glory of God. I shall ignore all worldly interests, placing them apart, sacrificing them."

To hold my imagination, I shall represent to myself the summit of Calvary, the bare rock, and the three crosses, our Lord's in the center.

I ask grace to understand the marvelous efficacy of the cross—an incomparable grace. Our Lord said that He came for the raising up and the casting down of multitudes. All souls who are saved will be saved by the cross. Those who are lost will be lost because they refused to be saved by the cross of Christ.

My dear friends, here is the plan, the lesson of Christ's Heart: He suffered and died upon the cross. It is thus that He saved us at the close of His life of thirty-three years.

Hell was open before humanity. Through the cross, Heaven was opened to us and the dreadful abyss was closed. The death of our Lord upon the cross was the decisive moment of our redemption. Our Lord recognized this so intimately that He termed it "My hour." Long before, He had said, "My hour is not yet come." Then, as He saw it approaching, He said, "My hour is here," and He advanced toward Calvary. Thus are souls saved. We must needs suffer, and carry our cross with Christ. Our holy vocation is, as it were, a guarantee of salvation for us; nevertheless, much suffering is to be expected along the way. If we reject the cross, we should fear that at the same time we are closing heaven, and, it may be, opening hell to ourselves, our beloved relatives, and friends.

Do you wish to save the souls of those with whom you live or work? Those whom you educate with so much prayer? Do you wish to save, to help, those whom you counsel, those who beg for your prayers? The salvation of souls must be paid for by the coin of suffering. We must needs complete what is lacking in the Passion of our Lord.

When the mother of James and John approached our Lord to ask: "Grant, then, that my sons shall sit, one on Your right side, and one on Your left, when You come into Your Kingdom," she was trying to reserve the first places for them. Our Lord replied, "Can you drink of the chalice of which I drink? Can you suffer yourself to be crucified upon My cross?"

St. Peter started along the Appian Way to leave Rome, where he feared the persecutions. Hurrying along in his desire to escape, he met our Lord.

"Lord, where are you going?"

"To Rome, to be crucified anew because you, Peter, refuse to suffer."

My friends, have you ever thought of how much of the blessed cross you have lost through your own fault? Have we rendered ourselves unworthy of the gift of those small crosses destined for us by our Lord? Perhaps you are even complaining that you have no big crosses to carry; carry first the little ones well. Our Lord will then decide whether you are worthy to be laden with greater ones.

We have rendered ourselves unworthy of the cross.

My God, give me my crosses, all of my privileges as Your beloved friend. Leave to me all the crosses that You destined for me, and through which I shall aid You to save souls!

The thief who turned away from Christ was a man for

whom God had destined incomparable graces. He was to be a witness to the death of Jesus, a companion to His Saviour who was extended upon His cross, consummating the redemption of the world.

This wretched man faced the adorable Victim. It was the supreme effort of divine mercy to save the unhappy soul from hell, from eternal remorse. He might have been the first to profit from Christ's Sacred Blood as it flowed upon the cross, but he hardened himself against divine Grace. The sight of our innocent Lord suffering upon the cross had no personal significance for him. All within his mind and heart resisted the divine mercy. Sometimes a great trial causes blasphemy—a great trial destined to sanctify that soul, to save it, but which plunges it into hell. The cross is offered us either "for the fall or the raising up of a great number." Woe unto us if we abuse the cross.

If the unhappy man had, at least, suffered less in consequence of his blasphemies, if they had resulted in some comfort to him, the cross might have been less hateful in his sight. But no, his sufferings were but doubled. They became sharper, more intense. See how he is convulsed in the intensity of his pain! See how different are his reactions from those of the good thief, who resigns himself. He is finding out the final torment of the cross, the sharpest, the most heart-rending pain of all, through the one act of blaspheming against it.

How they are to be pitied, these worldly people! Their crosses and sufferings torture them, fill them with bitterness, because they do not recognize the divine mercy when the loving Heart of Jesus apportions to them trials. These trials, accepted with gratitude and understanding, would win for them an eternal recompense.

The good thief, also, had commenced to blaspheme. He was at the summit of his crimes, of his guilt. He had joined his voice to that of the crowd in a delirium of reproach. Suddenly he heard, wrung from the Heart of his Fellow-crucified, these memorable words: "Father, forgive them, for they know not what they do." His heart was touched—for this man still possessed a heart. He was conquered; there shone a great light in his soul. This thief, wicked as he had been, had not entirely closed his heart to goodness. He grasped the full import of the words of the divine Sufferer at his side, and his own sufferings were mitigated, softened, made bearable, even desirable. He realized that he, the sinner, was suffering in company with innocence. With calmness, he accepted his pain. He resigned himself; his cross suddenly became a joy. If his divine Companion could beg for forgiveness for His torturers, doubtless He could also extend forgiveness for his sins. The good thief turned his eyes toward our Lord: "Master, when You come into Your Kingdom, remember me." And the instant, self-forgetting response: "Today you shall be with Me in Paradise." Oh, ineffable words! Even today, with Him in Paradise!

At one moment of time, a robber is being punished. The next moment he is an altogether different being, who gazes into the face of death with joy, who even looks forward to the parting of soul and body. How he blesses his sufferings! How they now appear to him in a new light, as good and desirable!

My friends, how happy are those who learn to suffer with our Lord! Their pains become light, inconsequential.

Let us throw ourselves at the feet of the Crucified One. Let us express our gratitude that He saved that poor thief, and beg Him to inundate our souls in His Divine Blood, that we, too, may find at His side our strength and our hope.

35. The First Easter

M<small>Y DEAR FRIENDS</small>, I beg of you, permit yourselves to be imprisoned in this Divine Heart, and never seek to escape. Our Lord usually reserves graces more intimate, more mysterious, for the last hours of a retreat, a mission, or a series of conferences. Let us, therefore, be more recollected, more closely united to Jesus. It is then, above all, that He speaks softly within our hearts. To be able to hear Him, to understand Him, there must be absolute silence. To hear and to understand our Lord is the result of an intimate union with His Heart.

Let us redouble our zeal for little things. The demon spies upon us from earliest daybreak, and it is at that time, above all, that he disputes with our Lord for possession of our first thoughts. Let us pay attention, therefore, to our first waking moment, to give our hearts to God. The demon knows well that if he can gain the first moment of the day, the remainder will most likely belong to him. Let us neglect nothing within our power to prevent him from robbing our Lord of what rightly belongs to Him—our hearts.

In one of our Houses, the biography of one of our saintly religious is carefully preserved. One detail of his last moments touched me greatly. He was at the point of death when he asked for his superior and, giving him two worn little statues, said, "Father, I am happy to die possessing nothing."

Before the close of this series of conferences, examine yourselves to see if you have any reservations as to poverty. See if, among the things allowed for your use, there are not some with which you could dispense. See if there are not some small sacrifices to be made.

There is one page in the Gospel that I repeat with deep respect, that I kiss each time it comes before my eyes. I read and re-read it with profound emotion, and each time I discover new truths.

This page of the Gospel is that which relates the details of the events surrounding the Resurrection of Christ. The Heart of Jesus manifests itself here with an excessive goodness which surpasses our imagination. May He accord us the grace fully to understand it.

On the day of the Resurrection, the Holy Women left their homes before daybreak. They sallied forth laden with ointments of great price, and went toward the sepulchre. Where were they heading? And with ointments? Was not our Lord to have arisen? He had said plainly, "On the third day I shall come forth from the tomb." Yet they were setting forth to embalm His body. Did these women lack faith? Let us listen to them as they converse on their way to the tomb, "How shall we manage this? Who will roll away the stone for us? It is so heavy and we are so weak."

Do you realize the significance of their words? They did not believe the promises of Christ. Doubtless there was true devotion to our Lord in their project, but what astonishes us is their utter incredulity.

Reaching the summit of the hill of the sepulchre, they were frightened. What! The guards had fled? The stone was rolled away? The Roman seal had been broken? The tomb was empty? Then an angel appeared. At sight of the angel, the women became really upset. This is the way we often behave. We are filled with fear even when an angel of God comes to help us. We are thrown into a kind of disarray. There is no reason for us to be plunged into trouble; an angel of God could only bring peace and joy to us.

The angel said to them, "Peace and joy be to you!" It is the blessing which our Lord so often gave to His disciples, "Peace be to you." In the holy writings, peace signifies the culmination of all good. It may even mean, in ordinary language, "I wish you health and happiness."

The women were still perplexed. I have no reason to be envious of the angel. He succeeded no better than I. I have only to say to a soul, "Peace be with you; fear no more," than I am apt to hear, "Oh, Father, I am more worried than before."

The angel admitted no discouragement. "You seek Jesus of Nazareth. He is not here. He is risen as He told you. Behold the place where He was laid. Go, say to His disciples and to Peter that He awaits them in Galilee. It is there that they shall find Him."

"Go, say to His disciples . . . and to Peter . . . ?"

"His disciples?" But they are apostates; they are all fallen priests!

Those poor aspostles! How desolate they had become! Without doubt, they had said to themselves, "Even if our good Master pardons us, we would no longer have the right to follow our vocation. We are no longer fit to become columns of His Church." But you have no right to doubt the heart of your Divine Master. Before you have made a move toward asking His pardon, He takes the initiative. He says to you that all is forgiven.

"Go, say to His disciples"—by these words they understand that they are still His disciples, that He has forgiven all.

But, oh, angel of God, what are you saying? "To His disciples and to Peter"? But Peter was even more unworthy than the others. He had committed a triple apostasy. Sins of men that are committed against God are more serious than all the infamies, the impurities, that could be committed. Apostasy is the crime of crimes. And Peter, column of His Church, had committed that crime.

Peter must have said to himself, "Even though my good Master pardons all the other apostles, could He ever pardon me?" He must have thought, "I have been so ungrateful, so proud, such a sinner! An apostate! Even if, through excess of love, my good Master would render to my fellow apostles all their former privileges, even if He re-established all their former rights, surely that would not include me. I am so unworthy, so guilty. A renegade!"

Peter, you have not the right to doubt. Through the ministry of an angel, He sends you a personal invitation, an invitation for you alone. He even calls you by name. He wants you to know that not only does He restore to you His confidence and love, but also He restores all of your privileges. See how the Heart of Jesus revenges itself!

But now behold the Holy Women all radiant. Their hearts are dilated, lightened. A moment ago, in sadness, they were slowly climbing the summit of Calvary. Now joy lends wings to their steps. They run; they fly. David, the holy king, said, "Lord, when You dilate my heart, I run in the way of Your commandments."

But here is one who does not obey the angel. She sits there weeping. Why, it is Mary Magdalen! Why does she weep? Why does not she, too, give over her heart to joy? She sits beside the tomb, weeping, when she should be radiant with joy. But no, she is heavy-hearted. She is even more incredulous than the others.

Our Lord had told His disciples many times that He would arise the third day. An angel appeared to recall this to them, but they still did not believe. They probably imagined that it was all some kind of strategy on the part of the Jews or the Romans. The soldiers must have taken His Body away and hidden it.

Now we behold Mary Magdalen arise and go forth to search anew for her Lord in the garden and at the sepulchre. In her persistence there is doubtless much love, but there is also incredulity. Does she not merit severe reproof? Yes, our Lord is about to revenge Himself, as always, by a fresh show of love. He approaches her first of all, because she is the most unhappy, the most culpable.

Unexpectedly, He shows Himself to her, but Magdalen does not recognize Him. Sadness acts as a veil which robs her of the clear sight of God. Sadness and worry are the devil's masterpieces. We are incapable of great deeds while we are sad. "A saint sad, is a sad saint," said St. Francis de Sales. The devil desires nothing so much as to rob us of our peace and joy of soul. Magdalen was sad; therefore, she did not recognize our Lord.

"They have taken away my Lord, and I do not know where they have laid Him. Sir, if you have taken Him hence, tell me where you have laid him." Surely she deserves a severe reprimand for her unbelief. But in that very moment, our Lord answers with but one word, spoken in a tone of His own mysterious tenderness, "Mary."

At that voice, Magdalen trembles. She recognizes the Master. Watch her throw herself at the feet of Jesus! Truly the woman is bold. Should she not hide herself, blushing with shame? Caught in a major dereliction, should she not strike her breast, beg forgiveness? Was it not an insult in the very face of Jesus? Not even to have recognized Him? She thought Him to be the keeper of the garden. "If thou hast taken Him hence, tell me where thou hast laid Him?"

Yes, if Mary Magdalen had been moved solely by conscience, had she but a religion of respect, I know well what she would have done. Frustrated by the sight of the figure of Jesus, she would have blushed to her eyes. She would have begged forgiveness. Do you think it would have made

our Lord happy to have beheld this poor sinner in adoration at His feet? How happy the good Master was to see
that this poor, guilty soul did not hesitate, that she was so
certain of His love that, completely overcome, she attempted to throw herself into His arms, crying, "Master."

Our Lord checked her. "Touch Me not!" But why?
We have seen our Lord more indulgent. Had He not once
permitted her to kiss His feet? Why then refuse a lesser
privilege today?

The Holy Fathers give this explanation, and a reason-
able one it is, "Oh, Mary, do not touch Me, for if I permit
this divine caress, your joy will be too great. Your heart
could not support such great joy. It would break from
excess of bliss. It is out of pity for you that I say, 'Touch
Me not!' "

Another interpretation is even more beautiful, more
worthy of the Heart of Jesus. "Mary, do not touch Me.
When I met you for the first time, you were guilty, unhappy, bowed down under the chains of your sins; therefore, you had need of encouragement and I permitted you
those holy embraces. But today you know what is in My
Heart; you have become stronger; you can advance from
those sensible consolations. No, do not touch Me. I reserve
My most intimate consolations for guilty souls."

The Saviour added: "Return to My brethren. . . ."
Your brethren, Lord? The angel termed Your followers
"disciples." Was not that enough? But You call them "My
brethren." Your brethren! Why, they did not have the
courage to watch one hour with You in the Garden of
Agony. The very day of their ordination to the priesthood, they betrayed You, abandoned You. Not one of
them made the journey to Calvary with You. Not one
aided You to carry Your cross. Oh, Lord, have You not
done enough when You said to them, "I no longer call
you servants, but friends"? Today they are even more

culpable. Yet now You give them the sweet name of brethren? "Yes, Mary, go tell My apostles that I now call them
My brethren." Poor apostles, how greatly dismayed they
must have been. They would have said to themselves: "Oh,
but the angel did not know how guilty we are. He was
ignorant of our crime of treason." But now you have not
the right to doubt. It is your God who speaks. He knows
all. He calls you not only His disciples, but His brethren.

"Go to My brethren . . . and to Peter." Our Lord
sent a special invitation to Peter. Surely that would appear
to be the height of weakness. He pardoned all, forgot all,
even before His disciples made any overtures for pardon.

"And to Peter"? My good Master, you are sending a
message to Peter? Poor St. Peter, how sad he must have
been! He probably said to himself, "The angel did not
know how guilty I am. Even if our good Master does pardon all the others, could He forget my triple denials?
Could I still be termed Head of the Apostolic College? I,
more culpable than all the others?" How stricken his heart
must have been! How he must have said to himself,
brokenheartedly, "What must my Master think of me now?
My beloved Master, whom I denied? And that on the
holiest day of my life, the day of my First Holy Communion, of my ordination to the priesthood!"

Oh, Peter, you have not the right to speak in those
tones of distrust. It is our Lord who speaks now. Is it
because you are Head of the Church that He displays more
mercy toward you? No, it is because you are the most
miserable, the most guilty. The Sacred Heart reserves
treasures of ineffable tenderness for poor, repentant sinners.

"Go, say to My disciples and to Peter, that I go before
you into Galilee." Oh, permit me, my good Master, have
you the courage to wait the forty-eight hours that it takes
to go from Jerusalem into Galilee?

Such was His intention, we know, for the angel announced it. Good Master, You will not keep to that decision, for Your Heart will overrule it. You are about to contradict Yourself. Can You wait forty-eight hours before consoling Your poor apostles? Your Heart will refuse the delay.

Mary Magdalen, in her turn, ran to the Cenacle, where the disciples were gathered. The other Holy Women had preceded her, breathless with fatigue and excitement. They were now describing, over and over, with excited volubility, what they had just experienced.

"They are deluded visionaries! They imagine these things." The apostles still did not believe, so the Gospel tells us. It was useless to attempt to convince them. They were incredulous.

Mary Magdalen arrived, more excited than the others. "I saw Him! He is risen! He appeared to me, spoke to me." This was too much. Believe a woman more foolish than the others? "What are these women trying to do? To upset us even more than we now are? Would that they would keep themselves calm, as we are!"

The apostles shrugged their shoulders and looked at one another, plunged in somber reflections. At last the apostles must have recalled some words of our Lord. He had twice promised that He would arise from the tomb. Even had they been completely forgotten, the words of the women might have recalled the words of the sacred prophecies to their troubled minds. But all was useless. The disciples could not believe, and doubtless, in their secret thoughts, accused our Lord of having deceived them. At last, glimmers of the truth pierced the minds of Peter and John. They decided to find out for themselves, and ran to the tomb. John outraced Peter. He had the lighter heart. He, at least, had stood beside the cross at Calvary. He felt himself pardoned; he could face his Master.

But the other—whom do I see? Peter running? Peter

trying to be the first to see his Master—if the women's stories are true. Was Peter at Calvary? Should he not hide himself for very shame? Should he not permit all the other apostles to outstrip him? Could he undergo the scrutiny of his Master's clear eyes? But now Peter no longer hesitated; he ran to meet the Master whom he had betrayed. How happy was Jesus to behold His apostles now running, in all haste, no longer hesitant, anxious to verify the stories about His appearance.

When Peter and John arrived at the place of burial, they looked about them. It was true, then; the seal of the tomb was broken. The linen cloths which had served to bind up the body of our Lord were there, neatly folded. All that pointed to some mysterious happening. Then, convinced, John returned to Jerusalem. Good St. John was pardoned; he needed no support for his good will. Our Lord permitted him to depart without revealing Himself. He reserves His tenderness for poor sinners. Good Master, do You not recall Your own words? You made an appointment to meet the apostles in Galilee.

But Jesus could not let the erring one return to the Cenacle without a word of love. No, He felt constrained to show Himself to Peter—to Peter, the most culpable of all His chosen followers, therefore the one who most needed to be consoled, reassured. What a moment! The Gospel furnishes no details of this appearance, but we can be sure that Peter threw himself upon the Heart of Jesus, reveling in His pardon, His goodness. Our Lord did not allude to his sin of betrayal; He spoke no word of reproach. Later it may be that Peter would ask forgiveness, but at that sacred moment there was room in his heart only for an immense joy at the presence of Jesus.

Yes, had Peter acted from motives of conscience alone, he would have thrown himself at the feet of Jesus, would have beaten his breast in repentance, have been plunged

into confusion. Would our Lord have been better pleased
to have seen Peter trembling at His feet? No! How His
Heart must have rejoiced to see His poor disciple, no
longer fearful or hesitant, throwing himself into His arms,
with not even a backward thought as to the kind of person
he had been before.

Peter in his turn, beside himself with joy, raced back
to the Cenacle, crying out to the assembled disciples, "I,
too, have seen Him. He is truly risen! I went to the sepulchre with John," he must have said; "then the Lord appeared to me. He spoke to me. I threw myself into His
arms," he would have added, with Oriental emotion.

The strongest personality in the Apostolic College was
now speaking. Did they believe him? Not at all. "Another
visionary! This is too much! This seems to be a day of
universal madness; Peter appears to be even more distracted than the others." It is so written in the Gospel. The
disciples still did not believe that Jesus had arisen. Their
unbelief is confirmed by the fact that two of them had
even left the Cenacle and were on their way home that
very day, returning to their families at Emmaus. They
were so discouraged that they resigned everything, including their vocations. All of the witnesses to the Resurrection
were looked upon as madmen, unworthy of credence. The
other apostles and disciples refused to believe; they had
been too discouraged over the events of the weekend. They
murmured among themselves upon beholding their hopes
for a successful Jewish revolt against alien and pagan rulers
fade away.

Behold, therefore, the two disciples who had deserted
their vocations and were returning to their homes and
families in Emmaus, complaining over the turn of events
as they slowly traversed the six miles from Jerusalem to
Emmaus. Should our Lord not have felt His patience completely exhausted by their blindness, their utter disbelief?

If the apostles had to deal with another than Jesus—had they been obliged to deal with us—they would certainly have been in for a bad half hour.

Would Jesus not punish these two deserters? Permit them to go to their ruin? Deliver them over to the unhappy end that awaits deserters? According to our standards, they would have deserved such treatment. Christ had multiplied miracles in their presence; He had sent a visible angel to the Holy Women, had appeared to Peter in person. Should not that have sufficed to win their belief? Would our Lord not have, justifiably, reached the limit of His patience? Its last extremity? Ah, if you think this, you do not understand His Heart.

Suddenly, the fugitive disciples, slowly trudging along, were joined by a wayfarer. They did not recognize the Stranger, because, as the Gospel says, "they were sad." Sadness forms a rampart, a wall, between the soul and Christ.

Our Lord made the advances. He was the first to address them, with a question, "Friends, what are these discourses that you hold, one with another, as you walk and are sad?" They, in bad humor, responded with small courtesy, "Art thou only a stranger in Jerusalem and hast not known the things that have been done there in these days?" Jesus acted as though He did not understand them: "What things?" He asked. They answered, "Concerning Jesus of Nazareth, who was a great prophet, mighty in word and work before all the people. . . . But we had hoped that it was He who should have redeemed Israel. . . . True, certain of our women affrighted us, saying they had seen a vision of angels who say He is alive." Doubtless they added, "But we ourselves have not seen Him."

Listen to their words: "We *had* believed"; "we *had* hoped." Actually, they did not then believe. They threw their insulting disbelief into the very face of the Saviour.

"Have I ever given you justification to withdraw your confidence? To mistake Me for an impostor?" He could ask.

But Christ did not reprove them as they deserved. He made but one gentle reproach, "Oh, foolish and slow of heart to believe in all things that the prophets have spoken." Beginning with Moses, He expounded to them the things that were written concerning Him in all the Scriptures. "Ought not Christ to have suffered these things, and so to have entered into His glory?"

By now, the two sullen travelers had softened in their attitude toward this stranger, so well instructed in the Scriptures and ancient prophecies, and who expressed Himself so well. Thus they arrived at Emmaus. Our Lord made as though to continue His journey. Out of delicacy, He acted as though He would not embarrass the two travelers by stopping when and where they stopped. He awaited an invitation, a prayer, that He would accompany them to their destination.

Then they constrained Him: "Stay with us, because it is toward evening and the day is far spent." Our Lord accepted their hospitality and entered with them into their humble abode. The Master willed to fill their cup of joy to the brim. They reclined at table for the evening meal. Jesus took up the bread, lifted His eyes to Heaven. He blessed and broke it.

Oh, my Master, what are You doing? Giving Holy Communion to these two renegades? Do they deserve that? Are they worthy of it, guilty of desertion as they are? Had we been sitting at that table in Emmaus, which one of us would have dared say, "Give them Holy Communion"? We would have thought it a sacrilege. They alone had this privilege: the first Holy Communion from the hands of their risen Saviour. In that act, they recognized Jesus. Our Lord disappeared after consoling them. He had restored their peace of heart, and went on to console others.

Now their eyes were opened; their minds and hearts were clean, full of the light of joy. Immediately, without taking time to await the morning, without resting, they set out upon the journey back to Jerusalem—six miles to traverse a second time. A short time before, they had been walking slowly, painfully. Now, transported with joy, they no longer sensed their fatigue. They walked briskly. How joy lends wings to our feet and our minds! When they arrived at the Cenacle, it must have been almost midnight. They found the disciples awake and more confused than ever, plunged into a gloomy silence. They were discouraged men, prey to profound sadness. What a contrast to the joy of the two disciples of Emmaus!

"We have seen Jesus!" they announced. "He followed us along the road and joined us on the way. For all of an hour He spoke with us; He entered our home. We recognized Him in the breaking of bread. With His own hands He gave us Holy Communion." Did the disciples believe their report? Alas, no. "Two more visionaries, like all the rest! Two more who have lost their heads over the happenings of the past week. This whole day is a day of madness."

The disciples were obstinate. They had hardened themselves in their disbelief. Was it possible that, at last, Christ would not become indignant at their stubbornness, their hardheadedness? Yes, our Lord was about to take revenge in His customary manner. He was about to appear to all of His disciples. His Heart would not allow Him to leave them longer in their discontent. Having consoled the disciples who were the most despairing, He hastened to the others. It is as if He said: "I hasten to speak to you, to console you, to restore your peace, your joy."

Suddenly, there He was in the midst of them, "the doors being closed." Now we see the entire group of disciples excited, upset; they thought they saw a spirit, a phantom.

Jesus spoke, "Peace be with you: it is I, be not afraid." But at these words, they were more disturbed than before. What, an apparition that speaks? Our Lord reassured His disciples, and they were even more fearful. Surely, by now our Lord's patience was completely exhausted. Surely, He would bring into play His justice, give them a sharp reproof.

What do I hear? Our good Master condescended to an act that totally confounds us. "Have you anything here to eat?" And they offered Him broiled fish and honeycomb, the remains of their own evening meal. Our Lord placed Himself at table and ate before them. "You see that it is really I, and that I am truly alive. A spirit does not eat. But if I eat, it is not that My risen body has need of food, but that you may believe."

At last the Heart of Jesus triumphed; the disciples believed in His Resurrection. They believed and feared no longer. Now see them reassured. They gazed with renewed wonder, love, and faith upon their Master. Their joy ran over. How good, how patient He has been, and how they love Him!

Jesus passed the remainder of the evening with His disciples. He gave them no reproof, not a single word to recall their unbelief. Far from that, this very evening He restored to the apostles all the privileges of their priesthood. He bestowed upon them the power to remit sins. Breathing upon them, He said: "Whose sins you shall forgive, they are forgiven them; and whose sins you shall retain, they are retained." Not only did He not deprive them of their vocation, but He did not deprive them of any of their privileges. He reposed His full confidence in them; and as the crowning act of His generosity, He accorded them new graces, greater favors. Tell me, could our Lord

have granted to his apostles more than He did? Could He
have been more generous to them?

Had we been at Jerusalem on the morning of the Resurrection, and had Christ said to us: "You know what
My apostles have done. They could not help knowing that
I would be wounded by their lack of faith, of confidence.
They rendered themselves guilty of sacrilege on the very
day of their ordination. Tell me what you think I should
do? What line of conduct should I follow with them? But
be generous; I want to be merciful to them."

I ask myself if there has ever been a human being so
confirmed in goodness as to say: "Not only should You
not revenge Yourself upon them—impose no penance upon
them—but You must pardon them before they have made
one movement toward asking for Your pardon. You must
take the initiative. You must restore to them their holy
vocation." I ask if ever a created heart could have devised
such a vengeance?

I know well that never would a human heart think of
saying: "Good Master, not only should You restore to
them all the divine graces which they once possessed, their
apostolic vocation, all of their privileges, but You must
add to them. You must revenge Yourself, yes, but through
even greater love than before. You must appear first to
Magdalen, the most guilty of Your followers, then to
Peter, the most criminal. You must follow the deserters to
Emmaus, to give them Holy Communion. Upon all Your
apostles, You must confer the power to forgive sins."
Behold the vengeance of Jesus, the sole vengeance known
to the Heart of our Lord.

My dear friends, had we been at Jesusalem on that first
Easter day, had our Lord been to us a complete stranger,
and had He given us the privilege of following Him, of
seeing Him in all the circumstances of that eventful day,
tell me, would we not have loved Him, won by so much

goodness? Would we not have been subjugated, fascinated, by the display of so much love? Before the close of the day, would our hearts not have been won, in spite of ourselves?

We have neither right nor reason to complain. Jesus has not changed. He is still our most loving, our most generous Friend. He is always with us in the tabernacle.

Oh, my good Master, when shall we come to know You truly?

Oh, Jesus, to know You even a little is already to love You. To know You better is to love You with an ever-increasing love. To know You perfectly is to love You perfectly; it is to attach ourselves to You by the most delicate, yet the most profound fibers of our heart.

Oh, my God, grant that I may come to know You, that I may love You truly. I give You free reign in my heart and in my affairs. I ask nothing from You. I refuse You nothing. I surrender myself blindly to Your good pleasure. All that happens to me will be but what your love has prepared for me. I ask of You but one grace: that I may not offend You.

Oh, Adorable Heart of Jesus, when the storm rages I want to make You hear the cry of my prayer. I desire that my trials serve only to unite me more intimately to You, my Companion and my Friend upon earth, while I await heaven and the intimate companionship of Your Divine Heart for all eternity. Amen.

A NOTE ON THE TYPE

IN WHICH THIS BOOK IS SET

This book is set in Janson, a Linotype face, created from the early punches of Anton Janson, who settled in Leipzig around 1670. This type is not an historic revival, but rather a letter of fine ancestry, remodelled and brought up to date to satisfy present day taste. It carries a feeling of being quite compact and sturdy. It has good color and displays a pleasing proportion of ascenders and descenders as compared to the height of the lower case letters. The book was composed and printed by The York Composition Company, Inc., of York, Pa., and bound by Moore and Company of Baltimore. The typography and design are by Howard N. King.